We, the People

By the same author

The Jail Diary of Albie Sachs (Harvill Press, 1966)

Stephanie on Trial (Harvill Press, 1968)

Justice in South Africa (University of California Press, 1974)

Sexism an● the Law (Martin Robinson, 1979)

Soft Vengeance of a Free●om Fighter (Grafton, 1990)

Protecting Human Rights in a New South Africa (Oxford University Press, 1990)

A●vancing Human Rights in South Africa (Oxford University Press, 1992)

The Free Diary of Albie Sachs (Random House, 2004)

The Strange Alchemy of Life an● Law (Oxford University Press, 2009)

ALBIE SACHS

We, the People

INSIGHTS OF AN ACTIVIST JUDGE

WITS UNIVERSITY PRESS

Published in South Africa by:

Wits University Press
1 Jan Smuts Avenue
Johannesburg, 2001
www.witspress.co.za

Cover photograph © Steve Gordon (www.musicpics.co.za)
Edited by Hazel Cuthbertson
Proofread by Elsabé Birkenmayer
Indexed by Marlene Burger
Designed and produced by Fire and Lion

Acknowledgements

Mind-wrestling with Alex Dodd has been a delight. Thanks, Alex; you are strong, agile, nuanced and stylish – the perfect editor. And conceptual engagement with Corina van der Spoel has been equally pleasurable. Thanks, Corina; you are simpatica, calm, focused, deft and authoritative – the perfect project manager. Between the two of you, what would have been just thousands and thousands of words became a book.

1988

Nineteen eighty-eight, and it's raining, drizzling – nothing unusual about that in Ireland. I'm sitting in the kitchen of Kader and Louise Asmal in suburban Dublin, feeling very, very at home – nothing unusual about that. And we're doing work that we know is historic. It was one of those 'pinch-me' moments (maybe the first real 'pinch-me' moment for me) – knowing that we were entering into a whole new phase, not simply denouncing, imagining, mobilising; but beginning to craft the foundations of a new society. What was unusual was that, for that whole weekend, Kader didn't smoke once inside that house! The way we put it, we were converting the Freedom Charter into an operational document that would protect the rights for which people in South Africa had been fighting.

2016

I was rushing to catch my plane at the airport when a middle-aged African man blocked my path and flung his arms around me. 'Thank you, thank you,' he kept repeating. 'It wasn't me,' I interrupted, 'I left the Court some years ago.' But he kept his grip and carried on offering thanks. I had to pull myself away to reach the gate in time. But then as the plane lifted off my heart swelled with emotion. The Constitutional Court had ordered the President to pay back the public funds overspent on his private home. There was hope. Millions of ordinary South Africans were celebrating. This book is dedicated to them all. It is they who ensure that the Constitution lives on, deeply rooted in the realities and ideals of the nation.

Contents

Figure 1: This portrait of Albert Luthuli by struggle photographer Eli Weinberg used to be displayed in modest homes throughout South Africa. Luthuli was president of the ANC from 1953 until his death in a restricted area in 1967. In 1958 he worked with the ANC's then Secretary General Oliver Tambo on drafting a new constitution which prefigured the organisation opening its membership to all. Through his integrity, courage, thoughtfulness, openness, warmth and lack of personal ambition, Luthuli became the model of what a president should be.

Figure 2: Oliver Tambo as a young articled clerk in the 1950s, before he and Nelson Mandela went on to set up the first black legal partnership in Johannesburg.

Figure 3: Albie [back], a second-year law student aged seventeen, gives the ANC thumbs-up salute as he is arrested, along with Hymie Rochman [front left], and Mary Butcher [Turok] [half hidden], for sitting on a bench marked 'non-whites only' at the Cape Town General Post Office during the Defiance of Unjust Laws Campaign in 1952. The magistrate declared that he was a juvenile and sent him home to the care of his mother.

Figure 4: Albie, aged 21 in January 1967, after being admitted as an advocate of the Supreme Court of South Africa, Cape of Good Hope Provincial Division.

Figure 5: Albie in exile during a visit to York, England, in 1967, where he had gone to thank the Joseph Rowntree Charitable Trust for a stipend which enabled him to do a PhD at Sussex University.

Figure 6: Albie speaking to poets, writers and photographers in his apartment in Maputo, c. 1980.

Figure 7: Albie at the ANC conference in Kabwe, Zambia, in 1985, introducing the ANC's Code of Conduct forbidding the use of torture on captured enemy agents. On the far left is Oliver Tambo, acting president of the ANC, and next to him, Tom Nkobi, the organisation's treasurer general. Zambian troops surrounded the building to protect it from possible commando raids by South African forces.

Figure 8: Albie marching on May Day in newly independent Mozambique in the late 1970s under the banner of the South African Congress of Trade Unions (SACTU). The ANC had an official office in Maputo but was not allowed to conduct political activity in the country. The only work it did publicly was attending funerals of members who had died, mostly as a result of actions by South African security forces, and cleaning the graves of comrades on 16 December each year. Members were permitted, however, to march under a SACTU banner.

Figure 9: Memorial gathering to honour Ruth First, killed in August 1982 when opening a parcel bomb in her office in the Centre for African Studies, the building in the picture. Albie is sitting in front of Ruth's picture, which is below that of Samora Machel. Ruth's husband, Joe Slovo, is seated to the right of the rector of Eduardo Mondlane University, Fernando Ganhao. Eduardo Mondlane, who had studied at the University of the Witwatersrand, was the founder and first leader of FRELIMO. He was killed by an assassin's bomb in 1969.

Figure 10: Albie on the pavement moments after his car exploded in Maputo, Mozambique, on 7 April 1988, causing him to lose most of his right arm and the sight in one eye.

Figure 11: Albie hugs Dorothy Adams at the Young Vic Theatre in London after a benefit performance of *The Jail Diary of Albie Sachs* had been put on by the British theatre community to assist him in his recovery from the car bomb attack in 1988. Adams had whistled to him while both were in solitary confinement in Maitland prison 23 years earlier. Peter McEnery of the Royal Shakespeare Company played Albie, while Simon Callow and two other actors who had played him in previous productions took other parts on this occasion. One of the other actors, Matthew Marsh, was to play Eugene de Kock in another play some decades later.

Figure 12: Albie with Louise and Kader Asmal and their sons Rafiq (left) and Adam in 1988 at their home in Dublin, where he and Kader prepared a draft Bill of Rights based on the principles of the Freedom Charter.

Figure 13: Chris Hani greets Cheryl Carolus as Albie ascends the platform of the University of Durban-Westville Sports Hall in July 1991 just after being elected to the National Executive Committee at the ANC's first lawful conference on South African soil after more than thirty years of forced secrecy, imprisonment and exile.

Figure 14: The ANC delegation disperses after having a group photograph taken at the Convention for a Democratic South Africa (CODESA) negotiations, c. 1992.

Figure 15: President Nelson Mandela presided over the swearing-in ceremony of the judges he had appointed to the Constitutional Court. His opening words were: 'The last time I appeared in court was to find out if I would be sentenced to death. Today I inaugurate a Court whose work will be central to our democracy.' Six months later the Court struck down two important proclamations issued by President Mandela as being unconstitutional. He immediately went on television to say that he, as president, should be the first to accept interpretations of the Constitution as made by the Court.

Figure 16: Albie raises his right arm as he is sworn in as a justice of the Constitutional Court on 14 February 1995.

Figure 17: An off-guard moment for eight of the eleven judges after being sworn in at the Constitutional Court on 14 February 1995.

Figure 18: Albie being greeted by Raymond Mhlaba, a friend from early struggle days, at a reception after inauguration. Mhlaba was sentenced to life imprisonment during the Rivonia trial and, decades later, became premier of the Eastern Cape. Phineas Mojapelo, later deputy-president of the Gauteng High Court, looks on.

Figure 19: Constitutional Court judges during a workshop, c. 2000, clockwise from centre: Chief Justice Arthur Chaskalson, Albie, Yvonne Mokgoro, Richard Goldstone, Kate O'Regan, Zak Yacoob, Johann Kriegler, Tholie Madala, [indistinct], Deputy Chief Justice Pius Langa and acting-justice Edwin Cameron. They workshopped together after almost every case, going round and round the table several times to reach consensus where possible and to write separate judgements when necessary.

Figure 20: Albie on the stairway to the library in the new Constitutional Court building, with Judith Mason's painting, *The Blue Dress*, in the background. The painting commemorated the last moments of Phila Ndwandwe, an MK guerrilla who was captured close to the Swaziland border and tortured and executed. As a result of the Truth and Reconciliation Commission, her body was found in a shallow grave, naked except for a piece of plastic covering her pubic area. The blue dress was the artist's tribute to the woman she called her 'sister'.

Introduction

To know the taste of an avocado pear you have to cut it in half. I'm reminded of this statement of Samora Machel's as I turn these pages. Decades ago, when I arrived in newly independent Mozambique, Samora would say that only when you let all the contradictions come out will you resolve problems in an open and principled way. Three contradictions in this book stand out for me.

Contradiction number one is personal and amusing in an 'Only in South Africa' kind of a way. My relationship with former apartheid president FW de Klerk had always been distant. When I was told that, in the Government of National Unity, he had bitterly opposed Mandela selecting me as one of the justices on the Constitutional Court, I was not surprised. Yet, early this year when I was asked to speak at a conference on multi-culturalism in South Africa organised by the FW de Klerk Foundation, I accepted. Our Constitution belongs to everyone. And if I speak about it to trade unionists, community organisations, faith groups, schoolchildren, student activists and NGOs, so should I engage with the multiple foundations that South Africa has produced.

When I arrived at the venue I was greeted warmly and spontaneously by Elita de Klerk, but more restrainedly with a stiff handshake and correct smile by the former president. Maybe it was the challenge of addressing an audience invited by his foundation that caused me to speak with special emotion about the crucial but virtually unknown role played by Oliver Tambo in establishing the foundations of our Constitution. I went on to pay particular attention to how, in the ANC, we had dealt with the manner in which the Constitution should protect Afrikaans as one of eleven official languages, an issue of some controversy in schools and universities today. I mentioned that my contact as a child with Afrikaans speakers had been most positive. In Cape Town it had been with the poet Uys Krige and the artist Gregoire Boonzaier, both lively, progressive and full of fun. In Johannesburg it had been with people like Johanna and Hester Cornelius, both members of the Garment Workers Union of which my father, Solly Sachs, had been the general secretary, and both lively, progressive and full of fun.

After making my presentation [see Section 10, *Unite♦ in Diversity*], I thought I would slip out quietly. But De Klerk suddenly placed himself in front of me, blocking my way, and began to speak to me in Afrikaans. In a serious voice he told me that his father, Jan de Klerk, had been a school principal in the Transvaal, and a successful one. But then he had been asked by the National Party to leave his job and work full time on something quite different. It was to destroy the leadership my father, Solly Sachs, was providing to the Garment Workers Union. Afterwards, De Klerk Snr had been made minister of labour, and was responsible for a number of the labour laws of the time, laws which, FW added, he had gone on to repeal. He smiled warmly for the first time, shook my hand and walked away. Only in South Africa, I thought, only in South Africa ...

A second contradictory moment occurred after a far more poignant and astringent emotion flowed from re-reading the chapter on the contradictions between Free Spirits and Ravaged Souls, adapted from a keynote address I gave at the Time of the Writer festival in Durban in 2011 [see Section 6, *Free Spirits an♦ Ravage♦ Souls*]. I think about how bitterly the tensions that lay at the core of this talk later manifested themselves in the terrible Charlie Hebdo episode in Paris. And also about what has happened in the intervening years to the two main protagonists of my presentation, the cartoonist Zapiro and the president, Jacob Zuma.

Zapiro, the brave, progressive and much-loved political cartoonist, had at the time insisted vociferously on his right to untrammelled free speech when depicting Zuma being urged by his political colleagues to open his fly and rape a prostrate Lady Justice. Yet, interestingly, since then Zapiro has modified his position. He has accepted, after a great deal of serious introspection, that he erred in not taking into account the injury his cartoons might cause [if quite unintentionally] through triggering painfully racialised stereotypes.

Meanwhile, for his part, President Jacob Zuma has since withdrawn his claim for huge amounts in damages from Zapiro. His popularity ratings have plunged dramatically in recent times. People I was close to during the struggle have expressed anguish at the thought that Zuma might succeed in doing something that Verwoerd, Vorster and Botha failed to do, and that is destroy the ANC. They are deeply concerned that he is providing a kind of leadership that could not only undermine the South African constitutional order through state capture, but could also rip out the heart of the ANC's constitutional ethos by means of branch capture.

As a former judge I feel it would not be appropriate for me to take any public stand on these issues. What I can ask myself is, if I make the assumption that these fears are justified, does it change my concerns about the appropriateness of the original cartoon? And my answer continues to be 'No'. The issue is not a purely legal one. Nor is it simply about the need to maintain civility and good political manners. Our Constitution might indeed permit the publishing of cartoons and artworks that are deeply offensive to large sections of the population. And there might be moments when controlled, focused and meaningful disruption of discourse can be justified. But here the basic question relates to the degree of cultural sensitivity required of artists in a country where many, many of its citizens have known (and still know) great pain simply because of who they were and who they are. Protection of human dignity lies at the heart of our Constitution. Artists should feel concern in their own souls if they become aware that their work is further ravaging the already ravaged souls of others.

This brings me to my third and final reflection, which relates to the central contradiction animating this book. It is the tension in any constitutional order between perfectibility and corruptibility, a tension that has been particularly pronounced in South Africa. My inaugural lecture at the University of Cape Town in 1991 was entitled 'Perfectibility and Corruptibility'. We had seen this tension in many countries where we had lived in exile, where brave freedom fighters had ended up as authoritarian and self-serving heads of state. We had seen the tension inside our own organisation, where not all members lived up to the values of people like Oliver Tambo and Chris Hani and Joe Slovo and Ruth Mompati. I had recently returned from exile and was heavily engaged in the preparations for burying apartheid and achieving a new democratic and non-racial constitution. Now, a quarter of a century later, people of all ages from all parts of the country are asking me the question: 'Is this the country you were fighting for?' They point to the continuing racism, the massive inequalities still associated with race. They refer to the vast unemployment and the unacceptable level of crime. Above all, they express shock at failures of leadership and the degrees of corruption in which a number of political leaders at all levels of government are involved. Has corruptibility triumphed over perfectibility? Is this, they repeat, the country I was fighting for?

And my answer is 'Yes, this is the country I was fighting for'. But 'No, it is not the *society* I was fighting for'. So the answer to the question is not to allow the deficiencies of our society to destroy the country, but to use the country to deal with the fault lines and failures in our society. This is not just a lawyer's play with words. When, in the days of oppression, we called for freedom in our lifetime and demanded universal franchise, we were told sneeringly to look at Africa; there would only be 'one man, one vote' once. We have in fact had four general elections. Our presidents step down after two terms, maximum. President Mandela voluntarily left office after one term and President Mbeki resigned before his second term had ended, not because of an army coup or huge demonstrations in the streets, but because a majority in his party had shown preference for another leader.

The institutions founded on the principles of mistrust and vigilance that we placed in our Constitution to protect ourselves from ourselves, have been working. The reports of the public protector in fulfilling her constitutional mandate have not only helped clarify issues of great public controversy, they have also given legitimacy to the whole constitutional project. Even more so, the creation of an independent, constitutionally minded judiciary has given the people clear points of reference in understanding how power should be exercised in our country. Protected by the Constitution she protects, and enjoying increasing public esteem, Lady Justice is far from cowed. And just as we have a new generation of judges upholding the central tenets of our country's existence, so we have a lively new crop of journalists using their constitutionally guaranteed freedom to investigate the doings of the mightiest and the meanest in our nation.

Black majority rule has not failed in our land, even if our society continues to fail in many serious respects. Black leaders achieved something that generations of white rulers never succeeded in doing. They integrated the Bantustans into one united country. They amalgamated armed forces that for decades had been bitterly fighting each other. They unified systems of health and education that had been segregated for centuries. We can all move freely and speak our minds. There are no holy cows in South Africa. We all have the vote and our elections are taken very seriously. We can take our disputes to court, challenge the highest and defend the humblest. Our books are not banned, there is no detention without trial. This is our country, South Africa. We have won our freedom and we are not going to let it go. We have mechanisms to hold our leaders accountable, and the opportunities to make use of the rights we have won.

Our problems are huge. It is true that nearly a quarter of our population has moved from shelters to brick or cement homes with water, electricity and sewage; that ninety per cent of our people have gained access to water and electricity; that almost a third of the nation receives social grants; that we have a large and growing black middle class that is both driving the economy and changing the nature of political discourse. We can and should take considerable pride in these accomplishments. But none of them justifies Marikana; the inordinate expansion of wealth for those already extremely rich while the majority remain poor; the failures to accomplish meaningful land reform; the racism still rampant in our society; or the corrupt dealings in the state and inside political parties.

We need to engage seriously with issues placed on the agenda by a new generation of students who are calling bravely and boldly for decolonisation of hallowed institutions like our universities, and not simply their deracialisation. The burning of buildings and paintings by some in their ranks should not stop us from opening our minds to what they are saying and responding to their idealism and passion. When I spoke to two hundred fervent law students at the University of Cape Town recently I couldn't help seeing myself as a young law student on that very campus sitting in their ranks. Our institutions are strong enough to contain and be strengthened by the turbulence that besets them. They are more likely to collapse from routinism, corporatisation and, in some cases, cronyism and corruption, than from having to find sustainable and meaningful responses to the tumult on their precincts.

And we have to listen to what the workers are saying. I was reminded of this when attending a conference recently to discuss twenty years of our Constitution. The hotel in which I was staying was filled with workers attending another conference. Speaking to one of their leaders at a lunch where we chatted more than we ate, I recalled the role that the unions had played in establishing democracy and non-racialism in our country. Long before trade union members had the vote they were electing their own leaders. Long before non-racialism and non-sexism were made foundational values of our Constitution they were breaking barriers of race, tribe, language and patriarchy in struggles on the shop floor.

I will end with another statement by Samora Machel: 'Leaders may come and leaders may go but the people never die'. Samora Machel was killed when his plane was lured to a hillside by a false beacon. His people and his country were severely wounded but they never died. In South Africa we have a people who are as determined as they are diverse. We, the People, made our Constitution. There is nothing in it that prevents a second major transformation of our society. Unlike transition, transformation never ends; our society needs constant renewal. It is We, the People, who produced our Constitution, and it is We, the People, who must ensure that its full vision is achieved. In our lifetime.

ONE

In the Beginning

The Future of Multiculturalism in South Africa: The vision of the Constitution

FW DE KLERK FOUNDATION CONFERENCE | CAPE TOWN | 2 FEBRUARY 2016

If we did a paternity or maternity test on the South African Constitution, whose DNA do you think would come up? It's no one in this room, although there are people here who made a major contribution. Nor is it Nelson Mandela. The answer is: Oliver Tambo.

I recall a moment in March 1988 when I was walking to the microphone in a room in Lusaka about a tenth of the size of this one. My topic was a Bill of Rights in a democratic South Africa. And my heart was going boom, boom, boom.

Oliver Tambo had set up the ANC Constitutional Committee which had organised a workshop to discuss a document we had prepared, titled Constitutional Guidelines. For years our legal skills had been used to denounce apartheid. A typical paper I had written had shown how every single article in the Universal Declaration of Human Rights was being violated in South Africa (with one exception, I should add – try as I might, I couldn't show that apartheid denied rights to intellectual property!) Now we were moving our focus from what we wished to destroy, to what we were determined to build. It was thrilling to work as part of a team with the quiet, thoughtful, principled and open-minded Oliver Tambo at the helm. My function at the workshop was to explain what a Bill of Rights was and why we needed one in South Africa.

About forty people were looking expectantly at me. Some might have been there directly from the underground at home, but most were comrades living in exile, a couple from the MK military camps, others from various political structures. I had three arguments, and my heart was racing. How would these comrades at the heart of the struggle, many risking their lives on a daily basis, take my reasoning?

The first argument, the diplomatic one, was easy. Being seen to support a Bill of Rights would put the ANC in a positive light. It would tell people, ourselves, the world, that we were not power-hungry terrorists waiting to seize power, to get revenge. On the contrary, it supported the idea that we were aiming to achieve a free, democratic and law-governed South Africa. The delegates nodded their agreement, no problem.

The second, the strategic argument, was a little more complicated. An entrenched Bill of Rights was our answer (note that I'm using the word 'our' – I was a member of the ANC until the 1994 elections, when I decided to be a candidate for the judiciary, and stepped away from political activity). It was, I repeat, *our* answer, developed primarily by Oliver Tambo, to group rights. This was a time when protection of group rights was being strongly promoted as the key to a constitutional settlement in South Africa. In non-technical terms, group rights were hailed as the foundation for creating a system of power-sharing between the white minority and the black majority. In more technical language, the principles of consociational democracy, as advanced by Arend Lijphart, were invoked in favour of adopting group rights rather than majoritarian democracy. Lijphart's central idea was that in deeply divided and segmented societies it is both principled and practical to grant as much autonomy as possible to the different community groupings. Each would then have a large measure of governmental control over its own special affairs, and all would accept governing by consensus at the national level. Even our closest friends internationally, from East, West, North and South, were urging us to 'get real' and adopt some form of power-sharing along these lines.

It is a nice term, power-sharing – but power-sharing between whom? Between racial groups? The problem wasn't only that the Constitution would in effect be entrenching a grossly inequitable status quo in which the 13 per cent white minority happened by law to own 87 per cent of the land and 95 per cent of productive capacity. It would also be placing racial identity right at the heart of all the structures of government. Thus, parliament and the presidency would be shared between persons selected as leaders of the different racial and linguistic groups. As we saw it, this would mean that a form of apartheid would be moved from the sphere of separate development and Bantustans right into the institutions of the central state itself. At the same time, race discrimination would continue to be shielded in the private sphere by the mechanism of constitutionally guaranteed property rights and freedom of association.

Oliver Tambo was the great proponent inside the ANC of a completely different vision. He took constitutionalism and constitution-making very seriously. His point of departure, however, was not that black and white groups should live side by side in separate communities protected by power-sharing arrangements. Rather, it was to secure the fundamental rights of all, black and white, in a united, non-racial South Africa. He had no problem in principle about accepting group rights for workers, or women, or children, or members of language groups and faith communities,

> ... but Tambo refuse∙ to 'get real' an∙ intro∙uce constitutionalise∙ markers of i∙entity, culture an∙ historical provenance into the very formal structures of government itself. Instea∙, people woul∙ have their fun∙amental rights secure∙, not because they belonge∙ to a majority or a minority, but because they were human beings.

Thus, the instrument to protect people from future abuse, humiliation and dispossession would not be power-sharing between ethnic groupings but an entrenched Bill of Rights guaranteeing the dignity, equality and freedom of all. The delegates cottoned on quickly. Once more I noticed nods of agreement. No need for my heart to go boom, boom, boom.

What was the third reason for having a Bill of Rights? It was advancing this, perhaps the most profound and deeply principled reason of all, that was causing my heart to race. We needed a Bill of Rights, I said, against ourselves.

What would the delegates think? It was easy for me, a lawyer who had grown up with the privileges that went with a white skin, to come up with these ideas ... I looked into the eyes of the audience. To my joy instead of hostility or repudiation, I saw looks of delight. It was as though they all felt a sense of reassurance that the Constitutional Committee, fulfilling the mandate given to it by Oliver Tambo, was urging the creation of institutional mechanisms against any abuses of power from any quarter whatsoever in our new democracy. This was not for us a matter of pure political or legal philosophy. We were living in societies where many people who had fought very bravely for their freedom had gone on to become authoritarian heads of state themselves. Jomo Kenyatta was held up as a prime example; jailed by the British for years, he had gone on to use his status as president of Kenya to seize land and amass a fortune for his family. Indeed, we had seen inside our own organisation how Oliver Tambo, with the support of people like Chris Hani and Joe Slovo, had from time to time been obliged to take firm and principled initiatives against unacceptable forms of conduct and abuses of power.

If anything, I had been a rights sceptic. Strongly influenced by critical legal studies ideas, I inclined to the view that it was wrong for essentially political issues to be decided by the courts.

I sometimes get praise for being the person who intro•uce•
the Bill of Rights into the ANC. It was completely the other

*way aroun•. It was the ANC, Oliver Tambo, who persua•e•
me that in South African con•itions, a Bill of Rights coul•
enunciate the quintessence of all we ha• been struggling for,
convert the Free•om Charter into an operational •ocument,
an• become the cornerstone of our country's new constitutional or•er.*

The judiciary would then become a crucial instrument for ensuring that
core elements of political morality would be maintained in the new
society. They could also see to it that the rights of workers, women,
children, the disabled and the poor were respected.

A month after urging acceptance of a Bill of Rights, I was blown
up. I can't help thinking that the real target was Mathews Phosa, who
was then deep in the underground in Maputo, with the code name of
Freddie. But they couldn't get him and I was a sitting duck, so they blew
me up instead. I'm not blaming you, Mathews; indeed, the operative who
planned the operation has stated on film that my name was on the list of
'those deemed important enough to be eliminated'. Anyhow, as soon as
I was out of hospital some months later, the Constitutional Committee
of the ANC flew to London. And, fantastic though the intervention of
surgeons and physiotherapists and occupational therapists had been, the
best, best, best medicine I received was of a different order: I was asked to
work with Professor Kader Asmal on drafting the first text of the ANC's
Bill of Rights for a Democratic South Africa.

The Bill of Rights for us, then, is not just another legal document.
It is life and death, it is who we are, it is the foundation of our
transformation in South Africa. It certainly acknowledges and embraces
multiculturalism. But it does so without allowing group rights to become
the foundation of the governing structures of our new constitutional
order. That was foundational. From a political point of view, our
institutions simply had to be non-racial.

Once the principle of non-racial democracy was accepted, then the
issue of multicultural diversity could be handled within that framework.

It took six years to get our Constitution an• it wasn't easy. It wasn't FW •e Klerk an• Nelson Man•ela getting into a room, •oing a little •eal; you give me this, I give you that. The process was robust, fille• with conflict an• setbacks.

It took us six hard years; we had breakdowns. Chris Hani was assassinated, we had rolling mass action, we had massacres. It was extremely tense but we never let go of the ideal, and we got it. We, as South Africans, got this amazing Constitution! And twenty years afterwards we can have the open, free debate that we're having in this City Hall Chamber.

The democracy we take for granted emerged in a situation where nobody in the world felt South Africa stood a chance. A racial bloodbath was seen as the inevitable outcome. It's not only that we avoided catastrophe, we established a strongly implanted Constitution with institutions, mechanisms, principles and values that enable us today to deal openly and robustly with the many, many things that concern us and worry us and ravage us. We do so with the knowledge that we've got the vote, we've got free speech, we've got an independent judiciary, we have strong political parties, open contestation. We take the openness of our society for granted. It's great we take it for granted, and it's sad we take it for granted. Great because it's normal, that's the country we're living in; and a little bit sad because we don't give ourselves credit for our enduring achievements.

We beat ourselves up too easily, I believe, too quickly, because many things are happening that many of us are very, very •istresse• about. But that shoul• be a reason for using the •emocratic rights we have won to bring about the changes we •esire, rather than to •escen• into •espair an•, at times, self-flagellation.

Once the issue of directly constitutionalising group rights in our institutions had been taken off the agenda, then issues of how to respect and balance out different community, traditional and cultural interests could come to the fore. This they could now do in their own right, and not as proxies for political and economic power. Problems of race, gender, disability, sexual orientation and so on, are ubiquitous and are dealt with by the equality provisions of the Bill of Rights. Similarly, unfair discrimination on the basis of language, culture and religion is prohibited.

The Original 'Pinch-me' Moment

LAUNCH OF THE KADER ASMAL HUMAN RIGHTS AWARD | UNIVERSITY OF
THE WESTERN CAPE | CAPE TOWN | 28 MAY 2013

Sitting at that kitchen table in rainy Dublin in 1988, Kader Asmal and I began the task of preparing the Bill of Rights – I'd actually imagined, that it was a wooden table, in my head it became a wooden table, but apparently it wasn't, it had a plastic-covered top. The Constitutional Committee, prompted by Oliver Tambo, had said, 'just draft an outline' – that was our mandate – 'of the fundamental themes that a Bill of Rights in the new South Africa ought to have'.

I recall we divided up the work – I would do the material side and Kader would deal with the enforcement, and then we would swop. I sat down at that table with a clean piece of paper – no books, no documents, no charters, no constitutions, no preambles – the idea being that a Bill of Rights should speak from inside of you, it should proclaim itself.

It's something human beings are entitled to. Something so fundamental; so central to what human beings are, and what they want, and what they strive for, that it shouldn't be derived from anything: it should just emerge. And particularly those of us who'd spent decades swimming, immersed in that environment, the phrases should come out. And I was writing with my left hand – I had to learn to write with my left – and I jotted down a number of fundamental rights that the people of South Africa would have. And afterwards, we checked; Kader went through it, he made some textual changes, and we checked it against the great instruments of the world, and all the fundamental rights were there.

It wasn't because we were particularly clever or astute. It was because we'd been so deeply immersed and involved in a struggle, with millions of people taking part, and expressing their demands, that we were able to find the language. And have that first 'pinch-me' moment: 'Is this really happening? Is it really true?' And we were to have many, many more …

TWO

Hope and Caution in Exile

The First and Last Word – Freedom

SOUTH AFRICAN CONSTITUTIONAL STUDIES CENTRE | INSTITUTE OF
COMMONWEALTH STUDIES | LONDON | 1990

We give the first and last word to freedom, yet we do not know what it is.

This is the central irony of the deep and passionate struggle in South Africa – that it is for something that exists only in relation to what it seeks to eliminate. We know what oppression is. We experience it, define it, we know its elements, take steps against it. All we can say about freedom is that it is the absence of oppression. We define freedom in terms of the measures we need to take to keep its enemy, tyranny, at bay. Tyranny is the negative indicator of freedom; freedom is what apartheid is not.

When the call went up in the 1950s, 'freedom in our lifetime', it signified the end of something very specific – colonial domination in Africa and apartheid tyranny in South Africa. The Freedom Charter, adopted in 1955, was conceived of as the reverse of apartheid. A product of struggle rather than of contemplation, it sought in each and every one of its articles to controvert the reality of oppression the people were undergoing. Its ten sections were based on the demands that a suffering people sent in, not on any ideal scheme created by legal philosophers of what a free South Africa should look like.

Any new constitution in South Africa must be first and foremost an anti-apartheid constitution. The great majority of the people will measure their newly won freedom in terms of the extent to which they feel that the arbitrary and cruel laws and practices of apartheid have been removed.

> *Freedom is not some state of exaltation, a condition of instinctive anarchy and joy; it is not sudden and permanent happiness. In fact, some of the freest countries have the most melancholy and stressed people.*

Freedom is indivisible and universal, but it also has its specific moments and particular modes. In South Africa the mode of freedom is anti-racist, and anti all the mechanisms and institutions that kept the system of racism and national oppression in place. Yet the Constitution has to be for all South Africans, former oppressors and oppressed alike. It expresses the sovereignty of the whole nation, not just part, not even just the vast majority. If it is to be binding on all, it should speak on behalf of all and give its protection to all.

The elimination of apartheid does not by itself guarantee freedom – even for the formerly oppressed.

> *History records many examples of freedom fighters of one generation becoming oppressors of the next.*

Sometimes the very qualities of determination, which give freedom fighters the courage to raise the banner of liberty in the face of barbarous repression, transmute themselves into sources of authoritarianism and forced marches later on. On other occasions, the habits of clandestinity and mistrust, of tight discipline and centralised control, without which the freedom-fighting nucleus would have been wiped out, continue with dire results into the new society. More profoundly, the forms of organisation and guiding principles that triumphed in insurrectionary moments, on long marches, in high mountains, that solved problems in liberated zones, might simply not be appropriate for whole peoples and whole countries in conditions of peace.

These reflections have led some people into arguing for inaction against apartheid because of their concern that removing one tyranny might lead to its replacement by another. From a moral point of view, it seems most dubious to refrain from dealing with an actual and manifest evil because of anxiety that its elimination might lead to the appearance of another evil. Sufficient unto the day is the evil thereof.

> *The best time for fighting for freedom is always now, and the best starting point is always here.*

The standpoint, the question of guarantees of freedom for all, is an important one that needs to be confronted now. It has a bearing on the character of the Constitution and the process whereby the new Constitution is to be brought about. There can, of course, never be absolute guarantees in history. What we do know for sure is that attempting to defend minority privileges by force of arms, whether through the present system, or by means of a constitution based on group rights, can only result in continuing strife and violation of human rights. The only system that has a chance is one based on non-racial democracy. What we need to do is strengthen the prospects as much as possible for it to be brought about as swiftly, securely and painlessly as possible. A democratic constitution is one and entire. It does not have 'own affairs' sections – one set of guarantees for blacks, another for whites.

> *A constitution is a document with an intellectual reach into the future. It is our generation that drafts it in the light of our historical experience and thought of our age, but we consciously attempt to produce something that will last.*

If we wish to break down the habits of thinking in racial categories and encourage the principles of a non-racial democracy, we must produce a constitution that contemplates the rights of all the citizens of our country, not just of a section, however large and however abused in the past. To be effective, the Constitution must be rooted in South African history and tradition. It must draw on the traditions of freedom in communities, not just those who at this historical juncture are in the forefront of the freedom struggle.

There is in fact not a section of the population, whatever its position to•ay, that has not at some time in history fought for free•om.

Many of the foreparents of the whites who live in the country today were refugees from persecution – the Huguenots who fled from massacre in France because of their faith, the Jews who escaped from pogroms and then from Nazi terror. Thousands of English-speaking whites occupying important positions in the professions and public life, volunteered for military service against Nazism and fascism in Europe and later marched in the Torch Commando against the extension of racist rule in South Africa.

South Africa has had an unusually large number of bishops who have been willing to go against the tide, usually stronger in their own churches than outside, as well as of writers and journalists and lawyers and academics and medical people (even at least one freedom-fighting dentist and two road engineers).

There is not an Afrikaans-speaking white family that was not touched by the struggles over the right to speak Afrikaans and to uphold their Afrikaner identity; Boer heroism against the might of the British Empire became legendary throughout the world, and is part of South African patrimony, just as the concentration camps in which thousands of civilians died are part of our shame.

Workers from all over the world, driven by hunger and unemployment, came to work on the mines in South Africa, where they died in huge numbers of lung disease; hundreds fell at the barricades, gun in hand, as they fought against reduction in wages.

*The tra*ition of singing free*om songs as patriots face*
execution was starte by four tra*e unionists who sang 'The
Re* Flag' as they mounte* the gallows.*

Many South African women joined the suffragette movement and challenged the physical, legal, and psychological power of male rule.

Apartheid has distorted this history, subordinating each and every action to its racist context, suppressing all that was noble and highlighting all that was ugly. The ideals of democracy and freedom are presented as white ideals, the assumption being that blacks are only interested in a full stomach, not in questions of freedom. Daily life refutes this notion. It is the anti-apartheid struggle that has kept democracy alive in South Africa. It is not just the number of organisations that have indicated support for a document such as the Freedom Charter that proves this, but the growth of a powerful, alternative democratic culture in the country. The culture of democracy is strong precisely because people have had to struggle for it.

In the last resort, the strongest guarantee of freedom in South Africa lies in the hearts of the oppressed. It is they more than anyone who know what it is like to have their homes bulldozed to the ground, to be moved from pillar to post, to be stopped in the streets or raided at night, to be humiliated because of who their parents are or on account of the language they speak. Inviolability of the home, freedom of movement, the rights of the personality, free speech – they fight for these each and every day. If the Constitution is suffused with the longing of ordinary people for simple justice and peace, then freedom in South Africa is ensured.

Constitutions can have many meanings. In the first place, they establish the structures of government, and lay down how political power is to be exercised. Yet a constitution does much more than indicate the political and legal organisation of the state. It serves as a symbol for the whole of society, as a point of reference for the nation. People like to feel that they have constitutional rights even if they do not exercise them.

The existence of a constitution is an in•ication that society is rule• by stea•y an• known principles an• not by the arbitrary whims of persons. Like the flag, the anthem an• the emblem, the constitution stan•s above everybo•y an• everything an• symbolises a share• patriotism bin•ing on all.

The Constitution can also serve as an educator. Its language is appealed to in all sorts of situations, it is studied in school, it integrates itself into the general culture of the society. The language of freedom in the Constitution becomes part of the discourse of the people. In South African conditions the Constitution will in addition be a compact, solemnly entered into by democratically chosen representatives of all the people, emerging out of strife, with the sense of and commitment to the creation of a set of rules in terms of which all can live together with pride and in peace.

Above all, the Constitution is a vehicle for expressing fundamental notions of freedom, at the conceptual, symbolic and practical levels. In South Africa this aspect has special importance. An effective Bill of Rights can become a major instrument of nation-building. It can secure for the mass of the people a sense that life has really changed, that there will be no return to the oppressive ways of apartheid society, while at the same time it can give to those who presently exercise power the conviction that their basic rights can be guaranteed in the future without recourse to a group rights scheme.

For many years, supporters of majority rule looked with suspicion on the idea of a Bill of Rights and the rule of law. On the other hand, proponents of entrenching fundamental rights and freedoms, balked at the notion of 'one person, one vote'. Two currents that for a long time tended to flow in different directions are now joined together. In turn, solving the questions of political rights and of fundamental liberties makes it possible to give guarantees in relation to the aspect of cultural diversity. All taken together make it possible to contemplate manifestly fair procedures for regulating the process of eliminating the inequalities created by apartheid. The envisaged provisions are not for black South Africans or for white South Africans, but for all South Africans; the last word goes to freedom.

THREE

We Have to Mistrust Ourselves

Preparing Ourselves for Power

FROM *TOWARDS A NEW CONSTITUTION FOR SOUTH AFRICA: ADVANCING HUMAN RIGHTS IN SOUTH AFRICA* | OXFORD UNIVERSITY PRESS | 1992

I start with two poignant sayings I brought back home to South Africa with me after years of exile elsewhere in Africa. The first is: the beautiful people are not yet born. It is the deeply sad observation of a Ghanaian novelist on the disappointments of independence in his country, applicable to Zimbabwe today. The second is even harsher: a rich man's fart smells sweet.

The Kenyan writer Ngũgĩ wa Thiong'o felt this phrase was so apposite to the situation in his country that he used it several times in a recent novel. Young Kenyans could not imagine that the Father of the Nation, Jomo Kenyatta, patriarch, autocrat and amasser of fortunes, had once been a famous freedom fighter who had spent a decade in prison for opposing British colonial domination.

Will the post-aparthei generation feel the same about us?

We who have spent all our lives fighting power, now suddenly face the prospect of exercising it. Many of us are as fearful at the prospect of finding ourselves in office as those presently there are alarmed about giving it up.

At the moment when we are about to see the achievement of what we dreamt of, a kind of sadness rather than joy settles upon us. Where there should be a feeling of elated accomplishment, there is an emotion of disenchantment, in some cases even cynicism. Can it be that apartheid, by depriving us of the satisfaction that should go with its overthrow, will be winning its last victory?

We cannot recapture the élan and conviction of the earlier period. We should not even try. It is as though the political and social pluralism that we now acknowledge in a diverse civil society reflects itself in a corresponding deconcentration and dispersion of our joy.

There is no moment of victory, no VE [Victory in Europe] Day (when we celebrated the defeat of Nazism and end of the Second World War). We move with emotional difficulty from the heroic project of insurrection on a certain day, to the banal scheme of creating good government over a period of time. Is this what all the dreams and pain were for?

Were we wrong in the dark and bitter days of the 1960s and 1970s to declare 'no middle road'? Today we are on the middle road, we help to construct it, eager to demonstrate the broadness of our vision. We even accept it as praise to be called flexible, though we might still flinch a little at being referred to as moderate.

And what is it about authority that causes so many of us to turn our backs on it? The truth is that a great number of us are as fearful of winning as we are of losing. We are confronted with crises of lifestyle. We find ourselves torn from old networks and plunged into new ones.

What is it that we are afraid of?

The dangers as I see them are of a subtle kind, as befits a country that is really far more sophisticated than one would believe from the bizarre caricatures of our people that still unfortunately seem to inhabit the imaginations of most whites.

I worry that the years of protracted struggle will have made us intellectually weary, so that our principal objective becomes that of getting into office and little more.

We should not, of course, underestimate the symbolic value simply of having a government based on majority rule. It is the visible embodiment of the achievement of our slogan: freedom in our lifetime. It is the foundation for allowing a country at peace with itself to evolve. It is the key to South-Africanising South Africa. Indeed, for many of us, taking part in the first democratic elections will be the highpoint of our lives. Yet voting, and even winning the elections, is not enough.

We need a programme, not just the words of a programme, but an actual programme, a coherent programme based on a clear vision, one that will function and that will proceed rapidly and systematically to improve the lives of those who have suffered the most under apartheid.

I fear for intellectual fatigue, a loss of imagination an• élan, a gra•ual •escent into an a• hoc approach an• improvisation.

We are correctly concerned about not making promises that we cannot fulfil. Perhaps this is the good that comes out of disaster, that emanates from the collapse of unsustainable dreams of perfection. Yet the poor are still poor, the oppressed still oppressed.

We enter the Union Buil•ings an• take our places in parliament, sing the longest anthem in the worl•, with verses from 'Nkosi Sikelel' iAfrika' an• 'Die Stem', win •ebate after •ebate, pass law after law, an• still the poor remain poor an• the oppresse• oppresse•.

We become masters and mistresses of defending our positions, explaining away our inability to tackle the problems of the country. We refer quite correctly to the terrible legacy of apartheid and the continuing resistance of the civil service, the selfishness of the business sector and the drag on progress imposed by all the many conservative elements in the country.

Deprived of the vision that we once thought would solve everything at a stroke, and reluctant to replace it with what we had formerly rejected as reformist solutions, we end up with nothing, and the poor remain poor and the oppressed oppressed.

We commemorate days of heroic memory, give each other decorations of one sort or another, remind the people of the years of struggle and sacrifice, launch campaign after highly publicised campaign to deal with all the problems of the country, and the poor still stay poor and the oppressed still stay oppressed.

Having resiste• the bullets an• bombs of lea•, we now face the bullets an• bombs of sugar, an• slowly we succumb to their sweetness. A job for a frien• here, a place for a relative there. A•vance knowle•ge of government •ecisions, buying up lan•, •irecting contracts.

After all, the Nationalists did it to great effect, not to help themselves, of course, but to assist the Afrikaner people. Now-it's-our-turn-ism takes over from ad-hoc-ism. There is no form of corruption that we will be inventing, every variety will already have been used in what will be referred to by some as the good old days. We will simply be carrying on the well-tried practices of previous governments.

If all power corrupts, then people's power corrupts in a popular way. A lucre continua! The poor become angry, the oppresse• chafe. We point out that it is not through a•venturist actions that they will get their rights, that they must take their place in the queue like everybo•y else. They are obstinate, occupy lan•, go on strike, refuse to pay taxes. We sen• in the police, lock up the persons who are agitating them, appeal for national unity, remin• them of the struggle.

We have achieved a great victory. We have deracialised oppression. We have done something that apartheid never succeeded in doing – we have legitimised inequality.

The rich man's fart smells sweet. May it never happen in South Africa that if a once noble veteran of the struggle passes wind, the people declare: what a victory.

The beautiful people are not yet born. Ayi Kwei Armah was right. He might have added: nor will they ever be. Each generation struggles to produce its own beautiful people. We can inherit riches or poverty, power or oppression, but beauty, never. We have to find it in ourselves, generation after generation.

Perfectibility and Corruptibility

FROM *TOWARDS A NEW CONSTITUTION FOR SOUTH AFRICA: ADVANCING HUMAN RIGHTS IN SOUTH AFRICA* | OXFORD UNIVERSITY PRESS | 1992

The human rights concept is based in its substance on human perfectibility and in its procedures on human corruptibility. That is why constitutions are optimistic and pessimistic at the same time. They encourage us to choose the best among us as our leaders, but prepare us for the fact that they may turn out to be the worst.

It cannot be repeated too frequently: all constitutions are based on mistrust. The more devoted we are to our leaders and our organisations, the more we have to be constitutionally mistrustful of them.

It is not only the rascals, corrupt persons and assassins from the past whom we have to mistrust. Nor do we merely have to beware of the millions of so-called ordinary people who have become so steeped in the values and assumptions of apartheid society that they automatically replicate them in slightly disguised form in the post-apartheid world.

We have to mistrust ourselves.

This is not to say that we must see our role only as that of critics permanently in the opposition. Someone has to take responsibility for helping our country regather its strength and begin to function in a decent way for the benefit of all. Nor should any of us regard ourselves as being somehow more holy, more sensitive, more progressive than anyone else.

We do what we are good at. Some of us are good at picking up the human dimension of a problem, at sensing dilemmas and difficulties. We enjoy searching through words and phrases till we find the ones we want. Sometimes we even invent new words if that helps us. We are not afraid to be called romantics and idealists. We know that we can afford to be soft because there are enough hard people around. We judge no one else, in fact we admire persons who have qualities opposite to ours.

What matters is that we do not pretend iron qualities we do not possess, nor do we eliminate any special characteristics we might have for the sake of blending unnoticed into the collective. Rather, we express our thoughts as they come to us. The pleasure lies in placing them in the mix of ideas, sure that they will interact and clash with the thoughts of others. We take our stand on the right to enjoy the right to be wrong; that is, the right to have the satisfaction of advancing an idea and seeing it refuted by a better one.

We are not against leadership, not against government. We are anxious to empower a new government to undo the damage of past governments and to undertake the responsibilities of all governments everywhere in the world to respond to the needs of citizens.

At the same time, we must ensure that the new government functions well and fairly, that it does not become a new source of oppression, alienation and abuse. Oppression can come under any slogans, in any colours, and with any anthem.

No one, neither king nor free•om fighter, has any •ivine right to rule. No one is automatically immune to the se•uctions of power.

Good leaders are conscious of this and struggle for good constitutions, aware of their own fallibility.

The biggest contribution our generation can make will be to provide an enduring link between our past aspirations for freedom and the lived reality of future liberty.

The Constitution should be a glittering shield in which we all see our faces reflected. It is our constitution, for everyone, protector of the weak as well as of the powerful, of the former oppressed and of the former oppressors. It lays down the fundamental terms on which we all live together as equals and compatriots in the same country. It is the document which establishes that everyone matters, everybody counts, that no one is born worthless, or to be the slave or instrument of another.

In South African conditions, a non-racial, non-sexist, democratic constitution is the ultimate antithesis of apartheid, the embodiment of universal sovereignty and the epitome of the equal worth of each one of us. This is so independently of how we look, what language we speak, or where our ancestors came from.

A constitution is therefore not a deal worked out between new victors and new losers about how to share the spoils of office. It is the fulfilment of an historic dream of the oppressed for irreversible deliverance from injustice; it is the reaching out for firm principles that will protect us all from mutual abuse and fratricide in the future; it is the declaration of a set of shared core values that will bind us together because we believe in them and not because they are imposed; it is the means for enabling us to pursue our different interests without knocking each other down, and to resolve our competing claims in a fair and non-destructive manner.

In preparing for the drafting of the terms of our new constitution, we try to involve the widest sections of the population. As Namibia showed, the process of constitution-making can bring out the best in a people and encourage a sense of shared nationhood based upon an acceptance of common values.

A constitution is not a product to be sold to the people through skilful advertising. It is something that emerges from our innar•s, that expresses our highest i•ealism while protecting us from our basest temptations.

For those of us working for human rights in South Africa, the idea of constitutionalism is something new. Our legal tradition, taken from Britain, is one of parliamentary sovereignty. Accordingly, the essence of our struggle has been for the right to be represented on an equal basis in parliament. We fought for the vote, not for a Bill of Rights. Now we recognise the advantages of a Bill of Rights as a means of providing the framework of core values within which parliament operates.

We regard the Constitution as an agreed compact enabling people to live together in a context of secure equality. A Bill of Rights guaranteeing fundamental freedoms for individuals does away with the necessity for special group rights, which, in the circumstances of a country emerging from more than a century of explicit racial domination, would inevitably mean protection of group privileges. We need to ensure that democracy and the Bill of Rights work, and not to seek bizarre constitutional mechanisms to make the whites more equal than anyone else.

If we draw on global principles of human rights we do so not to prove that we can read the documents, or that we are civilised, but because they really speak to and for all of us.

Each freedom struggle is unique, yet the basic human experience of suffering and resistance is the same. Just as there is terrible internationalism in torture and means of mass humiliation and destruction, so we can universalise the organised forces of hope and human goodness.

FOUR

Inventing a Constitution

South Africa's Unconstitutional Constitution: The transition from power to lawful power

SAINT LOUIS UNIVERSITY LAW JOURNAL | VOLUME 41, FALL | 1997

About one month ago, the Constitutional Court of South Africa declared the Constitution of South Africa to be unconstitutional, which I think is a unique jurisprudential and political event in the world. I want to explain how this unusual thing came to pass.

We go back to 1990. We had to shift our country, which at that time was the epitome of division, repression, and injustice – a point of negative reference for anybody who wanted to condemn anything in the world. It was a country that introduced the word 'apartheid' to the English language and international human rights discourse. It was a country that sent death squads across its borders to hurt and torture people to death and that had an organised system of repression that extended into every village and into every nook and cranny of society. It was a country that was racist, authoritarian, and narrow.

> *Whereas before, we ha⬧ the hour of the politician an⬧ the hour of the sol⬧ier, now we ha⬧ the hour of the lawyer. This was our big moment. An⬧ for some things you really only have one chance; for us it was this moment – quite a long moment – an⬧ we ha⬧ to make the best of it.*

This very harsh, racist South Africa had to be converted into a country – with the same people, the same physical terrain, the same resources, and the same buildings – into a country that was democratic and respected human rights. It had to be a country where people of widely different backgrounds would respect each other, where everybody would live in dignity, and where social peace prevailed. This was a not a small task. Just through language you can trace the whole constitutional parabola that followed as we made the best of it. In those days, we used to speak about 'the enemy', later 'the enemy' became 'the regime', then 'the regime' became 'the other side', and now 'the other side' is simply 'the opposition'.

At that same time, people like my comrade and later my colleague, Pius Langa, now Justice Langa [Langa served as deputy chief justice of the Constitutional Court from 2001 to 2005 and as chief justice from 2005 to 2009], were working, within the little space that the South African regime allowed, to bring progressive lawyers of all backgrounds together, not only to critique and challenge the apartheid legal order, but to envisage how law would work and how justice would be served in the new South Africa. All of us in our separate spheres were creating the germs of the constitutional order – in the lives, in the hearts and in the imaginations of countless individual people, so that it would not just be an abstraction when it came, but something already rooted, embryonic and growing.

The importance of a constitutional order was precisely to establish the appropriate relation between organised hope on the one hand, and structured caution on the other. These reflections were based on our life experiences, not on books or classroom lessons, or even talks like this one. We learned these things thinking about the heroism of the people around us, and also their setbacks and betrayals, and by looking at the inspiring emergence of new nations throughout the world, and seeing the difficulties they inherited as well as those they brought upon themselves.

While we were having these debates, Nelson Mandela, who first went to prison in 1962, was in contact with the South African regime, determined to initiate negotiations.

Leaping forward in time to the end of year 1991, I'm wearing this suit, which is the suit I wear for important occasions. I'm in the World Trade Centre outside Johannesburg, slightly different from the New York World Trade Centre – a real dump of a place, in fact, with gloomy, stale air and passionless carpets. I am in a space as big as this courtroom and across the way are other people in suits, perhaps more accustomed to wearing suits than I am. They are now the enemy/regime/South African government and perhaps they feel as strange looking at me as I feel when I look at them. These people had not even been on the scene when I went into exile; they later existed only as names to me, and now we were preparing to talk with each other. Not about whether or not to have a constitution, not 'talks about talks', the kind of talks in which Justice Langa had been directly involved in the past, but talks about the actual substance of an actual constitution.

Many outsiders can tell us how things are done in their country, what works there, what doesn't work there, what's useful, and what is not useful. But we have to look to our own needs, our own problems, our own possibilities and then we extract from other countries those things which we believe will work for us. We don't model ourselves on any other country, but rather absorb and benefit from the experiences and the techniques used in other countries.

We battled over every tiny detail before those talks started, and not just over the agenda. For example: who would control the finances for the talks? The South African government said, 'Well, we are in charge, we will pay for and manage the whole thing'. The side I was on said, 'No – we have to have joint decision-making over the finances'. Who would provide the security? Again the government said, 'Well, we have the security forces, we'll handle the security issues'. The ANC group said, 'No, it has to be joint security'. The ANC security forces and the South African government's security – which had been trying to destroy each other for a long time, trying to find out about the inner workings of the other side, and sometimes quite literally trying to assassinate one another – were working side by side, for the very first time, to protect the process and to make sure that nobody participating in the process was killed. When it came to administrative issues such as who would type up the agendas, the South African government said, 'Well, we've got secretaries, we'll do that'. The ANC side replied, 'No, we will have one, and you will have one'. It was like Noah's ark, we entered the building two by two. I think the only concession made was on the catering, where an outside firm was employed at government expense.

The psychological importance of the battle over these little ₹etails cannot be fully communicate₹; the more banal the issue, the more it represente₹ the unconscious habits of power.

When you have ruled a country, been the boss, been in charge, as your parents were and your grandparents were, and power came out of the barrel of a gun and then through a kind of intellectual/administrative hegemony for centuries afterwards – to suddenly have the formerly dominated and oppressed saying 'no' is quite a shock. When it came to negotiations, the structure and organisation functioned on the basis of engagement between equals. This helped right from the word go to establish the tone and the setting for the intellectual discussions that followed.

Then, there was a widespread assumption that the other side was more experienced in government and constitutional matters, and maybe the ANC required some help from foreign experts. We received many offers of assistance from governments throughout the world to 'level the playing fields'. Perhaps we were arrogant, but we had been through the mill. We had thought, studied, argued, debated, and lived in exile in so many different countries on all the different continents. We had seen how governments worked. Maybe this was one of the few benefits of exile. We could speak all the different languages. We were able to bring all of that together. We were much stronger intellectually, and much more strategically organised than the other side. We suggested politely that if they wished to 'level the playing fields', they should help the South African government.

Soon there was a crisis. We agreed on the process for decision-making and invented some rather interesting terms, such as decision-making by 'sufficient consensus'; that is, enough agreement for the process to go forward.

The negotiators consisted of self-constituted political parties, the South African government, parties inside parliament and all the different administrations and governments set up to support the apartheid policies. On the other side was the liberation movement in its various formations. We had no mandates. There was one party, called the Minority Freedom Front, which had one member in the racist parliamentary structure. This poor chap had to run around from one commission to the other to make sure his voice was heard everywhere. He happened to be a rather talkative person, so an outsider could be forgiven for thinking that he was running the entire negotiations. He came from the same city as Justice Langa – a city famous for the eloquence of its inhabitants.

The first crisis centred upon how the Constitution was to be drafted. Should all of us who were sitting around the table – coming from all the different backgrounds in South Africa – should we draft the Constitution and then put it to the nation in a referendum to give it legitimacy? That was the argument from the South African government and some of their allies. They claimed that that was the purpose of a Constitution – to protect minorities and to make sure the interests of everybody were recognised. The other faction, the ANC-led grouping, said, no, the fundamental constitutional problem in South Africa for centuries had been that the majority of the people were not allowed to decide the type of government they were to live under. It was essentially a problem of self-determination, and unless we held elections to create a constitution-making body that had a mandate from the entire nation, the product which emerged would have no legitimacy and no authority. Then the first group responded: 'But what about us? We will be handing over power to fifty per cent plus one of the people, and they will do what we did to them'.

*In other wor♦s, they argue♦ that because they ha♦ behave♦
so ba♦ly in the past, they nee♦e♦ to write the Constitution
to prevent retaliation in the future. Yet, they ha♦ a point,
an important point, because the Constitution is for the whole
nation. Everybo♦y shoul♦ feel protecte♦ by its character an♦
substance.*

How were we to reconcile these different approaches? They were not
just minor differences, they affected the whole character of the
constitutional negotiations. Our answer was to have a two-stage process
of constitution-making. The first stage was to agree on the process
of transition, including elections and the basis for the elections; to establish
a new government, a new parliament which would elect a new president;
and to have a Bill of Rights that would function in the meanwhile to
protect fundamental rights.

The second stage would be to entrust the new democratically elected
parliament [both houses meeting together] with a constitution-making
function within a framework of principles we could agree on in
negotiations there and then. A two-thirds majority of parliament would
be required for adoption. These agreed-upon principles would ensure
that the Constitution which emerged was a democratic one that
guaranteed fundamental rights and freedoms for everybody and took
account of specific interests and concerns of all the negotiating parties.

*We en♦e♦ up with thirty-four principles. Some of them rea♦
very, very o♦♦ly. You will fin♦ no clear logic to the whole set
of principles, except the logic of being as inclusive as possible
to make everybo♦y feel protecte♦ in the process.*

Four years later, it was the Constitutional Court of South Africa that had
to measure these thirty-four principles against the new text developed
over a two-year period in parliament. Parliament worked literally day
and night to draft the new Constitution. Two years were hardly enough,

yet if you didn't have a cut-off date the process would have gone on forever as people argued about every comma, every word. They were lucky it was a leap year – that gave them one extra day – maybe they would not have finished without that extra day! After working night after night, at the end of the two years, the text was ready to send up to the Constitutional Court.

Who were we, the judges of the Constitutional Court? I want to conclude with a coda of how we were formally inaugurated in a rather small and completely packed room with the eleven judges sitting in a row in the back. The president of the country was sitting with us. The former Minister of Justice, who had been responsible for locking up so many of us, for issuing the banning orders, was also sitting there, as was the new Speaker of the House, and the person who had been presiding over the Constitutional Assembly's drafting of the new Constitution.

Dignitaries, ju•ges an• their families, from all over the country, were jam-packe• into this room, an• Nelson Man•ela rises an• says: 'The last time I stoo• up in court was to fin• out if I was going to be hange•; to•ay I stan• up to inaugurate South Africa's first Constitutional Court'. To show our appreciation, eight months later we struck •own two presi•ential proclamations issue• by Nelson Man•ela.

These were important proclamations – dealing with the foundations, structures and institutional arrangements necessary for South Africa's first democratic elections at the local government level. To summarise a complicated argument [*Executive Council of the Western Cape Legislature an• Others v Presi•ent of the Republic of South Africa an• Others* (CCT 27/95) [1995] ZACC 8; 1995 (4) SA 877 (CC); 1995 (10) BCLR 1289 (CC)], in which a number of different decisions were given, we basically determined that the presidential proclamations were issued in a way that usurped the functions of parliament. Even if parliament had authorised the president to issue the proclamations – their subject matter indicated that they purported to do that – it was something that only parliament itself could do, following proper parliamentary procedures. Therefore the proclamations were unconstitutional. [This case is dealt with in greater detail in Section 7: *A New African Jurisprudence: From abstract judicial rulings to purposive transformative jurisprudence.*] President Nelson Mandela reacted by saying that he had acted on legal advice which he had accepted as correct at the time, but he could now accept that the legal advice was wrong. He then went on to say that he fully accepted the decision of the Court, and would reconvene parliament to pass the necessary legislation, adding that we now lived in a constitutional state, where no one was above the law.

> *Mandela said that he, as president, should be the first to show respect for the Constitution as interpreted by the Court. Some commentators observed that, with the great style and aplomb he had, he converted what others would have seen as a political defeat into a kind of victory, as if to say, 'you see what a marvellous country I am the president of?' It made everybody feel secure and it certainly helped to establish the legitimacy of the Constitutional Court.*

I opened by saying that in October of the next year, this Court of which I'm proud to be a member, declared the Constitution of South Africa to be unconstitutional. We did that because we saw that although the document was a product of the new South Africa – and it established a democratic organisation of our society, set up organs of accountable government and protected fundamental rights – it nevertheless failed to comply completely with the previously agreed-to thirty-four principles. In nine respects, it was deficient, and therefore we could not certify that this new Constitution complied with the principles.

> *The text went back to parliament. Provisions were made, amongst other things, to increase the powers of the provinces*

an• to more fully safeguar• the in•epen•ence of the Public Protector.

The amended text came back to us. We were now in a position to certify the text as meeting all the constitutional requirements.

On 10 December, which you know is Human Rights Day, at a moving public ceremony at Sharpeville, the scene of a brutal massacre in 1960, with many of the survivors of the massacre present, Nelson Mandela signed the new Constitution, and we now live under what we hope has not too inaccurately been called the world's most enlightened Constitution.

FIVE

With Clean Hands and Without Secrets

Why I Supported Amnesty

'HONOURING THE TRUTH IN POST-APARTHEID SOUTH AFRICA' | *NORTH CAROLINA JOURNAL OF INTERNATIONAL LAW AND COMMERCIAL REGULATION* | VOLUME 26, NUMBER 3, SUMMER | 2001

Today, we are still building our nation. Some of us are still learning that a nation is characterised by the diversity of its people. People who speak different languages and are from different cultures, still share certain basic understandings. If we allow bitter division and opposition to continue, even in terms of memories of the past, our future will be based on separation and mistrust.

To me, the biggest gain of our Truth and Reconciliation Commission created by law in the first year of our new democracy was the extent to which it exposed apartheid's so-called 'separate development' as having been something beyond institutionalised racism. The bitterly cruel methods used to sustain it, the lies told, and the misinformation and the deceit involved – all that has come out. It has changed the moral balance in our country and made other kinds of transformations possible. To me, that is the most significant gain. The Truth Commission itself did not create, restore, or established a balance of fairness and trust. Instead, it facilitated these processes. Unless the ideals of the Truth Commission are confirmed in reality by the South African people, so that whites are not living in relative affluence while blacks overwhelmingly are living in poverty, then the full story of the Truth Commission will never be complete. Still, the Commission was part and parcel of a much wider public process that, at the very least, created a moral climate in which it was easier to give social and economic transformation a chance to take place. The Truth Commission was not just an agency that recorded our history, but a landmark chapter in our history.

What are the international implications of South Africa's Truth Commission? Not every country can secure justice by these means. For example, I completely supported the prosecution of General Augusto Pinochet in Chile. There were differences of principle. First, General Pinochet gave himself and his regime amnesty. In South Africa, the main representatives of the oppressed people themselves negotiated and agreed to it. Secondly, General Pinochet never acknowledged the criminality of what had happened – the murders and assassinations. It is that total refusal to bend the knee which created such a profound sense of rancour, a sense of arrogant perpetuation of the denial of the cruelty. In South Africa, the Truth Commission was based upon the acknowledgement that terrible things had happened. Third, the amnesty given in Chile was a blanket one covering all actions perpetrated during a certain period. To receive amnesty in South Africa, each perpetrator had to come forward one by one to tell his or her story. This process put a face on the cruelty. In South Africa, the perpetrators acknowledged their crimes, and shame is/was their punishment.

It is not easy to go home to your children in the evening, who have seen your testimony on television about the bodies that you buried and the lies that you told.

Shame, however, gradually dissipates as one reintegrates into society. In Chile, the perpetrators have been shielded from their lies and their shame. These differences indicate that one cannot adopt a categorical position with respect to international criminal courts or truth commissions. Without the threat of prosecution in South Africa, no one would have come forward to the Commission. A simple calculation was made: 'I might be prosecuted. I might go to jail. I am given this opportunity'.

At the en▪ of the ▪ay, we learne▪ information that we woul▪ never have known otherwise, information that woul▪ have remaine▪ behin▪ a wall of total silence.

I believe that the international community should support the International Criminal Court. I would like to see all the nations of the world, the United States included, place themselves within its jurisdiction. At the same time, truth commissions (and there have been over twenty) have a considerable role to play alongside, and sometimes instead of, ordinary prosecution.

There are many circumstances where prosecution is impossible because history has move▪ on an▪ there is no one left to prosecute. But in these situations, storytelling is still necessary an▪ acknowle▪gment is still vital. It enables people to feel they are in the same country, not two, three, four, or five separate countries boun▪e▪ by separate memories.

Meeting the Man who Organised a Bomb in my Car

INTERNATIONAL CENTRE FOR ETHNIC STUDIES CONFERENCE | FROM
VIOLENT CONFLICT TO PEACEFUL COEXISTENCE | COLOMBO, SRI LANKA |
27 FEBRUARY 2014

It was about fifteen years ago; I'm sitting at the Constitutional
Court in Johannesburg in my chambers. The phone rings, and a
voice says, 'It's reception here, there's a man called Henri who says
he has an appointment to meet you'. I say, 'Send him through'.
And as I walk down the corridor to the security gate, my heart's
going *boom, boom, boom.* Henri had telephoned me a week before
to say that he was the security officer who organised the placing
of the bomb in my car, which blew up when I was in exile in
Mozambique, and cost me my right arm and the sight of an eye.

He was now going to the Truth Commission; was I willing to speak to
him before he went there? And I said 'Yes'. I open the door, and I see
this man; he's tall and thin like myself. A bit younger. He's looking at me,
and I'm looking at him. And I see in his eyes, 'so this is the man I tried
to kill', and he sees in my eyes, 'so this is the man who tried to kill me'.
We'd never met, we'd never fought, we'd never argued over love, money,
power, passion … But he was on that side, and I was on this side. And
he'd tried to kill me, and now he was going to the Truth Commission. As
we walk to my chambers, he is striding like a soldier, and I do my best to
use my judge's ambulation to slow him down. We come to my office, and

we talk, we talk, we talk, we talk, we talk, and eventually I say, 'Henri, I have to get on with my work'. I stand up, and I say, 'Normally, when I say goodbye to somebody, I shake that person's hand. I can't shake your hand. But, go to the Truth Commission. Tell them what you know, and maybe, maybe, maybe, we will meet again one day'. And when we walked back to the security gate, I noticed he was shuffling along, without that firm stride he'd had when he'd come in. He went out. Bye-bye Henri.

Now what was this Truth Commission to which he was going to go? The story goes back to six months before the first democratic elections, which I'm sure many of you would have seen on television in the programmes marking the death of Nelson Mandela. It was the first time black and white were voting together as equals in South Africa. About six months before that, the National Executive Committee of the ANC, of which I was a member, had a meeting near Johannesburg – about eighty of us at a very, very, very, impassioned meeting.

The issue was what to do about a report that had been transmitted to the National Executive prepared by what we called the Motsuenyane Commission. We had set it up to examine claims that the ANC had used torture during the liberation struggle; that we had held captured enemy agents in camps in Angola where the ANC guerrillas were, and that the captives had been subjected to very, very rough, abusive physical treatment. And the report said that prima facie evidence established that indeed this had happened. And it recommended in no uncertain terms that the ANC follow up against those responsible. The events would have happened in 1981–83. We are now speaking about it in 1993, discussing the recommendation that we must take steps to deal with the use of torture by the ANC in exile ten years before.

The ANC's position was to condemn torture unconditionally. We were freedom fighters fighting for life – how could we be against life? But what to do now, ten years later when we had got back home? Some of us stood up and we asked for the Motsuenyane report to be implemented. 'They've reported, we must follow through'. And others said, 'No, you've got to understand the circumstances. Our guards were young, they were untrained. They'd given up their studies to go and fight for freedom. They did what they thought they had to do in the situation, because that's what happened to them when they were captured by the South African Police. And it would be unfair to take action against them now'.

And I remember Pallo Jordan, one of the leading intellectuals in the movement, standing up and saying: 'Comrades, I've learned something very interesting today, there's a thing called "regime torture", and that's bad, and there's "ANC torture", and that's okay. Thank you for enlightening me!' And then somebody rose and said: 'What would my mother say?' Now 'my mother' was a figure we often used in our discourse in the ANC. 'My mother' would be an African woman with maybe four years schooling, not much knowledge about the world, but with a very strong sense of right and wrong. 'What would my mother say?' And he answered: 'My mother would say there's something very strange about this organisation. It's quite correctly examining its own failures, but what about what racist governments have been doing to us for decades, for centuries? Where is the balance, where is the fairness in simply picking on our people who misbehaved and not on the others?'

It was shortly after that Professor Kader Asmal stood up and said: 'Comrades, what we need is a truth commission'. Now this was one of those issues – how to deal with torture – that you can't resolve by a show of hands. This was a deep moral issue, requiring an understanding of the context and what it means for the organisation and who you are and how you stand on matters of principle. Kader said: 'There's got to be a truth commission in South Africa, when we have democracy, after we've voted, that examines not only what our people did to the relatively few captives in our hands, but also the experiences of thousands and thousands of people who were tortured, victimised, assassinated by the regime'. And suddenly we knew that was the answer. It wasn't a problem just for our organisation, it was a problem for the nation, the whole nation, across the board.

So paradoxically, ironically, the Truth Commission was set up not by an ANC government wanting to expose the crimes of the previous regime. It was set up by freedom fighters anticipating that they would sooner or later be in the government, wanting to help the ANC usher in our new democracy with clean hands; with no secrets; with nothing to hide.

We wished to find a way of dealing with the atrocities of the past, whoever had committed them, as a nation. That was element number one.

Element number two of the process also emerged in a surprising and paradoxical way. We have signed the interim constitution and are heading for elections. And I'm invited by a body in London called the Catholic Institute of International Relations, who'd given us a lot of support, to report to them on the new Constitution. I say, 'Fine', and fly to London. They put me up at a little hotel; a spartan little hotel in Kings Cross. And its quality is relevant to the story. I'm amused because as the constitutional negotiations advanced, our accommodation improved. For the last eleven days we had been in a Holiday Inn Garden Court Hotel. But now in London I'm back to my grassroots lodgings. I'm tired, I'm about to go to sleep, and there's a knock on the door. 'Terribly sorry to disturb you, Professor Sachs, but a fax has arrived from South Africa; it's very urgent, can you look at it?' And the fax said that there was a crisis that could jeopardise the elections. The generals and the leaders of the security forces in South Africa had said that President de Klerk had offered them an amnesty if we got democracy in South Africa. Then they read the text of the Constitution and saw nothing in it about amnesty. And they stated that they had protected the constitution-making process (and we knew that they had) and added that they knew of plans by extreme right-wing groups to bomb the elections to smithereens; many of their members were risking their lives to get information that would help protect the elections. But to ask them to protect the elections and then go to jail afterwards, that was too much. They weren't threatening a coup, they weren't saying they would take over the country, they weren't holding a gun to anybody's head. They simply said: 'We will resign our commissions, we'll go abroad, that's the only realistic alternative we have'. And the ANC head office fax, maybe even coming from Mandela, indicated a certain measure of sympathy implying that President de Klerk hadn't come clean in his dealings with his security people. I remember after reading the document – because this little hotel didn't have a fax machine; it didn't even have paper – I turned the paper over and wrote on the back: 'We can't give a general amnesty, a blanket amnesty. But could we not link amnesty to the Truth Commission? So that if people come forward one by one and tell their stories truthfully, then they can get amnesty on an individual basis'.

The fact is that we didn't set up a Truth Commission in some abstract way to deal with the problems of the past. It arose out of three very specific needs. 1. The ANC needed to come clean about its own failures. 2. Some mechanism had to be found to enable the security people to carry on protecting our process. 3. At a purely practical level, we needed to avoid having endless trials clogging up the justice system; where would you find the evidence, and who would you charge – the one who pulled the trigger, the one who switched on the electric machine, the one who ordered it, the one who made it, the politician in charge, the president of the country? The complicity was so wide that whole sections of the country would be engaged in endless prosecutions. So we had very strong practical motives for producing a process with a defined date of closure.

My friend, Dullah Omar, one of the lawyers on the National Executive, was made the first minister of justice. He spent almost the whole of his first year just working on the Act dealing with the Truth Commission. It was adopted in terms of a clause placed towards the end of the Constitution, called an epilogue, which I preferred to call the post-amble. And the post-amble was poetic, it wasn't in technical legal language. It spoke about acknowledging the untold injustices of the past, but responding to them not in a spirit of vengeance or retaliation, but in a spirit of ubuntu and reconciliation. Ubuntu is a word derived from African culture that that means 'I'm a person because you're a person'. My humanity is dependent on the recognition of your humanity. It implies that we don't exist as isolated human beings; though each of us is an individual person, we live in a society with other human beings. So my acknowledgment of your humanity enriches my humanity and does not diminish it. The word ubuntu was used in the epilogue to the Constitution, which said that the new parliament would establish the processes for dealing in the spirit of ubuntu with the crimes of the past committed in the course of the political conflict.

The Truth Commission as it emerged, then, had both a constitutional and statutory foundation. In drafting the law, we drew very heavily on Chilean experience. José Zalaquett, a famous human rights lawyer from Chile, came to South Africa to share that country's experiences with us. We learnt a lot from him about what they had done in his country, but we didn't copy the Chilean model and then add a few South African ingredients. Instead, we created our own Truth Commission, building on their experience.

It was structured around three different bodies. It was important that they functioned separately. The first was the one that heard the testimonies of people who had suffered. They came from all sides. This structure travelled around the country, headed by Archbishop Desmond Tutu. It didn't just sit in beautiful rooms, town halls. It went to little school rooms, church halls, into the communities. And it heard the stories of people who had suffered terrible trauma themselves, or who told of the loss of people close to them. It was so important for our country to listen to them. Ten thousand people testified, gave oral accounts. Another ten thousand sent in written testimonials. Overwhelmingly, they were people who had suffered at the hands of the apartheid regime. But it also included people who had suffered as a result of being placed in captivity by the ANC, or from injuries produced by bombs that the ANC had used. As Tutu said, 'it enabled the little people to speak.' This was for the people who had never been listened to. It's so much part of human dignity to have your pain, your suffering, the things you have gone through, the trauma you felt you could never get beyond, acknowledged. And we had very, very, telling testimony. It is important to note that you weren't relating your story to get damages, on the basis that the more you suffered the more you'd get. Nor were you telling your story to send someone to jail. You were telling your story just to tell your story. That was the one section of the Truth Commission.

The second section dealing with granting amnesty, was more formal. It had two judges and I think three lay people on it. The criteria for the granting of amnesty were laid down. Basically it dealt with conduct, usually secret, that had violated the law as it stood at the time. However bad apartheid law had been, it had never openly allowed the use of torture. It had never formally permitted assassination. In order to get an amnesty, you had to come forward and you had to reveal the truth of what you had done. And your actions had to have been related to the political conflict. Several thousand people applied. Most of them were in prison for things like robbing banks, who said, we were black people fighting the white racists, and we robbed the bank to help our people. They didn't get amnesty; their conduct might have had a political background, but it wasn't undertaken as part of the political conflict. The majority of the people who testified came from the security forces.

I still remember vividly Sergeant Benzien in Cape Town, my city, asking for amnesty.

This man ha• once ha• the power of life an• •eath over his captives. Someone he ha• torture• sai• simply to him: 'Sergeant Benzien, show us how you put a wet bag over our hea•s'. An or•erly went on the groun•, a bag, not a wet one, was put over his hea•, an• the sergeant kneele• on his back.

Tony Yengeni, formerly an underground operative of the ANC, now a member of parliament, told the Truth Commission: 'I thought I was suffocating, drowning'. And as Sergeant Benzien stood up, he started crying. We saw it on television, we saw his tears. This man who'd had power of life and death, was now crying. And he was crying because he'd been asked by Tony Yengeni, 'How can one human being do this to another human being?' Now the whole nation was asking this question, 'How can one human being do this to another human being?' The sergeant was crying because his whole world had collapsed. Before, he had got a medal, promotions. Now, he suddenly realised, 'No, this was not the way, I was doing it in defence of apartheid, and the very people whom I was torturing, are now giving me an opportunity to carry on with my life through telling the truth. And I thought I was doing this to evil terrorists who had to be destroyed.'

The third structure of the Truth Commission was the section that dealt with reparations. My own view is that it was the least successful of all three. It focused too much on money, identifying who the 'victims' were, and indicating how much money should be paid. I'm sorry to say, I don't think the South African government responded graciously and generously. The attitude was, 'we all suffered under apartheid, millions and millions over the centuries. To give a huge hand-out just for this one group that had come forward, somehow, we don't feel that's appropriate'. I feel they underestimated the moral, symbolic significance of the special form of suffering,

> ... but the real problem wasn't even about the money an• the timing. The real problem was that reparations shoul• have been in the form of actions that reache• into the imagination, the soul, the spirit of human beings. There will never be enough money.

You can never pay it quickly enough, and the money is soon spent. But gardens of remembrance, and assistance for people who have been disabled because of what had happened to them, and stipends for their children to get schooling to make up for loss of breadwinners, and creative things like libraries, and a bridge – these things are memorable things. One beautiful example was a bridge used by workers to get over the railway lines, named after one young guy who'd fought to the death as part of the freedom struggle. In Chile, President [Patricio] Aylwin [1918–2016], who wasn't even from Pinochet's group, sent a personal letter signed by himself to everybody who'd suffered under General Pinochet's military dictatorship, saying in the name of the new democratic Chilean government, 'I express my emotional feeling for you who have suffered so much in the conflicts of the past'. That was imaginative. It might seem like just a little piece of paper, but it's different from just money, just cash. I think we didn't equal the Chileans in that particular regard.

The value of the Truth Commission is contested in South Africa. People on the more radical side say that we allowed criminals to walk free – how could we let that happen? Or they say, 'You make the Truth Commission sound as if the only aspects of apartheid worth examining and exposing are the violations of rights by the security forces.'

But what about the system of apartheid itself that dislodged people from their land and their homes? And the deep systemic forms of economic exploitation? I think that's a powerful consideration, but an unfair critique. It wasn't the function of the Truth Commission to deal with the systemic violence and injustice of apartheid. The Truth Commission was there to deal precisely with atrocities. That was all.

If you can't get these extreme sources of pain out of the way, there's so much continuing rancour, so much pain, so much anger, so much emotion, that you can't even reach a proper historical analysis of the structured and institutionalised injustices. As for the deeper, more enduring transformations required, that's what the vote is designed to correct, and what parliament is for. It's the function of parliament then, of the whole society and civil society organisations, to deal with systemic structured forms of domination. But the secret, hidden atrocities of the past, that was for the Truth Commission to expose and manage.

Then there were people from a more conservative side who had a different critique. Their principal contention was there hadn't been due process of law in the Commission proceedings. Yet the strength of the narratives came precisely from their spontaneity. People could tell their stories without interruption. We did indeed introduce some due process elements. Thus, anybody mentioned negatively in a witness's statement had the right to bring counsel to question the testimony. But overwhelmingly the power and the glory of the process came from the manner in which it permitted people to stand up and tell their stories in their own voices in their own way.

An incontestable contribution of the Truth Commission was its role in preventing denialism. One of the worst features about covert atrocities is that the people responsible, and often their children and grandchildren, deny that they happened at all. They continue the denial for generations, and this keeps alive the pain, which never goes away. The society remains psychically divided. There's a kind of continuing insult and agony through the refusal to even acknowledge that these terrible things happened. Fortunately, no one in South Africa can now say that apartheid was simply a failed experiment. No one can deny its deep cruelty because we've heard about the evil things done in its enforcement from the mouths of the defenders of apartheid themselves. They testified in person, not because they were being tortured, not because they were being offered plum jobs, but simply because they wanted to come forward and tell the truth and get amnesty. It was vital to have at least the elements of a common understanding emerging about basic themes of our history. We couldn't have had a nation in South Africa without that. If you have a black memory and white memory, the whites saying, 'Well it wasn't so bad. We had a few bad apples, the system was unfair. But now, that's the past, let's move on'. And black people remember that it was their fathers, and aunties, and mums, and so on, who suffered terrible pain that's not even being acknowledged. It was a deeply cruel way in which human beings were treated by other human beings. If you don't acknowledge that, it becomes hard for us to find the generosity we are longing to express. Part of the freedom we fought for was to have freedom from anger. It is not easy to move forward if the pain remains with us.

In South Africa we have never had even a pretence of a common history. Even our history books were different; the history books for white kids, the ones I had in my school, were quite different from the history books for black kids. How can you build a nation, have a common citizenship, if people's memories are so totally divided, and there aren't points of commonality in the way we understand our past? At least let there be the ingredients of a common narrative, common appreciation. Otherwise the imaginative separation continues apartheid in our minds forever. So that was one aspect of the Truth Commission that is of enormous significance for us.

Can we say the Truth Commission brought about reconciliation in South Africa? Yes and no. Yes, it removed a huge impediment and blockage. We're beginning to live in the same country, to be on the same map. Getting the vote was a fantastic ingredient and symbol of common citizenship. But more was required. We needed to feel that the country belonged to all of us, and that we all belonged to the same country.

We're beginning to inhabit that same land, where the pain of some is the pain of all, where injustice is injustice, racism is racism, and cruelty is cruelty. That has been important. Because if you're living with suppressed rancour in your heart, you can't start passing legislation based on inclusive and comprehensive transformation. Everything you do is going to be coloured by your anger.

Whichever side you're on, you can't be objective, you can't have a nation-wide vision. In that sense the Truth Commission process helped remove huge impediments to developing that nationwide vision. That sense of facing our history was extremely important and we had the courage and strength as a nation to do it. It's not a sign of weakness to have a Truth

Commission. It's a sign of strength. A sign of great moral strength, that we have the capacity to examine, explore, come to terms with unacceptable things that we did, and to acknowledge what we, on all sides, had been responsible for, in varying degrees. So in that sense, it played a huge role in allowing processes of reconciliation to move forward.

> *And yet, and yet ... At the end of the hearings, overwhelmingly the people who had suffered the most would have to walk back to their homes, often shacks. And the security officials who'd done most of the torture, even if it wasn't easy for them to stand up and acknowledge on television what they'd done, would afterwards hop into their Toyotas and drive home. There's still a massive sense of inequality in our country, directly associated with race, reflecting who was advantaged and who was disadvantaged in the past. Until we really overcome those inequities, we'll never have full reconciliation.*

Pride in our nation's achievements came out very strongly at the time of Mandela's death. But massive problems still remain. Many we inherited but others we have made worse ourselves, and we've got to take responsibility for that.

What would I say were the key elements of our Truth Commission experience that could be replicated elsewhere? The first potentially transportable element is that no participants in a situation of conflict should automatically be assumed to be wholly without fault. The process has to be across the board. I might mention that when, many years ago, a truth commission for the former Yugoslavia was being proposed by civil society organisations, I suggested that it would be hopeless to simply look into the crimes of the Serbs, or the Croats, or the Muslims. Rather, the truth-telling had to be across the board.

The second possible exportable aspect of the process related to the public nature of the Truth Commission's proceedings. I tell the following story against myself. Following on the Chilean experience, I had argued that evidence should be given behind closed doors, otherwise you'd never get the truth, you'd never get the torturers and the killers and the assassins to come forward. However, civil society people like yourselves responded by saying: 'We don't like this Truth Commission thing, we want accountability; we want people to go to jail. But you seem to be insistent on having it, and if you're going to have it, at least let it be in public.' And fortunately, Albie Sachs was overruled, and fortunately, I repeat, the legislation provided for the proceedings to be held in public. That turned out to be absolutely vital. The report of the Truth Commission came out afterwards. It's a beautiful report, well worth reading. It's well written, it's vivacious, and not just a dull technocratic report. But, nobody reads it. Everybody remembers Sergeant Benzien crying, and moments like that. It was our people expressing themselves in memorable and totally recognisable ways, that's what we recall.

Even the security people giving evi•ence in their suits, with their little moustaches, intoning their wor•s robot-like as if giving testimony in a court of law – I wishe• sometimes they'• been more relaxe•, an• more open, an• more warm, an• more human – even they were true to form as they •elivere• their statements in a stiff an• formal way. It was important that they •i• ben• the knee, an• make some acknowle•gement that they'• •one awful things.

Participation in the Truth Commission processes was expressed in the body language of our people, we saw our nation there. It was like a huge drama unfolding in front of our eyes. I would say that's the second crucial element.

A third essential element that could travel well was good leadership. It was important to have people of the calibre of Archbishop Desmond Tutu, supported by Alex Boraine, who had also been a minister of religion conducting the Truth Commission. Their team was broadly based. It excluded prominent political activists, but included persons from many faith communities as well as people who were not religious at all. Parliament chose very carefully.

As Tutu woul• say, the commissioners were not neutral – you can't be neutral on torture, you hate it. But you're impartial in the way you listen to everybo•y.

You don't make up your mind about anybody in advance. The diversity and the balanced and wisely led nature of the Truth Commission was crucial to its success. The credibility of any truth commission will, accordingly, be dependent not only on the terms of its remit, but on the care with which its members are chosen, the integrity and wisdom of its public representatives, and the impartial manner in which it functions.

And the last and possibly the most important transferable feature of the Truth Commission was that it was not expected to carry the whole burden of our history and function in isolation from other processes of transformation in our country. If there hadn't been political transformation in South Africa – universal suffrage, the reconstruction of our vision of parliament, a whole new constitutional order that completely reconceived and reimagined South Africa – the Truth Commission would have got almost nowhere. Overall, what gave it its very special meaning in South Africa was that it was part of a wider process of dealing with the root problems that had led to the conflict.

So it's the end of the year, a hot day like today here in Colombo, and I'm tired. A friend of mine says we must go to a party organised by some film people, and I must relax. I go with her. The band is playing loudly. There's a big crowd. And I hear a voice shouting: 'Albie! Albie!' Wow, it's Henri [the security officer who organised the placing of the bomb in my car]! I haven't seen him for almost a year. He's beaming as he comes up to me, absolutely elated. And we get into a corner to be away from the music. Excitedly he tells me: 'I went to the Truth Commission, and I spoke to Bobby (it was Bobby Singh), and Sue (Sue Rabkin), and Farouk (Farouk

Mahomed) and I told them everything I knew. And that you said maybe, one day'. And I said, 'Henri, I've only got your face to tell me that what you're saying is the truth'. And I put out my hand, and I shook his hand. He went away absolutely beaming. And I almost fainted. And that should be the end of my story. But the truth doesn't end at any particular point.

I heard afterwards that he had been invited to the party given by film people interviewing him as one of the few soldiers who had gone to the Truth Commission. He was enjoying himself enormously, I was told, when suddenly he left, went home and cried for two weeks. And that moved me.

Henri is not my friend. I won't phone him up and say, let's have a drink or go to a movie together. But if I'm sitting in a bus and Henri sits down next to me, I'll say, 'Oh Henri, how are you getting on?' Somehow, this whole process enabled us to live together in the same country. We can acknowledge each other and feel some kind of connection. And to that extent I feel that the Truth Commission liberated me from the lurking mystery of that abstract thing, 'the enemy', that had tried to kill me. And now, it's this guy, Henri, who's struggling to get on with his life in the new South Africa. And somehow I feel just a little bit stronger in myself, thanks to the Truth Commission; just a little bit better and more human than I'd been before.

Soft Vengeance

JOURNAL OF THE AFRICAN LITERATURE ASSOCIATION [USA] | VOLUME 8, NUMBER 2 WINTER/SPRING | 2014

The three Ls: Literature, Liberation, Law. I'm going to add a fourth L. OK – and a fifth L: Love and Life. I'm going to tell you a story about a story about a story. And just to give you a little advance notice, there will be two diversions involving two great Americans who influenced my life. I'm going to give you their initials to see if you can anticipate. The one is PR, and the other is HW.

The story about the story about the story:

After the bomb, it took me some time to get better. I was flown to England. I travelled first class for the first time in my life, but I was unconscious. I ended up in a London hospital, which was quite amusing because I was under an assumed name, no one was to know where I was, so I would say I was in a London hospital but would refuse to give its name. Its name? The London Hospital!

And I got better. I learned to sit up. On a marvellous day after about six weeks – my heel had been shattered, and I was as nervous as anything – the physiotherapist says, 'Now you're going to stand'. I'm on the edge of the bed, I move forward – that moment of courage when you thrust through your fear. I'm on my feet, and I see my head in a mirror in front of me – shaven, scarred, bandaged, looking very, very serious – going up, and I see my head coming down again. Slowly, he's back! Look, Mummy,

I can stand! That same sense of doing it on your own for the first time as a little child. And then to walk. And I'm getting better.

But there were times early in the morning when I'd wake up feeling very alone. The painkillers are wearing off and I'm totally alone: no hospital people around, no cheerful nurses, and I feel isolated and a little bit sore. And I would be singing to myself [deepens voice, sings], 'It's me, it's me, Oh Lord, standing in the need of prayer. It's me, it's me, Oh Lord, standing in the need of prayer'. And this is where the first great American comes in – PR.

Paul Robeson. So, secular, secular, secular Albie is singing what used to be called a 'negro spiritual' from Paul Robeson. Robeson was our hero in South Africa. He had for us that same legendary status that Mandela has in the United States. And it wasn't just that he was tall and imposing and impressed people. There was something about his moral stature and his capacity for embracing everybody. So similar. We adored Paul Robeson in South Africa. And it's a bit off, you know, that you don't all even know who Paul Robeson was. It kind of amazes me, you know? And he had a very direct influence on our struggle. I discovered afterwards that when Professor ZK Matthews was studying at the Theological College in New York, he met with Paul Robeson and Paul Robeson said to him, 'You people in the ANC, the anti-apartheid struggle, are spending so much time denouncing apartheid – quite right. But what about projecting your vision of a future free South Africa?' And, I was told that the idea of the Freedom Charter, which ultimately became the guiding light of the struggle in South Africa, was born in New York during this discussion between Paul Robeson and Professor ZK Matthews, who went on to become the first African head of Fort Hare University.

'It's not my brother or my sister, but it's me, Oh Lord, standing in the need of prayer. It's me, it's me, Oh Lord, standing in the need of prayer. It's me, it's me, Oh Lord, standing in the need of prayer'. I thought I would get a few more voices to join in.

Now, in the youth movement I belonged to I had quite a deep bass voice, so I could sing the Paul Robeson songs. One of the songs I had learned was the Chinese national anthem. 'Arise! You who refuse to be bond slaves'. And what's amusing is we had the vice-president of the Chinese Supreme Court visiting the Constitutional Court in South Africa a few years ago, and his delegation was sitting on one side of the table – very, very serious. We were sitting on the other side of the table – very, very serious – and I suddenly sang, 'Arise!' and they looked at me in astonishment. They realised I was singing the anthem, big smiles came out and we got on quite marvellously afterwards.

The nurses would come down – 6, 6:30. Cheerful, my spirits were going up again – get through the day. And then one day, I got a note from my comrade, Bobby Naidoo, who could also have been a victim of the bomb in Maputo – ten years on Robben Island he had been.

> 'Dear Comra♦e Albie, we will avenge you!' An♦ I think, 'Bobby, what ♦o you mean? Are we going to cut off their arms? Blin♦ them in one eye? What kin♦ of country woul♦ we be living in?' An♦ I say to myself, 'If we get ♦emocracy in South Africa, if we get free♦om an♦ equality an♦ justice for everyone, that will be my soft vengeance. Roses an♦ lilies will grow out of my arm'.

And a couple of weeks later, somebody came to me very excited, 'Have you heard? They've captured one of the persons who put the bomb in your car, Albie'. And I think to myself, 'If he's put on trial, and if the evidence is insufficient to prove that he actually did it and he is acquitted, that will be my soft vengeance'. Because that meant living under the rule of law, and that is much more important than one rascal getting sent to jail.

I don't know if it's all of us South Africans, but this South African has spent a lot of time turning the negativity of disaster into the positivity of hope. So I'm starting to begin to think – I wrote a book about my jail experience, *The Jail Diary of Albie Sachs*, and I wrote a second book about my experience again in solitary confinement, sleep deprivation, torture, *Stephanie on Trial*. I had to write another book. And the ideas were slowly beginning to shape themselves into a narrative, and I knew what the title of the book would be: *The Soft Vengeance of a Free•om Fighter.*

And in fact the opportunity, my first chance to write it, came after I got out of the hospital. Several months later, I was at Columbia University in New York – the same university where Robeson had been – and I wondered, 'Can I do it?'

I've just got my left han• now, but computers, personal computers are coming in. I'm nervous as anything. I type out a couple of pages, an• I know. I can •o it. I can •o it!

And so the manuscript of *Soft Vengeance of a Free•om Fighter* was typed out high up in a flat on – I forget – the thirteenth, fourteenth floor or something – in a building near Columbia University. Title page: *Soft Vengeance of a Free•om Fighter.* We're still in exile, but now it's a time for envisaging and imagining a new South Africa.

First came *imagining* the soft vengeance, then *living* the soft vengeance. And we return from exile. Mandela's been released; the ANC, PAC [Pan Africanist Congress], Communist Party have been unbanned. We could come back home! It's part of that fabulous life that starts with surviving the bomb and feeling triumphant, and now we are returning home, not begging for anything, but returning home knowing we are on the road to achieving the things we've been fighting for.

The Constitutional Committee of the ANC is very active. We're invited to talk all over the world, to see different constitutional systems at work – interestingly enough, every country that invited us assumed that they had the best constitution. Even England, which doesn't have a constitution! And we come to the United States of America and this is where the HW diversion comes in. Any guesses? I'll make it easy. Chicago. Yes. Harold Washington! Sadly, Harold Washington had died, we didn't meet him, but his aura was there. The memories were there; they were memories of hope, of breakthrough, of possibilities. And a phrase that he used was passed on to us, I might not get it exactly right, but the sense of it was, and it was so relevant to us in South Africa: 'No one', he would say to the people of Chicago, 'no one – whoever you are – can escape my fairness'. And that's exactly what we're thinking in South Africa: no one, whatever you've done, whoever you've been, will escape our fairness. We don't want to be like you, only stronger; we don't want to say, 'Now it's our turn'. It isn't simply about getting into power. It is about transforming the very character of society, and feeling the power and strength of that transformation. It's not based simply on force. It's based on core moral ideals that can work in practice, and bring people together instead of dividing them.

And so the fable continues. Imagine you are helping to write your country's constitution! I heard from US Supreme Court justice, Harry Blackman, a story told to him by Thurgood Marshall about the time when people were writing the Constitution in Philadelphia: 'It's not true that my ancestors were not in on the constitution-making process. They were there in breeches and carrying trays'.

Now in South Africa, we are all making the Constitution. And look at us! All our skills are being used not simply to undermine apartheid, or to trip up the enemy, or to denounce the people who were aggressors, but to create the vision of the country we want to live in. It's why we would go to jail, it's why, in my case, I lost an arm. It's what makes sense of the pain. It takes on meaning, it's all validated, by the accomplishment and achievement of the ideals that brought us into danger in the first place.

And so we draft a new Constitution. Many people died before we got the Constitution, even while the Constitution was being drafted. But we got it. The whole world had predicted a total bloodbath in South Africa, and yet peacefully, if with difficulty, we negotiated a new Constitution.

And in fact, that's not enough to end the story of fables: we create a Constitutional Court. This is the body that's now going to ensure that the principles of the Constitution are applied in practice. And I'm one of those people called to serve on it. It's beyond a dream: the very things you've been fighting for in the muddy trenches of the struggle, and now you're one of the guardians of the product of that dream. And if that's not enough, we have to decide what kind of building we're going to work in, and where it will be. And we choose to place our new Constitutional Court building in the heart of the only prison in the world where both Gandhi and Mandela had been locked up. Now, if that's not an example of soft vengeance, then I don't know what is.

It's not denying the past, it's not saying it didn't happen, ignoring the history that shaped our despair and hope.

> I was reading a very nice brochure about this Marriott Hotel, saying: 'Oh what a beautiful place Charleston is!' But there's no mention of slaves here, no mention of struggles, no mention even of the Civil War which started here! You've just got details of pretty buildings and lovely gardens and this very important port, and I feel it's eviscerating your own history.

I urge you not to be ashamed of your history, but to find a way of facing up to it and making it present as part of your ongoing sense of who you are. And that's what we were doing as intensely as we could. If you want to have a court that is upholding the fundamental rights of everybody, you place it right in the heart of the site of the deepest pains society has had, unafraid. You have transformed the negativity into positivity. Turned the energy that's lying in the ground – you don't say cover it up, deny it, and suppress it, it didn't happen, forget it. You say, 'Yes, the energy is there, and now it must become energy for transformation and change'.

I often have the vision of a waterfall with the water thundering down, crashing down, and it gets caught in the funnels of the turbine and the turbines spin and convert the energy, the brutal kinetic energy, into positivity, turning it into light, into heat.

So my *Soft Vengeance of a Freedom Fighter* is having quite reasonable sales, and getting good reviews. I meet Vanessa. She comes from a different generation – hadn't herself been actively involved in the struggle. She has a brightness, a vitality, I find immediately attractive, and we get talking. We go our separate ways. She disappears and I forget about her. What I don't know is that somebody has told her, 'Albie seemed to take a real shine to you'. And she claims to have said, 'Who's Albie?' I must say that given my appearance, I find that hard to accept. But her story is that she was advised to read my book. So now my book becomes a chapter in the story of our lives.

And she said she had just come out of a very abusive relationship and she found that my book was speaking very, very directly to her: a man who could cry, who could speak about things inside of himself. As time passed, she placed the book next to her bed at night and when she was feeling a little bit lonely she would read a couple of passages.

And then we bump into each other by pure chance at possibly the least romantic place in the whole world: the business-class lounge of Johannesburg airport. And she decides to make a move. And the next thing we're meeting at a party that she'd helped to organise, and we just hit it off. More time passes, we start living together, and then another book comes out. It's called *The Free Diary of Albie Sachs*. And it describes the journey we take together in Europe where I'm reminiscing about a lot of the experiences I had had during the struggle. We travel to meet different friends in different countries, going to Ireland, where the Troubles were beginning to come to an end. And she writes a counterpoint to my *Free Diary*. She starts off by saying how she had read *The Soft Vengeance* and fallen in love with the narrator, but now she wanted to know if the guy who wrote the book corresponded to the narrator, to the writer. Fortunately, she didn't tell me that in advance, it might have made me self-conscious. She doesn't expressly say it, but it seems I passed the test. She goes on to study architecture and becomes an architect. We're very close together, and our son, Oliver, is born.

The work of a judge on a constitutional court defending fundamental rights in a country in the process of transformation, is exhilarating, it's testing, but truly, truly wonderful. Every, every bit of you is using your literary skills to find the language, to find the words to define what it means to be a human being in the twentieth century, now twenty-first century, in Africa, in the world. You're using your sense of history, your curiosity, your deep sense of fairness. Why, why, why? Why does Mrs Grootboom – and a thousand other people – have to sleep out in the open with their children, with the rains about to come, when so many people are living in beautiful homes with lots of spare rooms nearby? Why, why, why? And what can a constitution do about that? And what can we as lawyers do about that? And why, why, why do we take people who've killed others, and put a rope around their neck and literally kill them ourselves to show our abhorrence of killing? Is that permissible? These are profound questions of life and death.

In the last chapter of my ultimate book, *The Strange Alchemy of Life an• Law*, I state that judges have become the great storytellers of our age. They might not be aware of it. And the story they tell might be a dull, boring iteration of a technical set of phrases, detached from the real lived-in world, without any passion and without any sense of humanity. But that is a story in itself. It's a story about the law, it's a story about the society, it's a painful story because all passion, empathy is excluded. But the opinions (judgments) can be stories filled with heart and feeling, not just with emotion like happiness and sadness, anger and sorrow, but with a special kind of emotion related to fundamental rights, to humanity, to human society, to how power can be properly exercised. Writing opinions and judgments tests your literary skills, your emotional skills, your sense of history, your sense of society, your sense of your country, and your willingness to listen to your colleagues. We have to forge and shape something extremely precious and extremely pressurised, something durable. That was my job, my life, my way of earning my living.

To me that is part of the soft vengeance. And it's extremely powerful.

The power of vali•ating your life's aspirations, the power of having a society with strong moral foun•ations that unite people an• bring them together an• connect them, is well beyon• the power that comes out of the barrel of a gun or the placement of electro••es or the force of a boot, or even sen•ing someone to jail.

The story's almost over. Someone's making a film of my life, and she decides we must go to Maputo and film me at the site where I was blown up. And I say, that's fine, but Vanessa and Oliver must come as well. Oliver's now about three and a half. He climbs into bed in the morning, lies between Vanessa and myself, and we play a game with short arm and long arm. He loves short arm. And long arm is speaking to short arm, saying, 'Wakey, wakey, wakey!' and short arm jumps up in surprise. And I want him to understand why his daddy looks funny and different, and I want him to hear it from me.

We go to the spot, and the understanding is that if the film comes out corny or false, we're not going to use it. And I sit down on the pavement where my body lay on the ground, and hold Oliver with my left arm, and tell him how I walk down the stairs of that building, I'm on my way to the beach, my car is parked over there, and boooom! I'm hit, and I don't know what's happening. I find I can tell him about that, about the bomb, I can tell him all that, and also that some TV journalists happened to come by and put me in their van and took me to the hospital. I can tell him all that. I can tell him about the doctors deciding my arm is so messed up, that I'd be much happier and be in less pain, if they cut off and put bandages on the broken part. I can tell him about that. But I can't tell him *why* it happened. I find I can't.

I •on't want to tell him about aparthei•. I •on't want to tell him that his mummy an• I, his •a••y, woul•n't have been allowe• to live together, to love each other, to conceive him. I •on't want to. I •on't want to tell him about that worl• where everybo•y's lives were •efine• by race. He'll learn — of course he'll learn! Racism is still everywhere in the worl•. But I •on't want him to learn it from me. I feel it will be pulling

me back emotionally, an◆ pulling him back, from the worl◆
in which he's growing up as a young, free chil◆.

And I wonder to myself if possibly the time hasn't come to stop even talking about soft vengeance, and not to think of vengeance at all, not even in this benign, transformative form. Maybe the experience of living soft vengeance has become so pervasive, that even the ambiguous phrase itself should disappear. Maybe the time has come to just live in, explore and develop the society – enjoy the society – that soft vengeance has created.

SIX

Reconciling the Past and the Future

Archives, Truth and Reconciliation

1ST NATIONAL ARCHIVES LECTURE | SENATE HOUSE, UNIVERSITY OF
LONDON | 24 OCTOBER 2005

I woke up this morning feeling extremely queasy and everything
around me seemed a bit unreal. I would reach for something and
just as I was about to seize it, it seemed to disappear.

Naturally I was quite alarmed and I went to the doctor and the doctor
looked at me and said:

'You're from South Africa, aren't you?'

And I said, 'Yes'.

He said, 'I can tell from your accent, and I can tell from just the way
you're relating these symptoms to me; immediately I know what your
ailment is, it's endemic in South Africa, I'm sad to say it's incurable, but
it can be managed'.

And I said, 'Well what is it?'

And he said, 'It's archive fever'.

'I've had many patients from South Africa with that ailment', he
continued, 'and I'm not surprised, because people entering the realm
of archives feel they're entering a realm of security where facts are
facts, where things are collected and classified in a completely neutral
way, where there's no hierarchy of importance, and chunks – nuggets
– of social reality from one period are stored forever, for examination,
certainly for as long as the materials last. And instead of feeling more

secure as a result of entering this realm, they find themselves totally displaced. To begin with, the documents are as partial as you can get. They were documents that were collected by a ruling minority, confident and assured in relation to its right to rule, and not only to rule but to the right to record their own history, the story of the world in which they functioned, from their own point of view, which they saw as the natural point of view'.

'As for the majority of the population, they weren't agents of history; they were subjects of anthropology. They didn't live in time, but existed as units of unchanging social structures. And if any information at all was collected from what were called the native people, it was assembled not with the view to understanding their society as it understood itself, but with a view to more effective administration through control and subordination. And so this apparently neutral collection of documents called the archive immediately appears to be as partial as you can get. The silences become far more dramatic than the speech, the absences from the record more resonant than anything you read. You want to know what has been left out, but how do we find out what's not there? How can we interpret what is there without knowing about the silences and the gaps? And to make it worse, huge quantities of these documents that would seem to be particularly revealing were destroyed – deliberately, intentionally destroyed, to ensure that the picture that came through was a partial picture of a partial picture. Can you be surprised that your head seems split and your vision blurred?'

'If that's not enough', he continued relentlessly, 'Jacques Derrida came to Johannesburg at the height of the ferment and left behind him a blazing trail of contestation and irreverence. It was he who introduced the very words "archive fever". The very act of taking a document, a piece of information, and placing it in a file is, in its own way, betraying that document as a source of information. You're detaching it from its context, you're placing it in a different context, you're giving it an eternal real life of its own, when in fact it had a transitory, integrated, consequential relationship with the context in which it was generated.

A severed limb has all the physical features of an arm or a leg, but its formaldehyde immortality is its functional mortality. It no longer moves, feels pain, touches the ground or the arm or the leg of another.'

The doctor looked sadly and sympathetically at me. I felt disturbed. As anybody here would know, archive fever is very, very contagious. And if that wasn't enough, archivists found themselves confronted by people from the Liberation Movement, saying:

The only reference to us, fighting for the rights of the majority of the people, in the ꞏocuments that you claim to be neutral, are to us as a group of gangsters, terrorists. We are seen through the optic of police investigations aimeꞏ at ꞏestroying us. Everything we say anꞏ ꞏiꞏ is collecteꞏ, not with a view to honouring what we stooꞏ for, but with a view to prosecuting us, maybe senꞏing us to the gallows. The information is all ꞏistorteꞏ.

On the other hand, our own story of ourselves is not there at all: it was forbidden even to quote the whole list of banned people, it was a criminal offence to distribute their materials. One needed permission as a librarian to have a copy of *Justice in South Africa* by Albie Sachs, PhD, University of Sussex, my thesis, and it wasn't easily granted.

If that's not enough, other voices are coming forward: 'What about the oral tradition? That is how memory is transmitted amongst our people: stories, parables, through oratory, praise singers, multiple different ways of interpreting legends, family narratives and stories from the Bible, tales passed from grandparents to parents to grandchildren, from generation to generation. A rich store of information and knowledge, it's not in the archives at all'.

And then people say, 'Well let's go out and collect that information'.

You don't know where to start, it's millions of people with millions of stories and even if you concentrate, then the ultras will come along and say, 'But you're simply seeing these memory systems as potential evidence to be recorded in an archive, and you're destroying the orality, you're destroying their connection, you're detaching them from their own context'.

No wonder you feel in a state of crisis; even when you're trying to do good, people say you're not doing it well enough. And then there's a very strong women's movement, saying,

> 'We're looking through these archives, going back to written recor•s, from the Portuguese sailors, the Dutch sailors, the first Dutch settlers, the governors, the colonists, the missionaries; there's no voice of women at all. Women weren't there, one •oesn't know how chil•ren came unto the earth, how things were •one; it's a voice that's completely absent, even from the recor•s of the rulers, of those in charge of society. The so-calle• subaltern voices just aren't there at all.'

And so you're left with what looks like a rather pitiful collection of documents that formerly you were so proud of because you were guarding them for posterity and you feel in a state of crisis and you wonder, what can we do now? So much of the past has been lost. We have millions of people with their memories and their stories – how do we make sense of them? How do we integrate them? How do we give genuine dignity and equality to this precious function that we're undertaking?

And so the doctor said to me, 'You can see: it's endemic and it's incurable, but there is hope. It can be managed and I happen to have a very good medicine which I'm going to give to you … and I want you to open it at the right time, not straight away'.

And he said, 'I must warn you, the symptoms of archive fever can be quite bizarre. When you've got the fever you lose the certainties, even when you're giving a prestigious lecture at one of the top universities in the world, you're likely to start confusing fact with stories, with parables, with memories – and watch out, you might even (with a view to showing the multiplicity of influences that form part of popular culture and memory), you might even break out into song'.

'Sing,' I said, 'I'm a judge, judges don't sing!'

'I've warned you', he said, and he gave me the medicine.

After leaving him, my mind went back to the worst moment of my life. I don't know if it's good or bad to be able to identify with such certainty the worst moment of one's life. It wasn't when I was blown up: the survival – the recovery from the bomb was basically joyous. It was lying on the floor of Caledon Square Police Station, in Cape Town, during my detention without trial (solitary confinement), having collapsed after endless hours of interrogation, through the night, having been given some food which, subsequently I believe, had some drug in it. Trying to hold out, trying to hold out, trying to hold out, and eventually feeling my body is fighting, my mind, my spirit, my will, the sleep is so intense I just collapse onto the floor. And suddenly the security interrogators who'd been taking it in turns, coming, going, coming and going, working in shifts – there's a great urgency and they all collect.

> *I'm lying on the floor an• I just see these shoes, brown shoes, brown shoes an• black shoes moving quickly aroun• me an• I feel water pouring upon me an• I'm lifte• up an• I sit on the chair an• I close my eyes an• I feel heavy fingers pushing my eyes open an• I sit for a while an• I collapse onto the floor an• the same thing is repeate• three or four times an• eventually I just sit an• sit an• sit.*

And eventually they know their moment has come and something inside me has broken. My body is simply too weak. I've been overborne by the superior organisation, power, compulsion of those who are defending apartheid. And eventually a few hours pass and I'm trying desperately to control what I'm going to say, to retain at least a few shreds of my dignity, to betray as little as possible. It's hard to think, I'm desperate with exhaustion and Captain Swanepoel in charge starts, and I begin, like a well-trained lawyer, 'I'm making this statement under duress'. I describe the circumstances, the collapsing on the floor. He writes it all down, fairly patiently, and then he starts the questions and I give some answers, trying to control but feeling destroyed inside myself.

I've never got over that. I've got over the bomb, soared above and beyond that. I've never got past that moment of total personal humiliation. And what intensified it for me was a vague memory that somehow Captain Swanepoel had travelled those pages around, rewriting something, and getting me, in my tiredness, to sign something else. And afterwards I realise that even my rather feeble protestation that 'I'm giving this statement under duress' has evaporated. So on top of the humiliation, there's a kind of wounded macho feeling that he has outsmarted me.

A month ago I went to the National Archive in Pretoria, at the invitation of Graham Dominy, the chief archivist. I had been told a joke about archivists – and like many jokes it's a total stereotype – an archivist is somebody who found that being a librarian was too exciting; and then the joke went on and said the definition of an extrovert archivist is someone who, when he's speaking to you, looks at your shoes rather than his own. So I expected to see people in that mould, but in fact I saw in the archive, people like you see in South Africa; shes as well as hes, younger people, older people, very ebullient, very bright, very accessible, happy to have me there, staying after hours to give me information, and we had a marvellous free and easy dialogue.

And eventually I said, 'Well, do you happen to have anything on Albie Sachs?'

And they came back and said, 'No'.

And I felt quite dismayed, 'Am I not important enough to be in these archives?' And eventually they looked under Albert Sachs – my proper name on my passport, birth certificate, police record – and they gave me a file and I looked through the file with a kind of fascination. These were real documents from that time. Some of the earlier ones were from the Ministry of Justice, 'I place you under restrictions, you can't leave the magisterial district, you can't associate with more than two people at any time, you can't go to schools, you can't go to factories, you can't go to the docks, you can't, you can't, you can't'. And this was for five years. Then, at the end, 'I remain your obedient servant'.

And then I see there's a report from the magistrate, and I think it's a carbon copy and it says: 'The person I interviewed in his cell complained to me that ...' and there is the full report of being kept up all night, of collapsing on the floor with my eyes being prised open and I had forgotten that I had complained afterwards, when I had had a chance to see a magistrate. I felt quite wonderful. It made no practical difference: I'm still a member of the Constitutional Court, we've got our Constitution, but me, Albie, just felt a moment of my life that had been wiped out and denied, the worst moment of my life, where my voice had been silenced completely, where I'd been turned into an instrument against myself, where that tiny little bit of moral recuperation I had attempted at the time, had been recorded. It was on record. It was there. I thought, 'This is a most wonderful introduction to the brief I received: "Speak to archivists about the role of recorded documentation organised in exposing the injustice of the past, in achieving democratic accountability, in enabling the truth to flourish."' How I wish, how I wish, I could fulfil that brief. I thought about our Truth Commission, which was meant to be the centre of this whole enterprise, and without doubt, it did play an extraordinary role in our history, in the life of our country.

But the role of the archives was almost minimal. There were more fights about the archives than information coming from the archives; and that's partly because the key archives had been destroyed, but it wasn't just that. The strength of the Truth Commission didn't come from records; it came from personal testimony. It came from the voices of people who'd suffered pain and their pain was acknowledged. They had the chance – in front of the TV, which was one of the great validating mechanisms of our contemporary society, on the radio – to speak in their own language, saying, 'This is what happened to me, what happened to my son, to my neighbour, to my father, to my mother'. It was the strength of oral testimony, it was the tears, it was the hymns that were sung in the morning in the townships, it was the comforting of the people next to those testifying, it was Desmond Tutu putting his head down and crying at a certain moment, it was the texture of the voices, not just the words. And the truth just came pouring out, almost lava-like in one part of the country after the other. And it wasn't only truth about violations and crimes by the old security apparatus. It was truth about violations by the ANC, to which I had belonged ... violations by other organisations saying they were fighting for freedom, coming into a church and shooting at people. It was across the board – overwhelmingly state violence, but not exclusively. And it worried me as a lawyer, as a judge. My bread and butter came from due process of law. As lawyers we deal in truth; we earn our living, in a way, from the organisation, the presentation of truth, and deductions made from it.

Why does so little truth, reliable, convincing truth, seem to come out in a court of law? Here the truth was coming out in huge volcanic eruptions, flowing into our consciousness – our psyches – through this other kind of a process. And yet you have a criminal case and at the end of it you just don't know where the truth lies. This was round about the time of the OJ Simpson trial, which we all watched on TV – at the end, the jury acquitted him. Weeks of evidence, due process of law, and in the end, there's no clear understanding of where the truth lies. We didn't have formal due process of law in the Truth Commission, but we arrived at the truth.

To help myself through this, I invented – elaborated – four kinds of truth.

The first is what I call microscopic truth. You define a field, you establish the variables and you measure the interaction between them over a period of time. And that can be positivist truth in science; it can be legal truth in a court of law, where you determine the nature of the investigation; and the evidence is allowed in; and inferences are drawn according to certain degrees of credibility – reliability – to arrive at certain conclusions. And then you've got logical truth: that's the truth implicit in a proposition, a statement. And I assume logical truth really comes from the capacity of language to generalise from human experience, to come out with certain strong propositions that stand the test of time, of usage, so one and one makes two, and we can be fairly confident about that. And most legal work involves combining microscopic truth with logical truth, and it's not inappropriate because we are concerned with attributing forms of responsibility and so our concern is not primarily with truth, as such, but with proof – a well-tested and highly necessary condition for dealing with truth in a court of law.

But that wasn't the way the Truth Commission worked. If it had relied primarily on documentary sources, they would have been the main materials handed in and then there would have been some corroboration from eyewitnesses and participants. It didn't work that way. What we got was what I call experiential truth. It's story-telling. It's analysing your experience of a phenomenon in which you've participated. I got the notion from Gandhi, *My Experiments with Truth,* when he was locked up in the Old Fort prison in Johannesburg where we now have our new Constitutional Court. The prisoners of Indian origin were ordered to wear caps like the black African prisoners, and his colleagues refused and Gandhi said, 'We must wear these caps; if we want to understand what life is like for those who are the most marginalised amongst us, we must experience life as they experience it'. And they wore the cap and he said, 'We'll wear that cap with pride, as a badge of honour'. When he went to India he took the cap with him and the Gandhi cap became the symbol of the freedom struggle in India. He had interrogated, questioned his own experience, his own reaction to being subjected to a form of humiliation, and drawn certain conclusions from it, and for most of us, for most of our lives experiential truth is what guides us. We don't take out rulers to measure things. We act on our experience of life and we infer things from that.

And then the fourth is dialogical truth. And that is the whole mix of evidential, testimonial, experiential, the truths of many people being interpreted in many ways; and it's never-ending. So whereas experiential truth is very particular to an individual or community, dialogical truth is absolutely inchoate. And the Truth Commission was basically about experiential and dialogical truth, and that was its strength. It was its emotion, it was seeing on television people you could identify with, hearing voices that sounded like voices of your neighbours, people you'd been to school with – which you can't get from a document, you don't get from a document. The strength of the document is its impersonality, its objectivity. Its weakness in this context is that the voice, the texture, the emotion, the rhythm, the relationship to other materials, its place in the context of the story get lost.

It's been sai♦ that what a truth commission ♦oes, or what our Truth Commission ♦i♦, was to convert knowle♦ge into acknowle♦gment.

Knowledge is data, facts, information. There was very little that was actually new from that point of view. The number of people who disappeared, who had been killed, that they had been tortured: this was all known. It was known in a factual way. Acknowledgment meant acknowledging the pain, listening to the pain, responding to it. Acknowledgment involves doing something with the information. Connecting it with the world you live in: 'What would I have done? What can we do to stop these things from happening again? Where would I – which side would I have been on? Would I have had courage? Could I have done this to someone else? What makes human beings do these things?' It's a much broader kind of investigation that can be triggered and prompted by the facts, by the data, but won't be explained or understood, and can't be interpreted simply by the facts alone.

And so one comes across this whole debate on the difference between history, which states authoritatively, 'This happened, that happened, these were the causes'; and a counter-history saying, 'Well, it wasn't quite like that; the causes were different', but always with authority and certainty and memory. And memory, by its nature is fluid, it's full of contradiction and mystery, it's musical, it's intensely uncertain – uncertain by its very nature.

And so this is a kind of a dialogue, a contrapuntal relationship that to my mind runs through the whole analysis of the role of archives. If you claim the archives tell the story, that they do everything, and maybe you've got to fill in a few gaps and maybe with a little bit of astute interpretation you can correct some errors, I think you're involved in a futile activity and you're loading too much onto the archives and you'll crush what is there, what is stable, what should endure, what really matters under the weight of an interpretation that it can't bear and shouldn't try to bear. If, on the other hand, you simply rely on memory as something totally subjective, what everybody thinks and feels independently of verifiable information and facts, then you are also in the realm of a kind of a dream world, which has its own tenacity and its own significance for participants, but is also unreal.

I decided at this stage it's time for my medicine. I unwrapped it carefully and there was one of those little slips like you get in Chinese fortune cookies, and it said, 'The work of an archivist is based on paradox. The very act of abstracting a document from its setting to preserve it forever is to destroy a portion of its authenticity while creating a new kind of authenticity'. It wasn't quite as long as that.

And the doctor said, 'There are two ways of responding to paradox. You can deny it, at your peril, or you can embrace it. And that applies, I think, to all social sciences, and my advice to you, as your good doctor, is to embrace paradox. Don't try and suppress it, acknowledge that that tension is there, that it's built into the very nature of your endeavour and see how you can utilise that tension to achieve the objectives that brought you into this field in the first place'.

Well, I thought, 'That's lovely moral advice, but what's the elixir that's actually going to help me?'

And he said, 'There is an elixir. It'll work for you but not necessarily for other people. It's something that draws heavily on the past in a very intense way. It congeals; it reduces certain essential aspects of past experience in highly concentrated form and redeems it through that very act of concentrating that experience, placing it in a new context'.

And he said, 'It's called the Constitution. The Constitution's been called a bridge from the past to the future but it could also be seen as an archive, an archive of history up to a certain moment, organised in a certain way, to ensure that all that's valuable in the past can be retained and used as a basis for preventing repetition of the pain, the hardship, the injustice'.

Being a judge in the Constitutional Court, I was naturally very pleased to receive this advice and immediately I took out my copy. I wouldn't say I held it close to my heart; I just thought, 'What does this mean? What does this document mean to us in South Africa?' When we are sitting in Court, eleven judges with our long robes and counsel is arguing a point before us and the books, the heavy files, the leather-bound tomes are piled high, and they search through everything and they pick up this lovely little pocket book and I think, 'Isn't it marvellous that our Constitution is in this convenient form with a bright picture on the cover, accessible to anybody who wants to use it, and is indeed used all over the country?' Like any archive, if the Constitution becomes a monument, if it proclaims that it's recorded our history in a way that our history ends, we've reached it, we've got it, we are now living in a just society because we've got this Constitution, then it's guilty of that very objectification, of that very claim to eternal verity of the documents I'm speaking of. If, however, a constitution is a memorial that consecrates human experience at a certain moment, but opens the way to future development, to future interpretations, then it doesn't carry that risk. There might be certain values of freedom – human dignity, equality – that are eternal, but we can never say we've achieved justice, that it's there. The horizon of justice is ever-receding and never-ending, it has to be searched for; this document has to be interpreted; new life has to be given to it all the time ...

There is a sense of interconnection between all these different things. The often hidden archivist, who may not even be seen by anybody, gets our materials together, organises them and makes sure that they are not going to be destroyed by nature, copies them, conserves them, is doing something very beautiful in terms of our history, something very precious. It's linking up the generations. It's doing something intensely humane. The connections between our ancestors, and we speak a lot about our ancestors in South Africa in different ways, we become the ancestors of others through these material traces and remains, impressions that are kept by the archivists and they are doing it, not for political advantage, not because they are selling the documents, not because they get money. They are doing it simply because it's there, like Everest, because it's there. They are doing it for the unborn. They are doing it, not as we used to think, to guard certainty; but to protect uncertainty because who knows how the future might use those documents.

The Place Next Door to Number Four

FROM *MY/MEIN JOHANNESBURG* | WITH MARGIT NIEDERHUBER |
MANDELBAUM VERLAG | MAY 2014

I wondered why every single day as I entered the newly constructed Constitutional Court building on Constitution Hill, Johannesburg, I felt elated. It wasn't just that the work we were doing was enthralling, which it certainly was.

Appointed by Nelson Mandela as one of the first eleven justices on the Court after the first democratic elections in 1994, I found that being a judge was intellectually, emotionally and philosophically challenging. It was even physically exhilarating – we worked late into the night. The issues we had to rule on had profound meaning for our society: capital punishment, same-sex love, homelessness, and the provision of anti-retrovirals to people living with HIV, were just a few. But the work alone could not explain the very special emotion I felt. We had already been functioning in temporary court accommodation for ten years. There had to be something additional and directly connected with the building that lifted my heart and made my soul feel good every morning.

Could it be the character of the site where the building was created? South Africa possesses the dubious honour of having the only prison in the world where both Gandhi and Mandela had been locked up. When offered a number of sites in Johannesburg for what was going to be the first new building of South Africa's democracy, we judges had jumped at the recently decommissioned prison. What a site! Occupying extensive ground on a hillside close to the central business district and public transport, it would be readily accessible to the general public as well as legal practitioners. A big plus was that the development would help halt the spread of urban blight. Moreover, the precinct linked three sectors of Johannesburg that had been brutally kept apart under apartheid: on the eastern side was Hillbrow, filled with dense high-rise apartments, once salubrious and now overcrowded, vital, problematic and teeming with the energies of people from all over the continent. Go anti-clockwise ninety degrees and you could see the opulent northern suburbs nestling in what has been called one of the greatest human-made forests in the world – hardly a poor person in sight. To the west and south was bureaucratic Braamfontein filled with massive anonymous concrete buildings representing local state power. And to add an amusing personal note to it all, I had been born in the Florence Nightingale Hospital right across the way from the Old Fort prison – I'd been right around the world to come back to the site of my birth. Rather more significantly, three cities in one that had formerly been kept apart by the prison, were now to be linked by the Court: the embryo of a new Johannesburg that was struggling to be born.

Johannesburg had always been an improbable city. Most large urban centres have grown near to water – an ocean, a river, a lake. Not so Johannesburg. It sprang up in the late nineteenth century as a mining camp situated over gold ore deep in the earth. Even its name is meaningless – if you asked the three or four million people who live in the city today who the Johannes was after whom it had been named, hardly any would be able to answer that it was the first name of a minor official in local government who had something to do with registering the first title deeds [even I am not sure].

When the Union of South Africa was created in 1910, Cape Town was made the legislative, Pretoria the executive, and Bloemfontein the judicial capital; Johannesburg was totally left out. It was too unruly and too much of a threat to the dominance of the Dutch-descended Boers in the northern part of the country. Yet despite this official disdain, Johannesburg continued to be the economic powerhouse of South Africa. It was also its storm centre: the city of the Alexandra Bus Boycott as well as of the Soweto Uprising, and the place where the ANC underground leadership functioned before being captured at Rivonia.

And sure enough, where there was money and where there was trouble, there would be lawyers. Johannesburg quickly became the de facto legal capital of South Africa; today more than half of all South African lawyers practise there and two large law schools train future generations there. And once Johannesburg had been chosen by parliament to be the seat of South Africa's new apex court, the justices selected the Old Fort prison as the place where their new building would be erected.

The symbolism of choosing the prison as the site for the new Constitutional Court coul• not have been more intense. Everybo•y ha• locke• up everybo•y there.

In the 1890s the British sent an expeditionary force to seize the goldfields from the Boers. The expedition failed, and the Boers locked up the Brits. Many mining magnates found themselves behind bars on charges of treason. Though they loudly trumpeted their indignation at being treated like criminals, their conditions were far from harsh – the editor of the *Cape Law Journal*, who was one of the inmates, commented wryly afterwards that one of the prisoners' complaints was that they had suffered from sunburn while playing marbles in the yard.

Then, a few years later the British army defeated the Boer commandos. So now the Brits locked up the Boers. Some were executed there for treason. Next, the Boers won political power and they locked up the blacks. Albert Luthuli, president of the ANC and the first African to win the Nobel Prize for Peace, Nelson Mandela and his law partner, Oliver Tambo, immediately set up a choir that sang freedom songs inside the jail, while supporters stood outside with posters reading, 'We Stand by Our Leaders'.

Meanwhile, the so-called Native Jail, commonly known as Number Four, became notorious throughout the region. If an African man disappeared for being out on the streets after curfew hour at night, or for not being able to produce his pass book on demand by any policeman, or for any other reason, the first place the families would go to would be Number Four. The well-known singer, Yvonne Chaka Chaka, sang songs about Number Four.

So the new Constitutional Court was placed right next to Number Four. Anyone coming to Court would be reminded of why we had a Constitution, while anyone going to see the former prison would know that we were not trapped in the past.

Our history coul not be burie* an* forgotten. But its terrible negative energy coul* be harnesse* an* converte* into positivity. Living in a constitutional state meant that we stoppe* locking each other up. It presuppose* that we fin* principles an* rules for our society which woul* enable us all to live together in *ignity.*

Consciously or unconsciously, then, each day as I carried my documents to my chambers I would be sharply and happily reminded of the manner in which we were converting pain into hope. And yet inspiring though this was, I sensed there was something even deeper at work in my psyche. Could it have been the sheer aesthetic beauty of the building itself? Some young architects from Durban and a town planner from Johannesburg had won an anonymous international competition for its design. The theme they had chosen was 'Justice under a Tree', the traditional transparent and participatory manner of resolving disputes in southern Africa.

Two members of the competition jury ha themselves been locke* up in that very prison. Isaac Mogase, the Mayor of Johannesburg, ha* been in Number Four *uring the Alexan*ra Bus Boycott.*

He told us [I was also on the jury] if he had said to the warders that one day he would be the Mayor of Johannesburg helping to choose the architects for a new Constitutional Court building, they would have killed him. He loved the design, as did Thenji Mthintso, head of the Commission for Gender Equality, who had spent seven months in solitary confinement in the section called the Women's Jail. Thenji informed the architects on the jury that she did not favour the idea that the first major public building of our new democracy would be yet another of the big, powerful buildings of Johannesburg that had intimidated people like her mother [whom I knew had taken in washing from white families to send her to school and university].

*What was nee•e•, Thenji sai•, was a buil•ing that ha•
a face that woul• be smiling rather than frowning at her
mother.*

And when the international and local architects on the jury had been able to inform us that the Justice under a Tree design was technically assured, we had gone on unanimously to select it. Peter Davey, Editor of the *British Architectural Review*, said it was the best jury he had ever been on; normally the professionals argued amongst themselves, and the laypeople lined up behind one or the other, but in this case it was the lay people who made the running and the professionals, himself included, who all got on board with our preference.

Without doubt, then, the evocative nature of the building was a source of constant delight for me. Every detail was entrancing: the cladding of the Court chamber walls with bricks recycled from a demolished prison building; the installation of the Blue Dress, commemorating an executed freedom fighter whose naked body was recovered because of the Truth Commission; the dazzling carpets; the passive cooling system based on trapping cool night air in rocks in the basement; the openness, warmth and friendliness of the building.

It was a joy to feel that we were helping to reconceive the very character of courts, to make them places of beauty, thoughtfulness an• protection, rather than serve simply as grim an• •ispiriting cita•els of power.

And yet inspired though I was by the work we were doing, by the manner in which Constitution Hill helped the city knit together, by the symbolism of the site of conscience in which our building stood, and by the sheer brilliance of the architecture and artwork, I thought there was something even more profound at work, some extra element that invaded and spontaneously brought cheer to my unconscious. What was it? And then the answer came to me.

Everywhere I go in South Africa I am ma•e aware – even if only at the subconscious level – of the country's racial geography. The ol• aparthei• laws have been scrappe•. True, there is mobility in all •irections – upwar•, •ownwar•, lateral, even •iagonal. Formerly whites-only areas are becoming racially an• culturally •iverse. Yet the sense of white areas an• black areas is still pervasive. It's in the buil•ings, the streets, the layout of suburbs. Like it or not, almost wherever I am, I still feel that I am a white person in a white area, or a white person in a black area. But when I went into the Court, I felt •ifferent. In a worl• still heavily investe• with the fabric of racial •ivision, the Court was like a liberate• zone of the new republic of non-racialism.

We had conceived of, built and now occupied something pristine and imaginative that truly belonged to all who lived in the country. It had a new democratic aesthetic; it was open and welcoming to all; the people who worked in it were drawn from all strata of our society, and the leadership, management and functioning of the Court as an institution was truly non-racial.

I felt for the first time in a long life of fighting against racism that I was not a white person in a white area or a black area, but just Albie going to work. So simple, yet so profoun.

Sometimes the most banal emotions are the most wonderful ones, precisely because the right to experience them has been so hard to achieve. Thank you Johannesburg, and thank you the Constitutional Court, for making it possible for me to have that exceptional experience.

Nelson Mandela's connection with Number Four showed how, with grace and courage, the tragic could be transformed into the beautiful. Mandela first visited the prison as a practitioner, then as a prisoner, then as a president, and finally as a pensioner. It was as president that he found himself back in the prison yard, this time to announce the winner of the design competition for the Court building. He joked that he wanted the occasion to be handled as swiftly as possible since he had spent enough time of his life in jail. He then pointed to me and said how alarming it was to see ex-prisoners now on the Bench. This was his sly and humorous way of reminding everyone there that respect for human dignity, and not for status, lay at the core of our endeavours.

The last time Mandela visited the site [as far as I know], he did so as a pensioner. He walked through the building under construction, with Chief Justice Arthur Chaskalson, who had been part of his legal team at the Rivonia Trial where the main issue was whether he would be hanged, at his side. The two tall, imposing figures chatted animatedly to each other as they wandered through the low-hanging scaffolding. Fortunately, knowing how absent-minded both could be when deep in conversation, they were wearing hard hats.

So, the epitome of despair and the acme of hope, the old and new buildings on Constitution Hill stand side by side at the heart of Johannesburg and represent its quintessence. It is a lively, dynamic city, built on, driven by ingenuity and trying to overcome its many powerful contradictions.

Free Spirits and Ravaged Souls

ADAPTED FROM KEYNOTE ADDRESS AT THE TIME OF THE WRITER
FESTIVAL | DURBAN, SOUTH AFRICA | 2011 | PUBLISHED IN *AFRICA INSIDE
OUT: STORIES, TALES AND TESTIMONIES* | EDITED BY MICHAEL CHAPMAN |
UKZN PRESS AND CENTRE FOR CREATIVE ARTS | 2012

Everything suddenly was dark, totally dark. I knew something terrible was happening to me, but I didn't know what it was. And in that total obscurity, I hear a voice speaking to me in Portuguese, saying: 'Albie, this is Ivo Garrido speaking to you; you are in the Maputo Central Hospital. Your arm is in a lamentable condition; you must face the future with courage'. And in the darkness I say: 'But what happened?' And I hear another voice, a woman's voice, saying: 'It was a car bomb'. I fainted into euphoria.

That moment had come, that every freedom fighter is waiting for: 'Will they come for me today? Will it be tonight? Will it be tomorrow? Will I get through the day? Will I get through the night? Will I be brave?' They had come for me, and I'd survived!

Time passes, I'm suddenly conscious and I'm feeling very light. Joyous, happy. My eyes are covered, I can't see anything and I tell myself a joke. It's an old joke about Hymie Cohen who, like me, is a Jew. He falls off a bus, he gets up and moves his hands over his body as if to make the sign of the Cross. And someone says: 'Hymie, I didn't know you were Catholic'.

'What do you mean Catholic? Spectacles … testicles … wallet … and watch'.

I'm lying on the hospital be⦁ (after, I was to learn later, a seven-hour operation), an⦁ I starte⦁ with testicles. When the wor⦁ went roun⦁ the ANC camps, I who've trie⦁ without success all my life to be macho, su⦁⦁enly became a huge macho hero: 'An⦁ the first thing Comra⦁e Albie ⦁i⦁ was reach for his balls'. All in or⦁er? In or⦁er.

Wallet? If my heart is damaged, big trouble. Wallet seems to be okay. Spectacles? The bandages are there but there is no big crater; if my brain is damaged it can be very serious. Watch? My arm slides down and there's a gap. I say to myself: 'It's only an arm, it is only an arm, only lost an arm'. And I sink back into euphoria knowing that I've survived. And with a total, utter conviction that as I get better, my country, South Africa, will get better. This was in April 1988. When I came to tell the story of what it's like to wake up without an arm, to go through this experience, I ended the description with the words: 'I joke, therefore I am'.

Some months later I'm out of hospital, in London, and very weak. There's a ring at the door of the house where I'm staying. I open the door with some excitement. Two people sent by Oliver Tambo, leader of the ANC, are there to greet me on his behalf, the organisation's behalf, to find out how I'm getting on. One is John Nkadimeng, trade-union leader, who had known my dad, seen me grow up. The other is Jacob Zuma. We walk inside; Zuma has that big 'Zuma smile', Nkadimeng a long face, and I'm determined to make Nkadimeng smile. He has lost a son to a bomb blast, but I feel so joyous and euphoric that I'm sure I can get him to smile.

We sit down and I tell the story, not in a hurry, African style, enjoying all the nuances, the little flavours, the quirks of human nature along the way, not rushing to get to the climax. Nkadimeng with the long face, Zuma chuckling. A chuckle becomes a gurgle, a gurgle becomes laughter and when I tell him 'spectacles, testicles' he almost falls off the chair.

I sai⦁ to myself – this is how we are going to get a new South Africa, my Jewish joke meeting up with humorous storytelling in the African way. We ❯on't flatten our worl❯ to create a blan❯ non-racial society. We bring in what we've got; we share what we've got an❯ enjoy being members of a single, unifie❯ but ❯iverse nation.

Years later, Albie is now sitting in green robes as a Constitutional Court judge, during the '*Laugh It Off* Case'. Laugh It Off was a small firm. A graduate of journalism decided to challenge the dominion, power, of branding and logos by large commercial enterprises. He took several logos from big firms and he parodied them on colourful T-shirts. Most of the targets laughed and some actually bought the T-shirts and gave them to their employees to show that they can take a joke. But not Carling Black Label. Their logo was accompanied by the words, 'Black Labour, White Guilt'. They went to court; they got an order restraining distribution. The case went to the Supreme Court of Appeal which didn't think it was funny. You can criticise their policies as much as you like, but can't use the property, their logo, in order to do so, the judges felt.

It comes to the Constitutional Court and we unanimously decide that the free-speech values, which are clearly strong here, completely outweigh any possible commercial detriment. It's about the role of humour in democracy. Without humour, without the capacity to laugh at ourselves, to convert what are often very stressful and serious issues into the form of a joke, we bottle up our tensions, and democracy gets frustrated. So I wrote a concurring judgment which the magazine, *Noseweek*, absolutely loved and printed almost in full. The story went around the world and the property lawyers got into a state of extreme tension. Obviously they were quite right – the whole recession that followed afterwards could be blamed on my judgment!

The free-speech community think this is terrific and I'm basking in their good feeling – I sense that I'm 'Mister Nice Guy', and intellectuals like yourselves think it is wonderful to have a judge like that; until, that is, I come across some words in a poem by Mongane Wally Serote. It's a long poem, really a novel in the form of a poem.

The wor♦s that strike me are as follows: 'The ♦ogs bark an♦ bite, even in cartoons. They inflict woun♦s in the silent soul. They bark as they tear the soul apart'.

And I'm thinking: what's Wally getting at? What is the source of that extreme disquiet and hurt that he is displaying?

Somebody asked me once at a book-signing event about the Laugh It Off case and how I came to write it, and the background of humour and so on: 'Justice Sachs, what do you think about the cartoon by Zapiro depicting President Zuma about to rape the female form of justice?'

I said, 'I'm sorry but I'm a judge and President Zuma is suing Zapiro. I can't respond to that, the matter could come before the Court'.

To me it's the ♦ilemma create♦ by the poem of Wally Serote – how ♦o you reconcile expression of a free spirit, on the one han♦, with sensitivity to the ravage♦ soul of people subjecte♦ to historical hurt, on the other?

It reminded me of the distress felt on the occasion when the then Speaker of the National Assembly, Baleka Mbete, went to an exhibition at the Grahamstown National Arts Festival and saw pictures by a feminist artist which showed the vaginas of black women being used as ashtrays, and stormed out. She was indignant, and the artist couldn't quite understand why. The artist said: 'My whole point was to show how the bodies of black women are disrespected, how their sexuality is disregarded'. Yet Baleka, who is a noted African feminist and a very cultivated person, couldn't bear it. She was shocked and felt violated in a visceral way.

I see certain parallels between what Wally Serote was saying and what Baleka felt. Something is going on here, something we need to be aware of. Not to ban speech, not to send people to jail, not to prohibit the production of challenging artwork, but to engage in meaningful dialogue with a view to achieving mutual understanding. I'm not dealing with the legal questions at all, it would be quite inappropriate for me to do so.

I'm dealing with what seems to be a witty, sharp political observation by a satirist of great calibre and great personal courage. Can we laugh at or bring a smile or a sense of satisfaction to people looking at a cartoon that might be deeply wounding to millions and millions of other people out there, decent ordinary people who feel we might criticise President Zuma, poke fun at lots of things that he does, but still recognise that he is our president? In their view, you don't depict the president of the country about to open his fly, with ministers at his side urging him on, with a woman lying prone and helpless in front of him. For millions of people not familiar with metaphorical art, that kind of scene is reminiscent of the stereotype of the black male rapist. It ravages the soul, the issue is deep, it's hard, sharp.

It's painful for me personally. I mentioned Jacob Zuma coming to see me after I came out of hospital. I remember him on another occasion telling me how poignant it was when he came out of Robben Island prison and went to see his mother, a working-class woman, in a township in Durban. She had a tiny house and she got it tidy and neat for him. She was proud of it and so proud to receive him. He had to lie down there and he couldn't say: 'Mommy, Mama, conditions on Robben Island were better than your house that you want me to stay in'. She wanted him to promise that he would not get involved in the struggle anymore; because it would be too painful for her if he went to jail again. He had been torn between placating his mother and following the conscience that had brought him into jail in the first place.

I also remember scenes in London, at the time when he was married to Nkosazana [Dlamini] Zuma and I went to the apartment where he was living. He was very apologetic for taking the family laundry to the laundrette when we had a meeting to discuss something, but I suspect he was also apologetic in the way men are when they are seen to be doing what some might consider an unmanly thing.

I know Zapiro well, and hold him as a friend. His mother was a Holocaust survivor. When I came back from exile, at every ANC meeting Gaby Shapiro was there with little flags. There's always somebody with the buttons, the flags, the booklets, and she was there; as loyal, committed and anti-racist as you can get. Zapiro is a warm and brave person who was detained by the security police in the struggle days. He has taken positions of principle in relation to the rights of Palestinians that have made him unpopular among many members of the Jewish community. He is a good, decent person, with a brilliant pen and a sharp mind. Yet the imaginations, the feelings, the sensibilities of these two people whom I respect in different ways, came into a kind of collision. What's the role of the artist in a situation like that?

On the fence?

It's a funny thing, but in the English language to be sitting on the fence is always said as something negative, as though you're comfortable sitting on the fence, not taking sides.

Sitting on the fence, if taken literally, is actually a very uncomfortable posture. An I think an uncomfortable posture is goo for writers.

It's also precarious – and isn't writing about trying to get a balance where things are swaying, to find a centre, to find a connection? So while sitting on the fence is meant to be cowardly and negative, in fact to do so successfully requires positivity and courage. The main reason for urging writers to sit on the fence is to encourage them to be aware of both dimensions: on the one hand, the free spirit, the right to be able to say everything, not to be afraid; on the other, the need to plumb and be aware of the deep emotions, the sense of history, the personality, the being and significance of people. Not just of other writers and critics, but of people.

I'm dealing here with the conscience of the writer, not the duty of the judge. In some respects, the conscience of the writer might be more expansive than the limits of the law and even defy the law. In other respects, it's narrower than the law. You have a responsibility not just to stay within the limits of the law, but to be empathetic to fellow human beings, to your craft, to humanity, to ubuntu; it should animate much of what you're doing. Hopefully, your response should come out instinctively, intuitively, not because you feel bound by the strictures of being politically correct, but because it's right, because that's the kind of person, and artist, you are.

Towards the Liberation and Revitalisation of Customary Law

SOUTHERN AFRICAN SOCIETY OF LEGAL HISTORIANS CONFERENCE |
LAW IN AFRICA: NEW PERSPECTIVES ON ORIGINS, FOUNDATION AND
TRANSITION | PRETORIA | 13–15 JANUARY 1999

I will start with the words from the old song 'Wouldn't it be lovely'.

Wouldn't it be lovely if we already had a book, between two and three hundred pages long, that contained a comprehensive survey of the interaction between traditional African law and imposed state law?

Wouldn't it be lovely if this was a thoroughly researched work with references to existing literature, to commissions, to oral tradition, to the law reports of what used to be called the Native Appeal Court, as well as to the South African Law Reports? Wouldn't it be lovely!

Wouldn't it be lovely if we had a study that examined these questions in a social, economic, cultural and political context, breaking the narrow, self-referential bounds of positivistic legal analysis, that looked at the impact on law of the changing character of production and land tenure, and asked pertinent questions about political rights and responsibilities?

Wouldn't it be lovely if a book of that kind was written in elegant prose, beautifully shaped, showing how there had been a legal dualism in the Cape, with the Roman Dutch law system co-existing with partial recognition of African law in the Transkei; while the foundation of apartheid was laid for the first time by the British in Natal through the system of indirect rule, and not in the Boer republics, where there was a unified and integrated legal system, in which the master–servant relationship provided for separate levels of status within one code, and not for separate codes for separate people?

Wouldn't it be lovely if we had a book of that kind which focused specifically on the story of the changing role and legal status of African women? Wouldn't it be lovely!

The fact is, such a book already exists, and it is lovely! Its title is *African Women: Their Legal Status in South Africa*, and it was written by Jack Simons and published in London and Manchester in 1967. It's a wonderfully written and comprehensive book, which anticipates by thirty years the whole debate we are having today and all the dilemmas posed by the new constitutional order. Yet it is virtually unknown in this country.

Jack Simons was banne, *he was exile*, *his book was banne*, *it was a criminal offence to distribute it. The knowledge it contained was blotted out, just as other important studies done at that stage are virtually unknown today. We have lost three decades, and we have got to recover them.*

Jack Simons was my teacher, in the fullest sense of the word. He was senior lecturer at the University of Cape Town in a subject he inherited under the title 'Native Law and Administration'. ['Natives' were to be administered, and the law was the instrument for doing so.] Turning the course around, he called it 'Comparative African Government and Law', and critically analysed the different colonial policies in Africa. In those days the map of Africa was painted in colonial colours. Do any of you remember the colour for the British colonies? It was red for the real deep colonies, and pink for the protectorates! For the French colonies: green. There was schoolboy competition over whether there was more green or red on the map. And then, the Belgian Congo, as it was called, was a kind of mauve, while the Portuguese colonies were painted gold. In his lectures over the years Jack followed the disintegration of the colonial empires and the repainting of the map. Some of us were joyous as each colony gained independence, but he rejected our simple triumphalism, preferring to deal as an engaged and committed South African with the problems of postcolonial states in a scientific and questioning manner. In this way he prepared us for some of the difficulties that postcolonial states were later to encounter.

Perhaps as important as the content of his lectures was his teaching style. His classroom was always packed out. It was the only class I knew where students from other faculties came as volunteer listeners, and because the debate was so lively, there was standing-room only. This was right through the 1950s, the time of high apartheid. Today no one claims to have supported apartheid. Then it was different. Apartheid was being projected as the salvation of South Africa, separate development, rights for everybody in their separate spheres. Many of us had a very clear view: apartheid was rubbish, it was cruel, it was racist, end of matter. But Jack said our dismissive approach was not good enough. Apartheid had its team of intellectuals, it was getting a certain measure of international support, it had got a strategy. We had to deal with it as a set of ideas, not simply as the political philosophy of a ruling party, and he insisted that we get beyond denunciation and start considering alternative forms of government for South Africa. Could we live as equals in a common society? Was some sort of separation between black and white inevitable? What was meant by the concept 'government'?

I still remember him introducing the strange name of Max Weber to audiences in Cape Town in the 1950s. As soon as Weber's work came out in English translation in the United States, Jack was on to it, and we were discussing various forms of authority in different societies in the world. He always pushed us to use our own experience, problems, pain, conflicts, and debates as a foundation for examining the universal problems of what society was about, what life was for, why we were born, what it meant to live in the world, what it meant to be who we were, to speak our languages, to have our past and our hopes for the future. He took the ugliness of apartheid, its cruelty, viciousness and oppressiveness, as an instrument to compel us to engage in debate, discussion, evaluation, argument, argument and more argument.

There were supporters of apartheid in the class and he asked them to stand up and defend their positions, not in order to knock them down, but so that their arguments could be counter-posed by better arguments or different arguments. The right of people to speak their minds and to defend their philosophy was strongly entrenched and that is why everybody loved coming to his class.

It was precisely this kind of intellectual buzz we had all expected at university, but seldom encountered. In his own subtle way Jack would, of course, have the last word. He believed that, like everyone else, teachers had to take responsibility for the world they lived and taught in. Yet he would not mark down students because their positions were different from his. He looked for the logic, the clarity, the coherence, the sensitivity of their arguments.

When Jack returned to class after being detained without trial during the post-Sharpeville state of emergency, the whole class, to a person, cheered him. What really mattered, as far as he and they were concerned, was the honesty of the debate, not the fixity of the outcome.

We got our new South African Constitution through dialogue – intense, hard dialogue, interrupted by breakdowns, rolling mass action. Four years of hard, intense dialogue, and then another two. We solved problems one by one, two by two, three by three. When people call it a miracle, I get irritated. A miracle should come about simply through faith, it just happens spontaneously out of its own a-worldly logic, against history, against reason. In reality, we toiled nights and weekends, we met, we thought, we argued, we debated. I used to think that freedom meant a world with no more meetings; in fact, when freedom came along, we had meetings and more meetings and more meetings; there is certainly nothing miraculous about minutes and matters arising. There was hard work, intelligence, listening, sharing, learning to look into the eyes of the other, to see another person there, while that other sees you as a person too. How can we live together in one country? How can we learn to respect each other so that if I get on in life, if I can be what I am and enjoy living as I am, it doesn't mean you can't do the same? These were the fundamental questions. We had to find a framework for achieving all this, and in microcosm I had already seen the process at work in Jack Simons' class. That open debate, that not being afraid of ideas, that confidence that the truth would set us free.

Truth through dialogue; the dialectic of truth. One of the most wonderful sets of books I have seen in years has been the multi-volume report of the Truth Commission. It's vividly and passionately all over the place. One can argue about this finding or that, but as a narration of a deep, painful, and awful part of our history, it's intellectually and emotionally convincing, and once and for all precludes any future attempt at denial. One thinks: if only the British had had something like a Truth Commission after the Anglo-Boer War, how much this country could have been spared. If only ... If only there had been the kinds of free-flowing evidence and testimony ringing with truth, if only the many strands had been woven into a common narrative of the war, if only we hadn't ended up with separate peoples, possessing different histories and disparate memories, if only ... When people living side by side have different memories, whether of the Anglo-Boer War or of apartheid, then they stay apart, and the gulf remains as wide as the memories are incompatible.

There was one aspect of the report that left me as a lawyer and a judge particularly worried. My concern was the following: why does so little of what we call the truth come out in court cases while so much truth came out of this TRC process?

As Antjie Krog brought out so beautifully in her book, *Country of My Skull*: there isn't a single truth, only the experiences of many people put together, layered, interacting, which create a richer, deeper pattern, one which never is final, since there never is finality to truth. Dialogic truth is about listening, talking, interacting, hearing. It is not a search for supposedly scientific conclusions, for a unique, experimentally proved and logical truth, where one position annihilates another. On the contrary, it's about an open-ended interaction between positions, viewpoints, experiences, perspectives, imagination, empathy, observations and criticism.

There used to be an idea that the gateway to civilisation could be crossed by all, irrespective of colour, provided that they spoke English, ate with a knife and fork, had a Bible, comported themselves with appropriate protocol, and were male. 'Equal rights for all civilised men'.

Even to∙ay we are expecte∙, as Bloke Mo∙isane put it, to be eternal stu∙ents at the table of goo∙ manners – that is, to behave accor∙ing to rules set for the whole worl∙ by the West. Thus, we hear much about 'Western concepts' of human rights. I wish we coul∙ ∙rop that phrase. As far as human ∙ignity is concerne∙, the impact of the West on Africa was nothing short of ∙isastrous.

The colonial presence destroyed communities, undermined traditional agriculture, forced people off the land, introduced pass laws and used parliament – this wonderful instrument – to deny people their fundamental rights. It employed courts of law – these marvellous bodies – to oppress people. Gallows, corporal punishment and prisons were imported from the West. In our country hundreds of thousands of people were locked up every year simply because they didn't have the right documents. Inequality and division were promoted through the law, not in spite of it (and I am not even referring to the impact of the slave trade). There is no gain, only loss, in tying the origins of our human rights movement to the West.

By their nature, human rights belong to all humanity, not to any single continent. It is true that the term ♦emocracy emerge♦ in Greece which, by the way, was an African country, an Asian country an♦ a European country at the same time.

Some might even say that there was especially great theorisation of the human rights idea in Europe, precisely because of the specially egregious ways in which human rights were violated there – the Holocaust on European soil has yet to be surpassed in ugliness. Undoubtedly, there were freedom fighters in Europe who identified with those struggling against oppression elsewhere in the world, and due credit must also be given to the moral stands taken by committed philanthropists on that continent. But, in fact, the people who fought hardest in South Africa for the acceptance of universal principles acknowledging the essential dignity of all, and who searched the hardest to find the commonalities uniting black and white, were black South Africans. Not all black South Africans did so, and not all white South Africans opposed them. But overwhelmingly it was on Robben Island, in the trade union movement, in the underground and in exile, and not amongst those South Africans who called themselves Europeans, that what turned out to be the core values of our new constitutional arrangement were kept alive and nurtured.

This brings me to a theme that I wish would receive more attention, namely, the importance of international law as a point of reference for our debates. The principles of international law guided us in the quest for freedom and democracy in South Africa. The organised international community refused to countenance apartheid and firmly denounced the enforced separation of human beings. At the same time, those of us who fought against apartheid, not only derived support from international law, we contributed to and enriched it. Our Constitution is held up today as a model for the world. Before, it was a case of 'even in South Africa'. We were the extreme measure of oppression. If something was not done 'even in South Africa', it was truly beyond the pale. Nowadays people say: 'In South Africa they managed to do it, surely we can do it too.' Thus, our Truth Commission remains a source of global astonishment.

> *I travel often, an• the only thing people want to hear about is the Truth Commission. We've •evelope• something which is •eep in the African tra•ition, of listening, talking, bringing everybo•y in, of hearing all the •ifferent points of view an• affirming the •ignity of all through equality of •iscourse. Our continent then, is not only a universal recipient of values an• processes, it is a universal •onor as well.*

Equality is based upon acknowledging rather than eliminating difference. To say that if I suppress my language, culture, religion, appearance, my beliefs and way of seeing the world, then I can enjoy equality, is to deny me the right to be equal as I am. Any uniformity of treatment which comes at the price of suppressing my true self, involves the denial of the equal concern and respect for myself as I am, with my characteristics, that lies at the very heart of equality. Once more, we return to the concept of basic dignity, which means respecting people as they are and as they identify themselves in the world. This approach is so simple, and yet because of our racist ways of regarding others, we have made it so difficult.

The question then is how do we envisage the future of customary law in South Africa's new constitutional democracy? Here I think it is vital that we focus not on this particular or that special rule but on the core values and principles of traditional African law (customary law, indigenous law – the phrase is not crucial and the people to whom it means the most should be the ones to make the choice). These deep values – which derive from centuries-old African experience and are of significance for all of us, whatever our origin – have not changed, even though the institutional arrangements made for realising them in practice have altered substantially. We need to distinguish between these deep enduring and foundational principles which affirm orderly social cohesion, and the more ephemeral judicial institutions and legal rules which ensure meaningful day-to-day law enforcement in the concrete circumstances of the time.

Indeed, applying ancient mechanisms and formulae to rapidly evolving social life can result in the negation rather than the promotion of the core values we seek to protect. I believe that Professor Ronald Dworkin argues along similar lines when looking at how the centuries-old United States Constitution should be interpreted today. He suggests that mechanistic and literal application in contemporary society of the actual words used by the framers of the Constitution in the eighteenth century would frustrate rather than advance the core principles of the constitution-makers. As society evolves, so must the rules and mechanisms for defending those values develop.

> *In the case of tra*i*tional law, what nee*i*s to en*i*ure are the *i*eep principles of social respect, couple*i* with the all-embracing processes involving listening an*i* hearing, allie*i* to profoun*i* notions of restitution, of reintegration of* i*efaulters an*i* i*elinquents into the community, of attempting always to restore equilibrium, an*i* base*i* on the pervasive philosophy that something capable of improvement can be foun*i* in every human being.*

This profound and all-encompassing social philosophy has on occasion been summed up in the word ubuntu, a term which has both the strength and the debility of being open to many different interpretations. At the heart of traditional African legal concern is a sense of human solidarity, of regard for all. No one is cast out or left by the wayside. I am who I am because you are who you are; my personhood is inextricably linked up with yours. We all have to accept responsibility for ourselves, our family and our community [Do not ask for whom the horn sounds, it sounds for thee!]. Only in this way can we live together in the same social world.

Throughout the globe, people exist in atomise• an• anomic societies, where personal wealth an• in•ivi•ual autonomy have become inseparable from personal loneliness. By way of response there has •evelope• a universal ache for the experience of what our Constitution calls ubuntu. The concept of not being alone, of being part of the community, shoul• be seen as the central an• precious core of tra•itional African law.

The particular rules used to further social cohesion in the past were directly related to the social, cultural and family formations of the time. When production was done mainly by household members working together as a family, tending the fields and looking after cattle and the home, then the land and the home were centres of economic life. At the same time, extended families were centres of social and political relationships. The grand families of the traditional leaders became the leading families at the apex of the nation. As in England at the time of Henry VIII, constitutional law, or the law of the state, was in essence family law. From the highest to the lowest, rights and responsibilities were determined by land and lineage.

The situation of African life today is enormously different; the household is different, production is different, wealth is different and property is different. Two-thirds of households in the Transkei are effectively headed by women. They take all the day-to-day family decisions, not only looking after the children, but managing the family finances and property. Many are widows, others have been abandoned, while yet more see their husbands only every now and then. Both men and women in towns and countryside have ATM accounts, collect pensions, are owners and tenants with individual title, drive motor cars and tractors, receive wages for employment and participate in insurance schemes. They vote, study, play sports, take part in choirs and stokvels, and attend union meetings, all outside the framework of the household.

The particular detailed rules that applied to old forms of conserving family wealth and maintaining family cohesion are frequently quite dysfunctional now. If these rules continue to be applied mechanically, particularly in the way that they were formalised and frozen by magistrates, missionaries and patriarchal male elders in the colonial and apartheid era, they risk undermining rather than affirming the values of ubuntu and social solidarity.

They will be ignored, or implemented in opportunistic ways to serve new property interests, thereby undermining family solidarity, and creating new family resentments. They will result in unfairness and oppression, especially for African women and even more particularly for African widows, and will simultaneously violate the sense of right which lies at the heart both of traditional law and of the values of the Constitution for which the African people fought so hard. The strength of customary law lay in its organic connection with the lives and culture of the people. If customary law is to be revitalised it must accordingly link itself up to the new energies of a people in transition and be sensitive to the real nuances and contradictions of daily life. Its anchor must be the sense of justice and fairness of a community and its star the broad values of the Constitution.

The Constitutional Court has referred to the need to leave the complicated, varied and ever-developing specifics of how customary law should develop and be interpreted, to future social evolution, legislative deliberation and judicial interpretation. Does that mean that customary law is finished, archaic, obsolete? On the contrary. The above approach, focusing on core values rather than clusters of formalised rules, implies the liberation and transfiguration of customary law. It re-establishes its organic connection with the community. It ensures its revitalisation through imbibing the juices of daily life. It is important that democracy not be regarded as a blunt instrument that clubs customary law on the head. On the contrary, democracy finds protected space for customary law while freeing it at the same time from rigidly established (in colonial and apartheid times, frequently invented) and increasingly out-of-touch formalised codes. To recover its original vitality, customary law must respond to the lives that people lead now, to their sense of justice and fairness, and to the multifarious and at times contradictory ways in which an actively and evolving culture impacts on the actual lives of actual people. People are not being forced willy-nilly to 'modernise' or to 'develop'; they are being freed to enjoy all the aspects of the modern world to which they voluntarily choose to have access.

I have seen that approach work. During eleven turbulent years when I lived and worked in Mozambique, I witnessed the government there trying out a great variety of new modern institutions, none of which functioned, except the community courts. At one level, they were modern courts rooted in contemporary community life, at another they tapped deeply into ancient African tradition. The composition of the courts and the kind of solutions they arrived at were completely new. They were made up of people of standing in the local community, who were called upon to resolve disputes by applying their sense of justice and the principles of the Constitution. Yet the language, process, feel and underlying objectives were ancient. The community streamed to these courts with their problems, looking for practical and fair resolutions of their disputes. They felt embraced and comforted by the informal, African way in which the courts functioned. Although brief records of the proceedings were kept, the oral tradition reigned supreme. The judges always sat in a panel of at least three so as to reduce the scope for corruption, and at least one woman would sit in every court.

They ⋅i⋅ not ask: are you Tsonga, Nyanja or Makon⋅e; are you Catholic or Muslim, were cattle transferre⋅ when you got marrie⋅? They saw in front of them not tribesmen or tribeswomen, or a⋅herents of particular faiths, but husban⋅s an⋅ wives in trouble, families broken ⋅own, chil⋅ren to be care⋅ for an⋅ property to be ⋅ivi⋅e⋅.

I spent hours, weeks and months with these courts, wrote a book and helped make a BBC film about them. Their solutions were eminently fair and practical, and, I might add, always accompanied by African-style homilies on the responsibilities of good family members!

I am convinced that something roughly along similar lines would work well in South Africa. It could be that in many rural areas traditional leaders would be at the helm. Such leaders would link the wisdom for which they have been prepared with the creativity and inventiveness of ordinary people, so as to find practical solutions for practical problems. Men and women of standing in the rural areas might not be scholars, they might not even be literate, but in terms of finding balanced, down-to-earth and culturally sensitive ways of settling disputes, they are without parallel. To my mind it is in their creative and practical hands that the real future of customary law in this country lies. Enabling them to work properly in association with traditional leaders, would require an appropriately balanced institutional framework, softening some of the boundaries between formal and informal courts, and giving informal courts appropriate plasticity and scope for their work. Such courts would be guided both by the evolving values of the community and by the enduring principles of the Constitution. Let us, the professors, help with designing the institutional arrangements and legal framework, and not try to codify rules and attempt to determine outcomes. Then, once the courts have functioned and come up with their decisions, and our ranks have been broadened by scholars with their own community-based backgrounds, we can happily explore the new material, attempt to discern patterns and precedents, and write our scholarly works.

Let no one be alarmed. I am not proposing that community courts in the rural areas, headed by traditional leaders and functioning according to the informal procedures of customary law, be given powers to send people to jail. Nor should they be permitted to impose corporal punishment. If anybody is threatened with loss of liberty, there must be due process of law, defence lawyers, charge sheets, a system of appeal, and formal procedures. That is what the Constitution requires. But resolving family and neighbours' disputes and dealing with petty assaults and small thefts requires other techniques and processes.

> *We nee▪ new local courts. You may call them tra▪itional courts, customary courts, or community courts, or whatever, but they are courts. They are not just alternative ▪ispute resolution mechanisms, or me▪iation or arbitration bo▪ies, they are courts.*

They form part of the judicial system, they exercise judicial power, enjoy compulsory authority over those within their jurisdiction, and act on behalf of society as a whole to keep the peace and secure justice for individuals. They need to be carefully developed and monitored, starting with pilot schemes that may well vary from rural areas to urban areas and from one province to another. The experience of the five hundred traditional courts presently recognised by the law would be of special value. Attention would have to be paid to the fact that the boundaries between custom and common law have long become soft and permeable. I know that these terms are used separately in the Constitution. Yet they can be seen as having been employed in a descriptive and fluid rather than in a normative and categorical manner. By *common law* is meant that body of law that has been regarded as common law; by *custom* is meant that body of practices, rules, institutions and values that has been treated as customary law. Both need to be infused with the values of the Constitution. In the days of segregation, they were kept apart, both conceptually and institutionally. Today there is no reason not to recognise and welcome the fact that each has osmotically and irreversibly seeped into and reinforced the other. Furthermore, both have been profoundly and irrecuperably affected by legislation; if ever pure fonts of common law and customary law existed, they do not exist any more today.

Take the case, for example, of a woman who has been thrown out of the house with her children by their father, whom both she and the community at large regard as her husband. The circumstances might be varied. In some cases the judges might feel that the principles of customary law as they understand them are quite sufficient to provide an adequate remedy, that is, one which, in the context of the relationship between two families, will restore social equilibrium and provide adequate protection for the women and the children. In others, the de facto manner in which the conjugal partnership was established, the lack of inter-familial connections and the absence of cattle or other wealth transfers, could result in remedies derived purely from the common law, such as ordering that the woman be allowed to stay on in the house and the father be obliged to pay maintenance for the children, either in cash or in kind. In most cases, one could expect elements of traditional and common law to be fused in the quest for a just and fair solution.

> *What I am suggesting is that law in practice be allowe· to ·evelop in conformity with life in practice. This implies that the law be ma·e to fit the people an· not that the people be compelle· to ignore active parts of their lives so as to squeeze themselves into the categories of the law.*

This requires not rigid and formulaic doctrine, but open participatory procedures and the application by the local judges of clearly understood and firmly enunciated principles of equity and effectiveness. It also presupposes abandoning the strict legal dualism coupled with choice of law approaches that have been adopted in many postcolonial countries. It is not only that as a matter of principle we need to move away from the settler/native dichotomy highlighted by Professor [Mahmood] Mamdani. From a purely pragmatic point of view, it becomes increasingly difficult to separate out the customary and common law dimensions of law as they actually impinge on the lives of rural communities.

> *What appears to be nee·e· is appropriate fusion rather than artificial separation. Such interaction an· engagement between custom an· common law an· legislation shoul· be*

brought about gently rather than robustly, an• on a case by case basis rather than through an aggressively •octrinaire approach.

The goal must always be to reconcile and harmonise different legal concepts so as to provide solutions that are regarded as eminently fair and meaningful to the litigants and to the community as a whole.

Similarly, I think it is important to avoid an unfortunate but prevalent tendency to put customary law and the constitutional principle of equality on a collision course, that is, to say that for the one to live, the other must die, or to use a less dramatic metaphor, if custom triumphs, equality must fail (or vice versa). I think this is a profoundly mistaken view. Our Bill of Rights is not based on a hierarchy of rights, nor is it an assemblage of categorically defined rights sealed off from each other. Rather, it contemplates the interdependence of mutually supportive rights. Everything depends on the concrete circumstances which trigger the disputes, on their wider significance and impact, and on the intensity with which the underlying values of the open and democratic society as envisaged by the Constitution are promoted or breached in a particular case.

Where the exercise of one right inevitably involves trespassing on another, the notion of proportionality becomes central. Thus, it might be difficult to uphold a precept of custom or religion which required different penal treatment for men and for women who committed adultery; the injury to equality would be grave, while the religious rule infringed would be relatively peripheral to the core elements of the faith. On the other hand, if people follow a faith which only allows men to be clerics, it would be hard to justify a court injunction requiring women to be ordained; the state-enforced intrusion on freedom of belief and association would be massive in circumstances where the state as such was not being made directly complicit in sexist practices. Any remedy would have to lie in internal transformation, not external compulsion. The position might be different, however, if the state is directly implicated through being asked to use its machinery to give effect to patriarchal-type discrimination, that is, if the courts are called upon to apply rules of customary or religious law which, looked at from the point of view of constitutional rights, discriminated unfairly between men and women by means of overtly entrenching patriarchal subordination.

It is important in this regard to recognise that what has severely undermined patriarchy in African society is not the law or the Constitution, but the changing character of African life.

Thus, the practical question facing the courts today is not so much whether to perpetuate patriarchy as whether to rescue it. It has been undermined by the migrant labour system and by the fact that household farming has ceased to be the centre of production for the great majority of African families. It has been undermined by the reality that there are millions of women who work outside the home and bring in their own income and who have achieved a certain measure of autonomy and independence which they are not easily going to give up. Thus, the constitutionally created Commission for Gender Equality strives precisely to ensure that actual gains made by women in practice are not reversed or taken away by law.

I was at a judicial conference in Bangalore in India recently. One of the women speakers, a lawyer from Pakistan, dressed in a sari, told us how angry she got when she heard men saying that in defence of 'culture', we had to accept this, that, and the other, and resist the desire of some women to destroy 'our culture' with their allegedly Westernised claims for equality. And she said indignantly: 'Look around this room, look at all the men, dressed up in their modernised, Western-type suits, and look at the women'. (All the Asian women were wearing saris.) She said: 'We defend culture in our lives, in our languages, in our daily practice. We are the deepest defenders of culture, but the minute we ask for equal rights, then people suddenly start throwing culture at us'.

Jack Simons would have patted me on the back for telling that story. He died a few years ago [on 22 July 1995]. People who saw this frail, old figure, this boereseun become boere-oupa, being carried onto the stage to receive belated honours from UCT, couldn't have imagined the vigour and the fire of the once great teacher. Yet beautiful eulogies were delivered to him at St George's Cathedral in Cape Town by persons from the many different generations he had taught. This was after the choir had sung *Onwar♦ Christian Sol♦iers* followed by *The Internationale* (Jack's last pedagogical joke – he had asked for both of them to be sung). The warmest tributes came from former members of Umkhonto we Sizwe. They spoke about Uncle Jack, their wise, humane and humorous teacher, who had told them never just to accept ideas, but always to debate and always to argue – there they were in the Angolan bush, in danger of ambushes, short of food, threatened by mosquitoes and snakes, by everything, and they were discussing what it meant to be a human being on this earth, what it meant to live in society, what was meant by the concept of government, what was meant by tradition and culture. And let me say, one reason we've got the Constitution that we've got today, is because we had intellectuals like Jack entering into dialogue with the Black Consciousness generation; the streams of passionate young men and women who had crossed the borders as much in search of ideas as of military training, and who welcomed him as a brilliant intellectual freedom fighter in their midst.

The then South African government pai♦ Jack the highest accola♦e that any intellectual can ever receive: they sent bomber planes to try an♦ ♦estroy him. I am happy to say that he receive♦ the accola♦e in absentia.

Jack Simons is one of our heroes. I think when you read his book, you will see that I have not been exaggerating its virtues. We already have a strong platform from which to work. What is needed now is that dialogue, that input of ideas, experiences and values that will enable us to distil the most precious elements from our rich and varied experiences. We have done so much in South Africa already. I believe that, provided participation is extensive and honest, this is another area where we will prove to ourselves, to Africa and to the world how creative and sensible we can be.

Values, Nation Formation and Social Compacting

PRESENTED AT A CONFERENCE JOINTLY HOSTED BY THE MAPUNGUBWE
INSTITUTE FOR STRATEGIC REFLECTION AND THE THABO MBEKI AFRICAN
LEADERSHIP INSTITUTE | 20 YEARS OF SOUTH AFRICAN DEMOCRACY: SO
WHERE TO NOW? | UNIVERSITY OF SOUTH AFRICA | 2014

Nineteen eighty-one, the 20th anniversary of the launch of the
armed struggle, and Joel Netshitenzhe in his capacity as editor of
the ANC magazine *Mayibuye* asks for people to contribute stories
about their participation in the armed struggle. And I'm sitting at
my desk working in Maputo and I say to myself I am going to offer
something special: the most trivial contribution made by anyone
to the armed struggle.

It was in fact made some months before the armed struggle was launched
in 1961. I'm sitting in my chambers as an advocate in Cape Town.
There's a knock on the door, somebody comes in and he bends down,
saying very little. He then takes a little piece of paper out of his sock. He
holds it up, gives it to me, and tells me that in half an hour somebody else
is going to come in for that piece of paper. So I put that piece of paper
in my sock and wait. Sure enough after half an hour, there's a knock on
the door and somebody comes in. I take the piece of paper out of my
sock, I give it to him, he puts it in his sock, we say nothing and he goes
out. That, I later discovered, was the sum total of my role in the armed
struggle. Something I overheard suggested that the little piece of paper

probably contained the Umkhonto we Sizwe oath. And so, by keeping the oath in my sock for thirty minutes I made my contribution to the armed struggle.

I sent this story off to Joel thinking it would merely raise a smile. But Joel published it! And I was impressed because I thought it was important to have a sense of humour and understanding of the huge diversity of participation in what was so often simply reduced to abstract incantations about 'our glorious people's army'.

In any event, reflecting on the question of values, I began to think of a butterfly. It's a beautiful creature that flutters with lovely colours. You take that creature and you capture it and you pin it on a board and put it in a glass box. Is it still a butterfly? It's got the wings. It's got the colours. But it's not fluttering, there's no motion, no beauty. And values are like that. If you over-define value you are somehow taking the value out of value. It's got to have an element of poetry, of longing, of dreams, of selflessness, if you like. And yet it cannot only be poetic in a way that makes it free-floating and ineffective. Values have structure, logic. So now I want to talk about poetry and science, science and poetry. Taken together they are the foundation of values.

Social compacting is not something that you bring about through a National Development Plan. The plan could well have the indirect result of producing it. But you don't put social compacting as such in a plan, you create the conditions for it to emerge through a plan. I still remember when I was in Mozambique at a meeting with a guy from the GDR, the German Democratic Republic, responsible for culture. There were hardly any people there. I felt he'd come a long way and they were giving us a lot of support. I wanted to offer some delicate hint about culture in the GDR. So I said from a cultural point of view there was tremendous support for theatre, such as the Berliner Ensemble of Berthold Brecht. But wasn't there a lack of lightness, of humour, of variety? And he confidently answered: 'Don't worry, comrade, we have a plan for culture, and it provides that in the coming year we are going to train four comedians'.

What I am going to urge today is that we avoid that kind of approach, that we don't think we can produce a genuine and deep sense of all being South Africans by simply running up the flag and getting everybody to salute it.

Maybe we shoul♦ regularly salute the flag, maybe not. But that's not the way real cohesion between South Africans will be brought about. It's when we are ♦oing things jointly that we all believe in that we come together. We come in to the new evolving consciousness not because we are obeying some kin♦ of comman♦ to the effect that thou shall be compacte♦ an♦ thou shall love thy neighbour!

The shared consciousness emerges because we believe there's a credibility to the very actions that we are doing. Sometimes with the best intentions but uneven methodology, we end up with inadequate results. I was thinking of the different sites of memory of the apartheid era. Driving up here last night, I saw the beautiful lights up on the hill. I just wonder how many people in this room have been to Freedom Park. It's beautifully conceived and developed. Yet it's not working. It can work. I believe it will work. The framework is there. But now it's not working. We should ask what is the missing ingredient. There are lovely constructions in that extraordinary place with great symbolic meaning, what is lacking?

Part of the answer may come from Freedom Square.

Free♦om Square, a big monumental place built on the site of Kliptown where the Free♦om Charter was a♦opte♦, is ♦eserte♦. It's actually sa♦ to see. The only energy there comes from the people braaing meat, selling oranges an♦ knitting un♦er the enormous arches.

The idea was to bring about a sense of development and national memory and so on, and it's not working. Occasionally commemorative meetings are held there, but it all seems too forced, too imposed, a representation of an idea. The empty monumentality severs us from rather than connecting us to the past. As one of those who was there when the police surrounded us at the Congress of the People, I feel saddened rather than elated when I go there. We must learn from what is lacking. I'm sure Freedom Square will still have its day. But to do so it has to be connected organically to the life of the community and not remain as an empty, grandiose and monumental space.

Constitution Hill and the other institutions connected with the defence of the Constitution – these things are working and functioning. Some might like to see them working better than they do, but somehow that's a form of memory and a site of memory that brings people together, reminds us of the past and uses the past in a way that helps us to develop the future. The Commission for Gender Equality straddles the walls of what was once the Women's Jail and the jail now buzzes with meetings of civil society organisations. That's what is totally lacking at Freedom Square, and begging to be invoked in Freedom Park.

Solemn incantations of the past impose• on the present actually become alienating an• un•ermine inclusion an• social cohesion. They lack true vitality an• community involvement. They seek •utiful obe•ience rather than genuine empowering respect.

This morning Dikgang Moseneke asked me on the way down here, 'Comrade Albie, how do you feel about all these things happening in the country; do you feel this is what you were fighting for?' And I say when I look at this country, 'Yes, this is the country that I was fighting for, but many things that are happening here are not at all what I was fighting for. Lots of things are awful and impermissible and indefensible'.

One of the sa••est things to see these •ays is people •efen•ing the in•efensible, rather than saying how can we overcome the indefensible? You are in a hole, you dig in your heels, you dig deeper and deeper and you get deeper and deeper into the hole and you don't get out of it. But for all the shocks and setbacks, we've not got what happened in Mozambique where I lived for eleven years after independence. Huge transformation followed by a terrible civil war, millions of refugees, thousands of limbs lost to landmines. I was in Tahrir Square in Egypt after Mubarak fell, the jubilation in the streets was wonderful. Now the prime minister is in jail, the army took over. We have a functioning country. We have elections every five years. The president steps down after two terms maximum. We have a strong independent judiciary.

I feel so proud of having been part of that judiciary and to see the judgments that are coming out today and to see the way in which people from all sectors of our society feel that they can take a matter to court. Although I agree that we shouldn't send all our problems to the judiciary, it is one institution that at least saves people from feeling they have to go out into the streets and try to kill each other to get their point of view across.

I think it's a huge achievement, in the world, not just in South Africa. There is something about the style, the manner in which we on the Court worked – the fact that we were seated at the level of counsel, not high up there. Lots of little details went into making this an acceptable South African institution. The very building itself. We have created a new paradigm for courts in the world. We haven't copied an English court or the American supreme court. We have built our own type of court that is rooted in our culture, in our society, so that people feel comfortable and welcomed when they go there. The place, the process, the style of work, the openness, the seriousness, the warmth and the direct and ongoing connection with the Constitution all ensure the continuing evolution of new South African values in a most productive and meaningful way. Yes, the Court does settle disputes. But most importantly, it also deals with deep issues of public morality, with what it means to be a South African today. And the very composition of the Constitutional Court, the way it works, promotes the values of unity in diversity.

The German political philosopher, Habermas, round about the late 1980s, dealt with an issue that had cropped up very powerfully in his country. Lots of people were saying, 'We Germans must dig deep into our traditions and our culture and the history of Germany to create a shared patriotism so that everybody who is German could feel proud to be German'. Habermas rejected that approach. He said, 'What we need is constitutional patriotism. What makes us proud to be Germans is that we reconstructed our country after the defeat of Naziism, we found ways of expressing in the German language the values of constitutional patriotism, that draw deeply from our culture and history, but emphasise above all the pride that comes from the fact that we have dialogue, that we have debate, diversity, that we recognise freedom of expression, that we regard each other as equals, respect the dignity of all and take joy from the multiplicity of voices in the country'.

What gives me great pride in being a South African is precisely the fact that we have diversity, we acknowledge it, we don't try and suppress it to make everybody stand to attention and salute in a particular way. We have a lot of humour. Indeed, our biggest growth industry is stand-up comedians. And they come from all communities. We recognise the importance of dialogue. Dialogue, dialogue, dialogue. We got our Constitution out of dialogue. I don't like the word compromise. I like the word accommodation.

Accommodation is principled. Accommodation recognises there are other people there with their views, their positions, their longings. How can we live together? How can we find a common foundation rather than looking at the other and saying, if you do a deal with me, I'll do a deal with you? It's not that at all. It's a deep, principled way in a very diverse society of finding the means of living together. So, the three Ds then, this would be my answer: Dignity, Dialogue and Difference. [This approach is explored further in Section 7 of this volume, *A New African Jurispru•ence: From abstract ju•icial rulings to purposive transformative jurispru•ence*].

The Constitution is a value-laden document; it's not just a technical document about structures of government. It's about the value of being a citizen, of being a human being, being a South African, being a man, being a woman, being gay, being straight, being Zulu-speaking, being Tswana-speaking, being English-speaking, being whatever you are, all of that is recognised in our Constitution – affirmatively, positively. Rather than trying to reconfigure and re-jig our Constitution, we've got to realise its full promise. We've got to find ways and means of living out everything that the Constitution promises. There's no problem about saluting the flag from time to time. In the main chamber of the Constitutional Court, we have a large, beautiful flag made of porcelain beads by women at the African Art Centre in Durban. I used to love brushing my gown against it when I took my seat to hear a case. But the most important way we can foster values, nation formation and social compacting is to honour our Constitution, both in practice and in our hearts.

SEVEN

Living Constitutional
Law and Ubuntu

Constitutional Court Simulation, Case No. 2: The constitutionality of the death penalty

NATIONAL TAIWAN UNIVERSITY LAW SCHOOL | TAIPEI | 1 MAY 2015
[PRESENTATION AS INVITED EXPERT WITNESS TO A SIMULATED
CONSTITUTIONAL COURT HEARING ON THE CONSTITUTIONALITY OF
CAPITAL PUNISHMENT]

A number of men surround a person, drag his arm behind his back, march him to a platform, put a rope around his neck, pull away a trapdoor. The trapdoor opens, the person goes down, and the rope strangles him to death. A number of people surround a person without his consent, move him to a table, tie him to the table, inject him with poison, and he dies. A number of men surround a person, against his will – he is not fighting or resisting. They put him against a post, pick up rifles, and shoot him in the heart. This would be murder, cold-blooded murder. Except if done by the state. The real question, I believe, before this Court is: 'Is the state entitled to kill its citizens in cold blood?'

That was the question we had to face in South Africa when the new Constitutional Court was inaugurated in 1995. Our country had known an enormous amount of violence and was still plagued with high levels of crime. It was also a country with a new Constitution, a new president, and new values. The very first case which the Constitutional Court heard was whether or not capital punishment was consistent with our new constitutional order. Nelson Mandela, our first democratically chosen president, had no doubt about where he stood. He sent an advocate who had defended him when he himself had been on trial for his life, to urge the Court to abolish capital punishment. For their part, the state law officers argued resolutely in favour of retaining it. Four hundred people were on death row – there had been a moratorium on capital punishment – and they wanted to know whether the rope would be put round their necks. The cost-efficient gallows in Pretoria would have allowed for six of them to be hanged simultaneously. So their lives depended on our decision. This was not simulated, it was a real court experience.

In making up our minds we had to decide what kind of a country ours would be; what we aspired to be like as a nation; what the core values of our society were; what it meant to be a human being in South Africa. And generations of us were dreaming of, imagining and longing for a country where the state would not be seen as a source of violence itself, but rather as the guardian of the right of people to be protected from violence. This would mean that in a hostage situation or if there was a war or in the face of an armed attack, the state could and should use proportionate lethal force in defence of life. But did this entitle the State to kill a captured and trussed criminal in cold blood?

The arguments for and against the death sentence were very similar to what we have been hearing in Taiwan. The phrases used in our Constitution may have been different. But the crucial elements, the basic themes, were much the same.

We justices didn't discuss any case ahead of the hearing. We didn't want to be influenced by each other; we just wanted to study the documents in advance and then hear the arguments in court with an open mind. But as soon as we sat around the table after the three days of the hearing, it became clear that we all felt the same way. The full legal arguments we used in our judgments varied. Most of us had been in legal practice; many of us had been judges. In one way or another we had all been confronted in a hands-on way with the implications of capital punishment. And based on our experience of what the death sentence had meant in our country and on our understanding of what the Constitution envisaged for the new South Africa, we unanimously declared the death penalty to be unconstitutional. In essence, the death sentence profoundly violated the core notion of human dignity that lay at the heart of our Bill of Rights.

I'm going to outline the core elements of the Court's decision in *Makwanyane [S v Makwanyane an. Another* (CCT 3/94) [1995] ZACC 3; 1995 (3) SA 391 (CC); 1995 (6) BCLR 665 (CC)]. I'll follow that with a discussion on the place of public opinion in a case like this. Next I will deal with the respective roles of the Court and the legislature, and finally I will discuss the significance of proportionality.

> *Mr Makwanyane ha. committe. horrible crimes – that was not conteste.. He was somebo.y who ha. brought .ishonour on himself. He was a pre.ator in society. He .eserve. to be punishe., an. punishe. severely. But that was not the issue. The issue was whether it was permissible, un.er our Bill of Rights in our new constitutional regime to punish him by means of killing him.*

The chief justice of our Court, Justice Arthur Chaskalson, writing the first judgment he had ever written – he had not been a judge before – dealt with all the many issues raised in argument by the litigants. It was a beautifully crafted judgment, in my view one of the great legal decisions of our era. His basic line of reasoning was as follows: the only possible theory of punishment that could justify capital punishment was that of deterrence. There could be no chance of rehabilitation if the convicted person was dead. Prevention could be achieved by locking up the person for life. This left deterrence as the only possible legal justification for the death penalty. He underlined the drastic nature of taking a human life and the uniquely irrevocable consequences of error. In these circumstances, only clear evidence that capital punishment had a significant deterrent value that the threat of long terms of imprisonment did not have, could justify capital punishment. Such evidence had not been produced. In these circumstances, the severe, irrevocable impact of capital punishment did not pass the test of proportionality and was accordingly unjustifiable and unconstitutional.

I was proud to sign on to the chief justice's magisterial argument. Yet I wasn't completely comfortable with it. Technically speaking his argument was irrefutable, and based on classic legal reasoning. Yet my personal view was that there was only one honest argument in favour of the death penalty: vengeance. Society wished to express its denunciation of horrendous acts by applying what is called the supreme penalty, namely, exterminating the source of the public sense of injury. And if that was regarded as a legitimate objective of punishment, we should perhaps have said so, and dealt with it, and not have centred the debate on the instrumental value or otherwise of the deterrent effect of the death penalty.

But in any event my objection as a judge to capital punishment went well beyond the issue of no proof of its deterrent effect. What if there had been some form of statistical proof that the threat of capital punishment did indeed have a special deterrent effect and thereby save future lives?

When the Cape was under the rule of the Dutch East India Company the authorities used to nail the bodies of murderers up in the main street – they weren't even dead, and the birds would eat the dying carrion – a slow, painful and visibly shocking death. If you want to deter, then do it in public.

Well, when the British took over they abolished torture as a recognised form of criminal procedure and outlawed what they regarded as cruel forms of execution as well. For another century and a half, however, they retained hanging in secret as a civilised form of punishment before deciding that it too was inconsistent with the values of their society.

Why hang murderers in secret, as if there were something cruel and shameful in hanging that had to be hidden away? To this day, most countries in the world that still have capital punishment don't decapitate, electrocute, hang, poison or shoot the murderers in public. Yet logically if the objective was to deter they should carry out executions in the public sphere. The question arises then: if there is something barbaric in making the public view the act of execution, is there not something uncivilized and inhuman in the act itself?

My personal view is that there is something constitutionally obnoxious in a very profoun• way, in the i•ea of the state playing go• an• exterminating one of its own in col• bloo•.

It violates the values of the humanity, the sense of community, what it means to be a human being, the sense of human interdependence. It converts a human being into an object who is to be put down either for the sake of terrorising others or else of making members of society feel satisfied in their desire for vengeance.

What was needed was a different constitutional imagination. The role of the court in a matter like this was not simply to make factual findings and resolve a particular dispute. It was to establish the basic core norms of justice and public morality in a society seeking to transform itself.

I turn now to the role of public opinion, an issue raised very strongly by the state lawyers in *Makwanyane*. There was no doubting the support by the great majority of South Africans, then as now, for capital punishment. [Interestingly enough, white South Africans were more strongly in favour of it than black South Africans.] The main judgment made it clear that though the Court was sensitive to public opinion, it could not allow itself to be ruled by it. The whole idea of having fundamental rights is that even the most marginalised, the most despised, the most unpopular persons in the community are still human beings and still have fundamental rights. It is the very nature of fundamental rights that they inhere in you because you are a person, a human being. They were not given to you by the state. They came to you from birth. And it is particularly important that unpopular minorities – they could be migrants, aboriginal people, people who speak a different language, who come from a country that was once an enemy, people who have a different appearance or lifestyle, whoever they might be – should have their basic rights protected.

That was precisely where the issue of fundamental rights came in. As some of my colleagues pointed out, if we can't defend the basic fundamental rights of the most unpopular in our society, it's the beginning of not defending the basic fundamental rights of us all. That is why in principle it was so important to guarantee the rights of persons among us who were unpopular, people who made us angry.

I will now deal with the question of what appropriately belonged to the Court and what to the legislature in deciding on retention or abolition of the death sentence. During the period of negotiations for a new constitution, the ANC had been firmly against capital punishment, because it wasn't compatible with the free, democratic, humane country for which its members had been fighting. On the other hand, the then whites-only South African government had been strongly in favour of capital punishment. They couldn't imagine a state which did not execute its citizens. The two sides had been unable to agree. And you couldn't have a compromise, a half-way house, just a little bit of capital punishment. Either you had it, or you didn't. And we couldn't postpone the democratic elections indefinitely just because we couldn't get agreement on the question. So the general understanding arrived at by the negotiators was to leave it to the new Constitutional Court to decide whether the terms of the Bill of Rights permitted capital punishment. And, as I have pointed out, one way or another, all eleven judges on our Court decided that the basic normative structure in our Bill of Rights forbade the death penalty.

Twenty years have passed and although demands to restore capital punishment through a constitutional amendment are made from time to time, no serious effort has until now been made to do so.

To extinguish a person is to show total disrespect for that person, whether it is done by poison, strangling, shooting, electrocution, beheading ... it's inhumane. When the state kills people for what they have done, the state itself becomes a killer. As one of my colleagues put it, 'the state is not punishing the crime; it is repeating the crime'. It is reducing public abhorrence at the notion of cold-blooded killing. It is actually giving a perverse victory to the killer by saying in effect that the state is no different from the killer in its willingness in a deliberate and inhuman way to take life.

Looking back, I think that fundamentally underpinning our reasoning was the notion that the state was different, and that death was different. Capital punishment is not just another extremely severe punishment. All punishment can be inhuman, hard, and cruel to a certain degree, and society acknowledges that. But state-sanctioned killing of convicted people oversteps the mark of what is permissible in an open and democratic society that respects human life.

The state sets a terrible example to society by killing in col♦ bloo♦. It un♦ermines what it is seeking to preserve, namely, reverence for life. An♦ it weakens respect for public morality by asserting that the en♦ justifies the means.

To my mind, the defining question in this matter is where this Court feels Taiwan should place itself in terms of how best to express a deep judicial conscience on the core values of evolving Taiwanese society. Taiwan has reached the stage where it says 'whipping is inhuman, we just don't do it, whatever the person did. Whatever the deterrent value might be, we don't whip, because we are not like that'. 'Torture is inconsistent with the values of our Constitution, whether or not it is expressly outlawed in the Bill of Rights, because we just don't do that, even if it produces results, even if it enables us to get information that saves lives, we just don't do that'. In South Africa our Court decided in effect that capital punishment was on a par with torture and whipping, and did not belong to a society that placed human dignity at its core.

The statement I heard this morning that 'most countries acknowledge capital punishment' just isn't true. The whole of Europe has decided that capital punishment is beyond the pale of permissible state conduct in repressing crime. Most of Latin America, and a very large part of Africa has decided the same. Significantly, when the International Criminal Court was established to deal with the most horrendous crimes – genocide, mass murder, crimes against humanity – the Court was given power to order heavy jail sentences, but not to impose capital punishment. Organised humanity, in trying to protect the core values of the twenty-first century, decided we don't kill the killers, because then we become killers ourselves. We want to show the distinction between their morality and our morality. It means for the most horrendous crimes, on a mass scale, involving thousands, maybe millions of people, no capital punishment. I would urge this Court to take that into account in deciding whether or not it is appropriate, in the case before you or in any other case, for the state to impose capital punishment.

A New African Jurisprudence: From abstract judicial rulings to purposive transformative jurisprudence

INTERNATIONAL CONFERENCE ON INTERPRETING AND SHAPING A
TRANSFORMATIVE CONSTITUTION | NAIROBI, KENYA | 2014

I remember when we started the new Constitutional Court in South Africa. Although we were all lawyers and all strongly anti-apartheid and pro-democracy, we could not have been a more motley group. Some of us had been in prison, in the resistance, in the underground. Others had been on the bench during the time of apartheid. One had defended Mandela in his famous treason trial.

Some were deeply religious, others firmly secular; some had come from very privileged backgrounds, while others had suffered all the indignities that white supremacy imposed on the great majority of our people. Eleven in all, five sitting judges, four law professors and two advocates at the Bar – we had to mould ourselves together into a functioning and creative team and invent a key instrument for the development of our new democracy.

A couple of us had been involved in the actual elaboration of the Constitution. Yet we weren't even tempted to label ourselves the Original Intenders. All of us accepted that the Constitution was a public document that had to be interpreted with a public meaning, that it was deeply rooted in South African history of trauma and hope and that it needed to be implemented in a manner that was responsive to our country's socio-economic reality.

Getting the Constitution had been a hard, abrasive, difficult process. In an act of assisted suicide, the old racist parliament had given technical force to the newly agreed constitutional text that terminated its own life. Ironically, the first breath of the new constitutional order had been the last gasp of the old. Everything was new. The new democratically elected parliament had gone on to choose Nelson Mandela as the new president. And following a complex process of interviews by the newly created Judicial Service Commission, Mandela had nominated us to undertake the extraordinary, wonderful and taxing job of upholding the Constitution that was ushering in a new South Africa. This was not just a wonderful job for us to have. It was a dramatic moment in the lives of each one of us, and an extraordinary time in the life of the nation.

We were a completely new court in a totally new democracy having to function in an utterly new manner. We debated everything; big matters and small. Should we wear gowns? We decided, yes. How should we be addressed? We chose to drop the titles 'My Lord' or 'My Lady' and instead be addressed simply as 'Justice'.

We even debate, our seating positions on the bench, agreeing eventually that only the head of the court would have a fixed place (in the centre) while the rest of us would rotate our spots every session. In this way the legal profession and the public at large would know that there was no hierarchy on our Court, that we were all equal.

We also had to decide on our methodology. We workshopped, we brainstormed and we debated. I don't think there is any court in the world that has workshopped as much as we did. And when we actually started hearing cases we carried on with the practice of workshopping. This was partly because our caseload was not all that heavy, so we had the time to go round and round the table several times. But the main reason was that we knew that each decision would be foundational to the new jurisprudential order. We couldn't rely on the precedent of the old apartheid courts. Each case would be a landmark. And even if, of necessity, we employed many ancient, well-honed and internationally accepted tools of the legal trade, we had to do so in a particularly modern and creative way. This meant developing a new manner of looking at the material we were handling, as well as new ways of thinking about what the role the judiciary should be in an evolving constitutional democracy.

At the same time, we did not want the legal and judicial fraternity, as well as the general public, to regard us as exotic creatures parachuted in from Mars to perform arcane or miraculous judicial functions. We were lawyers. We had been trained as lawyers and had practised as lawyers and judicial officers in courts throughout the country. The challenge, then, was with careful deliberation to combine discontinuity with continuity, to destabilise old ways of thinking while laying down firm foundations for new ones.

When I cast my mind back to that foundational phase of our jurisprudence, three cases jump into my mind. Each brought something special to the judicial table. One is very well known; one I am personally trying to make well known; and the third is virtually unknown, and likely to remain so outside of this presentation.

I begin with our very first case, the very well-known one of *Makwanyane* [explored in the previous chapter]. With one main judgment and ten separate concurring judgments, we declared that capital punishment was inconsistent with the basic dignitarian values of our new constitutional order.

I should add that many years later the issue of safeguarding the basic rights of another extremely unpopular minority came before the Court. The issue was the right of prisoners to vote. The government had argued, when defending a law which denied prisoners serving jail terms the right to vote, that prisoners were unpopular and that the public would prefer the limited electoral resources to be used for special facilities for the elderly and the sick.

Our Court hel♦ that the right to vote was a fun♦amental right of particular importance in South Africa where the majority ha♦ long been ♦isenfranchise♦. The universality of the vote meant quite literally that every person counte♦. The fact that prisoners were unpopular was accor♦ingly not an acceptable justification for ♦enying them access to this basic constitutional right.

The second case is not very well known, but you will see from its facts why I always refer to it whenever I travel to other countries. It is the *Western Cape Local Government* case [*Executive Council of the Western Cape Legislature an♦ Others v Presi♦ent of the Republic of South Africa an♦ Others* (CCT 27/95) [1995] ZACC 8; 1995 (4) SA 877 (CC); 1995 (10) BCLR 1289 (CC)]. A few months before that case was heard, all the eleven judges of our Court had been sworn in in the presence of Nelson Mandela. I can say that, like most South Africans, we had all loved, admired and honoured Mandela as a person, public figure and lawyer. And how did we show our appreciation? In the first case before us to which he was a party, we struck down two important proclamations he had issued! Why, then, do I speak about this case? It is not to show off how powerful our Court was – after all, we struck down both the act of parliament that had authorised him to adopt the proclamations and the presidential proclamations themselves, two branches of government with one stone. It is rather to underline the way in which this case cemented the foundations of constitutional democracy in our country as well as to highlight Mandela's response.

The proclamations had undoubtedly been manifestly progressive. Their function had been to provide a legal framework for the holding of the first democratic, non-racial local government elections in South Africa. But by a large majority our Court held that under our new Constitution it was parliament itself that had been given the authority to adopt legislation. Parliament could not abdicate its responsibility by entrusting the law-making power to the president. The resultant declaration of unconstitutionality was trumpeted as a victory for the main opposition party. More important, it was extremely inconvenient in practice. Parliament was in recess and had to be specially reassembled so that it could itself adopt the law. Yet the principle at stake was of extreme constitutional significance. If I remember correctly, in my judgment concurring with the result, I pointed to the disastrous consequences that had flown from the passing of legislative power to Hitler by the German Reichstag.

We wondered how President Mandela, the least Hitlerian figure one could imagine, would respond. The majority of the members of parliament would specially have to travel down to Cape Town. The substance of the law had been patently for the good of the country. Would he understand that it was the principle that mattered, one that would be binding on all presidents in the future? So when we learnt that Mandela would make his views known on television, we tuned in with special interest. Addressing the public in his characteristically rich and dignified voice he stated that in issuing the proclamations he had acted on the basis of legal advice. He now accepted that that legal advice had been incorrect, and he added, as president of the country he should be the first to accept the interpretation of the Constitution as given by the Constitutional Court.

To my mind, that day was as significant in the life of the nation as the day when we all voted as equals for the first time. It marked the moment when South Africa affirmed itself not simply as a democracy but as a constitutional democracy. And once Nelson Mandela had responded with such conviction and grace, the postmaster general, town clerk, or minister of justice was not going to feel personally affronted by an adverse decision of the Court. Indeed, Nelson Mandela emerged with added and not diminished prestige. It was as if he was saying: you see what a marvellous country I am the president of? He was in effect reminding us all that no one was above the law. Rather, each one of us, however exalted or humble, was part of a grand new constitutional project founded on principles of human dignity, equality and freedom.

It was exhilarating to feel that constitutional democracy was firmly implanted in our country.

The third case seems not to have become well known at all. I think I am the only person who talks about it today. Yet for those of us involved in it, it turned out to be a watershed. It is known as *Mhlungu* [*S v Mhlungu an• Others* (CCT25/94) [1995] ZACC 4; 1995 (3) SA 867 (CC); 1995 (7) BCLR 793 (CC)] and dealt with the question of how to go about interpreting the words of the Constitution. If I remember the facts correctly, Mr Mhlungu was pursuing an appeal against the death sentence that had been imposed upon him. Our Court had not yet handed down its decision on the constitutionality of capital punishment. The problem before us was how to interpret a provision tucked away in the concluding sections of the Constitution dealing with Transitional Arrangements.

What turned out to be important in *Mhlungu* was that Ismail Mahomed introduced the notion of purposive rather than literal interpretation into our jurisprudence. And from then on, all the other judges came round solidly to accepting the purposive approach. To non-lawyers the distinction between a literal approach and a purposive approach to interpretation sounds like a typically arcane legal dispute of the kind lawyers love. In practice it made an enormous difference to the way the Court worked and the outcomes it arrived at. It humanised the law and located the Constitution in the heart of our nation's history, paying special attention to our people's pains and hopes for a dignified life.

As a result, we gave up the practice of using the Oxford English Dictionary to find a definition of a word such as 'pending'. Rather, when trying to understand a constitutional provision we began to look at the context in which the word was used. This included the social and historical context in which the Constitution had been adopted. We took account of the overall design and normative structure of the Constitution. We gave special significance to the preamble, as well as to foundational principles and principles of interpretation which the Constitution itself required us to respect. Finally, we looked at the specific textual context in which the relevant words appeared. Viewed in the broader context, what was the specific purpose or objective of the word/s in question in their immediate textual context?

Having come round to a purposive rather than a purely literal approach to constitutional interpretation the next step followed relatively easily. It was the adoption of the notion that our Constitution was intended to be a transformative one. In some countries the basic, unstated assumption of those in the highest court is that the country is basically on the right track. From this it follows that the basic function of the judiciary is to ensure that government does not spoil things by over-reaching itself and interfering unduly in the lives of the people. That was not our starting point nor how we envisaged our role. Although South Africa might have had one of the most advanced constitutions in the world, South African society was still manifestly and grievously unjust. Centuries of colonial domination and apartheid had established structures of privilege and subordination that kept our people divided.

If the full promise of the Constitution was to be achieve., constitutional interpretation ha. to take .ue account of the legacies of lan. .ispossession, force. removals an. .is-enfranchisement that lay heavily on the majority of people in the country. Similarly, it ha. to grapple with the reality that well-entrenche. structures of patriarchy continue. to impose unacceptable .isabilities an. subor.ination on women. The nee. for transformation was therefore the pivot on which the Constitution turne..

When, some years later, I was asked at a luncheon in the US Supreme Court whether I would say that the South African Constitutional Court was an activist court, I was able to answer, 'Yes, we were an activist court'. But, I was able to add immediately, we were working with an activist Constitution. It might be that in other countries where basic rights were not expressly spelt out, judges who were eager to uphold such rights might seek to invent a ghostly constitutional order immanent in the constitutional text. Alternatively, and with perhaps less discomfort, they could cite international human rights conventions to which their country had adhered as aids to interpreting their constitutions. In our case, however, a value-intense and explicit text left us with no alternative – we were obliged to work with the idea of the Constitution being a living tree that sheltered and promoted an emancipatory vision of democratic rights.

Even a most cursory reading of the Kenyan Constitution suggests that it too has an overtly activist character. Both the use of specific words and the thrust of the Constitution as a whole would seem to require judges to move decisively away from the old styles of overly formal and ultra-technical reasoning. To this outside eye at least, it seems that the Constitution should be interpreted in a rich, expansive and purposive manner that takes full account of the circumstances which led to its adoption. That, of course, will be a decision for the Kenyan judiciary to make. I will simply mention that in South Africa we found it necessary to treat the language used in the text of our Constitution in a manifestly progressive and transformative way. Naturally, in doing so, we judges did not suck purposes from our thumbs or impose our subjective predilections on the words used in the Constitution. Rather, we allowed the value system in the Constitution, both explicit in the language used and implicit in its overall design and socio-historical context, to dictate its meaning. In this respect, Ismail Mahomed's concept of a radical rupture with the past fed quickly into our vision of what the Constitution required us to do. What took rather longer to evolve was an appropriate jurisprudential methodology to give effect to the transformative vision.

We had all been brought up in the traditions of the British common law approach to legal interpretation. This had required us to start our inquiry by looking at the intention of the legislature as the authoritative source of law. And then the interpretive dance would begin. It was agreed that if the language of parliament was clear and unambiguous, you had to give effect to it, however unjust or irrational its consequences might be. Yet some judges would find ambiguities in the words used, others would not. Then, once you'd detected a degree of ambiguity you could find canons of construction either to limit the ambit and effect of the measure, or to give it maximum force. Thus, on the side of cutting down, you could refer to the presumption that the legislature intended to uphold as much liberty as possible. In South Africa we all knew that in reality our white supremacist parliament wished precisely to suppress dissent and that its actual intent was to compel people to submit to its racist and authoritarian will. Yet some judges in some courts would use fictional conventions to soften the impact of the vicious laws. At the same time, more authoritarian judges would cite canons of construction that required the courts to give as much efficacy as possible to the law under discussion – same words, different judges, different interpretations, all purporting to use the same methodology.

In a much-commented case in point I personally happened to be the subject of the litigation. While I was being held without trial in solitary confinement under the draconian ninety-day law, colleagues of mine on the outside applied to the Cape Supreme Court for an order allowing me to receive reading matter and writing material. The two judges hearing the matter (before whom, incidentally, I had frequently appeared) said that as a non-convicted prisoner I should at least enjoy all the rights of an awaiting-trial detainee, save for being cut off from the outside world for purposes of interrogation. This order actually helped me to preserve my sanity, and fortunately for me, by the time the decision was overruled in the Appellate Division of the Supreme Court, I had already been released.

Sadly for other detainees, however, the judges in the highest court in the land emphasised that the purpose of the law was to induce the detainee to speak, so that reading matter and writing materials could be withheld. The chief justice commented that if the detainee had been accustomed to having cigars and champagne before his detention, this did not mean that he would be entitled to enjoy these comforts once in custody. A number of commentators referred to *Rossouw v Sachs* [*Rossouw v Sachs* 1964 (2) SA 551 (A)] as constituting the high-water mark [or rather the low-water mark] of the judiciary using canons of construction to voluntarily lean as far as they could in favour of repressive legislation adopted to maintain the system of apartheid.

Now, in the new constitutional era we found ourselves in a completely different conceptual arena. We had to find new ways of working, thinking and expressing ourselves.

*When our first ju*gments came out many of our colleagues in other courts *di*n't regar* us as real ju*ges at all. As they saw it, we were not following the patterns of reasoning that, until then, ha* been entrenche* in South African jurispru*ence.*

To be sure, we were no longer focusing on deciding what parliament had intended from the language it had used. Rather, the primary investigation was whether the Constitution actually permitted what parliament had tried to achieve. If at first blush a straightforward reading would result in unconstitutionality, we had to determine whether the language could nevertheless be stretched a little so as to make the measure constitutionally compliant. We ceased to use the canons of construction derived from the common law, and instead created a vocabulary and system of judicial thought congruent with the demands of a functioning constitutional democracy. Instead of automatically and obediently giving effect to the primary meaning of the words used, we would, in appropriate cases, see if the words used could, with some but not too much strain, be read in a manner that was consistent with the Constitution. If they could not even with some degree of strain be so read, then we were duty-bound to strike them down as unconstitutional. Sometimes we would read the words down, that is narrowly, to limit their effect so as to preserve constitutionality. Eventually we even began, in a limited number of cases, to read words into an under-inclusive text. Far from intruding on the work of parliament, this would free parliament from having to squeeze in to its legislative programme a special amendment in circumstances where the text could easily be remedied by the Court itself adding the requisite words. The criteria for judicial 'reading-in' were that the duty on parliament was clear, the textual change was easily fitted in and there would be no major budgetary implications.

The concept of proportionality became fundamental to our work. Judges in South Africa had never expressly used proportionality as a key concept. What did it mean? One prominent English judge, trying to find a nice simple way of expressing it (and often common-sensical British judicial wisdom can be really useful) said: 'You don't use a sledge hammer to crack a nut'. That's certainly a good start. But in actual cases you don't get nuts and sledge hammers. You deal with intricately mixed bags of competing claims. You try to find points of conceptual purchase and repose, of principled intellectual intervention, before you do the balancing.

As I saw it, we were not so much dealing with determining the cut-off point between right and wrong, as handling the tension between right and right. In a modern pluralistic society there are divergent groups that all have genuine claims under the Constitution. What happens when these legitimate claims collide? That is where we have to harmonise and balance them out as well as we can, guided by the text, context and values of the Constitution. And this is where proportionality comes in.

The issue is not one of yes or no, right or wrong, black or white. I am reminded of the old popular American song, *Is you is, or is you ain't, my baby?* This, more elegantly expressed, is what legal interpretation had required in the past. Today a better ditty would be, *Please don't say no, say maybe.* It all depends. By its very nature proportionality is contextual. It all depends on the circumstances, the facts, the extent to which protected rights are engaged and the degree to which elements of public interest must enter the scales. It also puts into the scales the means used in the measure to advance the public interest – was it really necessary to go that far? And finally it involves an overall balancing of all these elements.

Classificatory logic on its own will not provie the answer. Nor will a reference to Oxfor English Dictionary. A egree of weighing an of making a value jugment is inevitable. Proportionality.

To use proportionality is not to sacrifice the objectivity and dispassion required of the judicial officer. On the contrary, it demands candid explanation from the judge of the weight which she or he feels should be attached to each and every objectively established element in the equation. Indeed, far from proportionality being based simply on a hunch or mere say-so of the judge, it should be founded on the transparent seeking-out of the actual factors which guided the judge in coming to her or his conclusion. In the past, technicity was used by all judges, whether enlightened or reactionary, to mask and justify the real but hidden reasons for their decisions. I believe that, even if tactically useful at times for progressive lawyers working in an oppressive legal environment, in its overall effect formalistic straight-jacketing of the law undermined its congruence with justice and inhibited its organic growth. In an open and democratic society, on the other hand, judicial integrity is maintained not by abstracting rules from the setting in which they are applied and purporting to give them a decontextualised and entirely self-referential autonomy. On the contrary, the law thrives and justice is best served when it is rooted in lived reality and demonstrably imbued with the values of an open and democratic society.

These thoughts came vividly to mind when our Court was dealing with the case of *Van Heeren* [*Minister of Finance an Other v Van Heeren* (CCT 63/03) [2004] ZACC 3; 2004 (6) SA 121 (CC); 2004 (11) BCLR

1125 (CC); [2004] 12 BLLR 1181 (CC)] which was concerned with affirmative action. In preparing my judgment which largely concurred in the majority decision by Dikgang Moseneke, I cited what is considered to be one of the great judgments in modern times, written in dissent by US Supreme Court Justice Thurgood Marshall. In poignant terms, he expressed his sadness at the manner in which the majority of his Court were using formal reasoning about equal protection to strike down socially progressive measures that the city of Richmond had been using to ensure that minority contractors received their fair share of municipal contracts. Sometimes, he said, a page of history could provide more legal wisdom than a thousand pages of logic. He pointed out that the city of Richmond had been at the centre of the slave-holding Confederacy. It was now taking practical steps to overcome the deeply imbedded racially based injustices of the past. Yet far from supporting these necessary and progressive measures, the majority in the Court was using the language of formal non-discrimination to strike them down.

Similarly, in South Africa, we judges found it necessary not only to look at the history of our country, but also to take account of the inequality that marked the lives still being led by our people today. To us it was clear that the very existence of the Constitution owed much to the struggle of the great majority of our people to get a more just society. This required from us replacing the formulaic and intellectually lazy judicial thinking of the past with a jurisprudence oriented towards transformation.

In retrospect the new approach now seems obvious and self-explanatory. At the time, however, we struggled, moving step by step to find the right conceptual footing. Some of the counsel who appeared before us had great difficulty in making the necessary adjustments. But eventually they got used to the new style of argument. I am happy to report that today the judiciary receives extremely helpful inputs from advocates deploying sensitive and thoughtful argument. And I am even happier to report that many of our former law clerks are now prominent amongst them.

I've spoken about the way in which the Constitution expressly affirms many of the values of an open and democratic society. I turn now to describe themes that, although not expressly identified in the text, gradually emerged in the course of our work as important organising principles. Anyone in Africa will immediately recognise them. I call them the three Ds. They are Dignity (ubuntu), Difference and Dialogue. None of them had featured in forensic discourse under apartheid. As mentioned above, in a wicked society different actors had relied upon formalism with different purposes in mind. The positivist approach had been convenient for everybody. The judges who had applied overtly racist and repressive laws could evade moral responsibility by saying that they had simply been carrying out the law. At the same time, although those of us resisting the laws could never in court challenge the injustices of the apartheid state as such, we could use technical grounds to try and trip up or delay the application of manifestly unjust laws. Thus we had made administrative law as technical as possible. We had used legal fictions to interfere with or at least temporarily limit the nefarious impact of the law. Thus, one of the principles of judicial review on which we had relied was that the legislature had intended that administrative functions authorised by the law would be carried out in a manner that respected the *au*●*i alteram partem* rule, that is, that persons who stood to be affected by the administrative action would be given a prior hearing. So we had become experts at technicalities.

Now, as new judges we had to abandon that whole way of thinking. Rigorous respect for the constitutional text was still required – we could not simply make up the law as we went along. But the foundations of legal reasoning had become different. Previously, the progressive lawyer had been somebody who had been smart at applying technicalities. Now, however, the forward-looking lawyer had to understand what the Constitution was about, the purpose of the Constitution and why it should be a principled and effective agency for transformation. It was in this setting that the new legal concepts of Dignity, Difference and Dialogue came in an inter-related manner to enter our judicial discourse even though only Dignity appeared in the constitutional text.

Dignity relates very much to the principle of ubuntu. As mentioned above, ubuntu emerged strongly in our first case which dealt with the death sentence. It then disappeared from our jurisprudence for a number of years before coming back quite strongly in the Court's reasoning more recently. The concept of ubuntu is something that our people can recognise and understand. It is especially strong amongst the poor who have looked out for each other, helped each other in the most difficult times. It underlines the spirit of human interdependence. In this sense it is very different from what a distinguished US Supreme Court judge described as the most fundamental of all rights, the right to be left alone. The right to personal autonomy has indeed been one of the great achievements of human civilisation. What has been called the firstness of the First Amendment was born out of people fleeing from Europe coming to America to get freedom from religious intolerance. Yet if pushed to an extreme, the result of the right to be left alone could be that you are dying of hunger, but with your last breath you have a constitutional right to curse the government. Thank you very much, but this is not the vision of freedom that we feel is appropriate for South Africa.

Ubuntu encapsulates what I might call the holy trinity of our Constitution, namely, human dignity, equality and freedom. All three notions are indivisible and mutually supportive. Thus, dignity combines the individual right to personal freedom and autonomy on the one hand, with the understanding that we live in communities that are meaningful in the lives of our people, on the other. The dignitarian approach to interpretation accordingly seeks to achieve an appropriate and organically interactive interaction between purely personal aspirations and societal responsibilities.

The second of the three Ds is Difference. In South Africa difference was used to divide our nation. The whites claimed that they were different from blacks not only in appearance but also in culture and level of civilisation. Colonial domination, segregation and apartheid were all buttressed by the principle of White Supremacy. The result was that by law the whites ended up owning eighty-seven per cent of the land and in practice ninety-five per cent of productive capital. By law, whites ran everything. They dominated every aspect of government and made and enforced the laws. So, the imposed difference based on skin colour became our enemy. We fought against discrimination based on this artificially constructed difference.

> *We struggled for the right to be the same, to be equal. But to be the same did not mean that we had to be identical. It did not require suppressing our own characteristics to fit into the mould created by the dominant minority. It meant the right to be treated equally, as you were, whoever you were.*

It presupposed the right to come into diversity and enrich an evolving common society. So we also fought for the right to be different. The key was the right to be treated with equal concern and respect.

This right was important not only in relation to race but also to gender. Thus, women had the right not to be discriminated against because they were not men. But there were important respects in which they were different from men. Thus men cannot bear and suckle babies, women can. And in our society women more often than men find themselves pursuing double careers, combining jobs and family. In these circumstances equal treatment does not mean compelling women to submit themselves to legal rules and principles created by male legislators and judges who only had male breadwinners in mind. On the contrary, combining the notions of dignity and difference required that the law be adapted to enable women to lead dignified and productive lives with guaranteed time off from work for maternity leave, which would not, it should be underlined, be equated with illness. From that flowed the rights of fathers too to take time off to assist at birth and look after the baby.

Similarly, our Court dealt frequently with the right of gays and lesbians to be different from straights. The Court emphasised that equality meant being treated with equal concern and respect across difference, and not the suppression of difference. At the same time, the Court recognised that there was difference about the significance of difference for different groups.

> *When the Court affirme• the constitutional rights of same-sex couples to marry, it also acknowle•ge• the constitutional right of faith communities not to be compelle• to perform an• celebrate marriages that went against the tenets of their religion.*

It accordingly emphasised that opponents of same-sex relationships should not be castigated as bigots. Thus the same constitution that protected the fundamental rights of people to have their love and intimacy publically recognised by the law, protected the rights of opponents of same-sex marriages to conduct their own lives in accordance with their firmly heterosexual beliefs. For gays and lesbians who had been discriminated against and subjected to hateful indignity, this was a strong example of the right to be the same coupled with the right to be different, that is, of the same rights being accorded to members of a sexual minority. On the other hand, the right to be different could also be claimed by those whose belief systems place them in opposition to same-sex relationships.

> *What the Constitution envisage•, then, was not war between the secular an• the sacre•, but a respectful an• principle• co-existence between them.*

The issue of the right to be different also cropped up in a poignant manner in the case of *Pillay* [*MEC for E•ucation: KwaZulu-Natal an• Others v Pillay* (CCT 51/06) [2007] ZACC 21; 2008 (1) SA 474 (CC); 2008 (2) BCLR 99 (CC)] where Chief Justice Pius Langa wrote what I consider to be a particularly eloquent judgment. Ms Sunali Pillay, a scholar at Durban Girls' High School wanted to a wear a nose stud. In the days of apartheid the school had been for whites only but now roughly a third of the girls were of Indian origin, a third of indigenous African origin and a third belonged to the group that would formerly have been classified as white.

The school ha• issue• a general prohibition against the wearing of jewellery by the girls. Sunali •i• not challenge the general prohibition, but sai• that she shoul• be exempte• from it because in her case wearing a nose stu• was not simply an a•ornment but part of her culture an• religion. The Court uphel• her claim. The principle to be applie• was that of reasonable accommo•ation.

Where a very close aspect of a person's identity based on culture and religion was involved, the school authorities were obliged to do what was reasonably possible to accommodate the diversity. To do so would, in fact, enrich rather than degrade the learning environment of the school. If the other schoolgirls had difficulty understanding why an exception to the jewellery ban should be made for Sunali, the school should take advantage of their queries to explain the educational importance of tolerance in a multi-cultural and multi-faith society.

Thirdly I come to Dialogue. At the time of transition, Professor Etienne Mureinik memorably declared that the new constitutional order represented a bridge from a culture of authority to a culture of justification. Central to the concept of justification is the notion of dialogue.

The three branches of government – the legislature, the executive an• the ju•iciary – are neither intrinsically monolithic nor essentially at war with each other. On the contrary, the separation of powers un•er the Constitution requires that each one of them serves the same constitutional goals, but •oes so with •ifferent core, though overlapping, functions. This in turn necessitates constant constitutional conversation between the three arms of government.

Similarly, the Constitution presupposes an active, ongoing relationship between government and the people. The ambit and implications of this relationship became central in the *Doctors for Life* case [*Doctors for Life International v Speaker of the National Assembly an● Others* (CCT 12/05) [2006] ZACC 11; 2006 (6) SA 416 (CC); 2006 (12) BCLR 1399 (CC)]. Doctors for Life described themselves as a family oriented organisation associated with the Catholic Church. They said that they had principled objections to a proposed law that would allow certain experienced nurses as well as doctors to perform terminations of pregnancy. They acknowledged that they had been given an opportunity to present their views to the Portfolio Committee of the National Assembly. Then, after finding that their objections had not been accepted at that stage, they had asked the second house of parliament namely the National Council of Provinces (NCOP) to give them a further hearing. The NCOP had informed them that it would not be necessary for them to come to parliament in Cape Town. This was because the NCOP would in fact have hearings in all the provinces on three medical Bills, including the one in respect of which Doctors for Life wished to make representations. It should be mentioned that the second Bill was of a purely technical kind affecting the organisation of dentists. The third Bill, though, had a wider sweep. It related to traditional healers and the manner in which they should be registered, and what their relationship with scientific health practitioners should be.

As things turned out, however, at some stage before the proposed hearings in the provinces could be held, the NCOP stated that pressures on the parliamentary timetable obliged it to cancel the hearings. The three Bills were then duly adopted by the NCOP and signed into law by the president. Doctors for Life responded by approaching the Constitutional Court for a declaration that these statutes were unconstitutional because they had not complied with a constitutional requirement that the legislature take reasonable steps to involve the public in the adoption of legislation.

The application raised novel questions concerning the relationship between parliament and the public. All the requisite internal procedures required for parliament to adopt a valid law had been complied with. Moreover, parliament had rules that allowed the public to attend hearings and make submissions to appropriate committees at different stages. Could it be said, though, that the failure to follow through with the promised public hearings in the provinces invalidated the law? By a large majority, the Court said yes. In a wide-ranging and pioneering majority judgment Justice Sandile Ngcobo highlighted the difference between periodic representative democracy and ongoing participatory democracy, and emphasised that both were important in our democracy. In my concurrence I emphasised the significance of constant dialogue between government and the people. I stated that the Constitution had itself been the product of national dialogue, and should be interpreted in a manner which upheld the importance of dialogue in our public life.

In an open, democratic and pluralist society it was particularly important that the voices be heard of sections of the population that might not be strongly represented in the more powerful political parties.

The law was of momentous importance to tra•itional healers who were, for the first time in the country's history, being given a •egree of legal recognition. Their knowle•ge an• practices were essentially local in character, •epen•ing on the roots, bark, leaves, waters an• animals of the areas they inhabite•. Consulting •irectly with them in the languages they un•erstoo• an• in the places where they felt comfortable, woul• make them feel inclu•e• in the national polity.

In addition, they could make valuable contributions to the texture of the law and promote its understanding in the communities where they functioned. Dialogue, I stressed, and democracy went hand in hand.

The theme of dialogue also found a central place in the Court's approach to eviction law. In South Africa some of the most acute legal tensions and dilemmas have emerged in respect of the use of the courts to order evictions. All over the country, desperately poor black families had found shelter in shacks on vacant land or in overcrowded apartments in abandoned inner-city buildings. Actual and potential owners had then called upon local authorities to have them evicted to make way for development. But where were the poor families to go if no alternative accommodation was being provided? The Court decided that the issues could not be resolved simply by applying the ordinary rules of property law. On the contrary, it was necessary to look at land law in the context of our history of dispossession, as well as of the rights of all persons to have access to adequate housing.

How to balance the needs of the homeless, then, against the importance of ensuring respect for legal title? How to discourage land invasions and permit appropriate economic and social development, on the one hand, while acknowledging that these were human beings with a right to have a home somewhere on this earth, on the other? We came up with the requirement of meaningful engagement.

This had to take place between the owners and local authorities on the one side, and the unlawful occupiers on the other. The purpose of this engagement was to get the parties themselves to find as fair and practical solutions as possible. They would then have to report back to the Court, which would make the final ruling. The Court pointed out that the occupants should not be looked upon as being an anonymous poor mass required to make way for development. They had names, lived in families and each had personal histories. For their part, however, the poor could not simply dig in their heels and insist that they would not be moved. They had to be as creative in finding solutions to their housing situation as they were each day when seeking to survive.

The practice arose, then, of the Court giving fairly precise directions to the parties with regard to the issues with which the engagement should deal. It would require the parties to file affidavits by a certain date setting out the progress made, if any, as well as proposing solutions that they believed the Court should adopt on the date established for the next hearing. Key issues would be the length of the occupation, the timing of departure and especially the existence of alternative accommodation in areas reasonably close to where the occupants eked out a living and sent their children to school.

The process of meaningful engagement has come to be used extensively in many socially fraught eviction proceedings. It has both a procedural and substantive dimension. At its heart lies the notion of principled dialogue informed by the values of the Constitution and supervised by the judiciary. Ultimately the court will decide, but only after focused and significant dialogue between the parties has taken place. The notion is beginning to insert itself into other areas of enforcing social and economic rights, such as education.

It taps into the African spirit of bringing parties together so that in the context of constitutional values they can talk, talk, talk their way to a realisable and sustainable consensus.

Lastly, dialogue is central in terms of our relationship with parliament and the Executive. As judges you can be too cosy and you can be too combative. We don't want to be either. Too cosy means you look after us and we'll look after you, we trust everything you do. Too combative means you are the enemy, we are the great defenders of rights and we'll keep you in your place. Parliament has the same duty to defend fundamental rights as we have. The Executive has the same responsibility. We are all part of the same constitutional project aimed at improving the lives and happiness of the people.

This brings me to observe how important dialogue is in relation to remedies for the protection of rights. Where there is a right, there is a remedy. Without a remedy, there is no meaningful right. And much of the debate on rights and fundamental rights turns on what are appropriate manageable and meaningful remedies. We found in South Africa that we had to be very expansive and exploratory in developing remedies.

In this connection our relationship with parliament became specially important. We characterised this relationship as one of conversation, of dialogue. We give parliament opportunities to correct failures of the legislation, as required by our Constitution. When we strike down legislation, we will frequently issue an interim order to prevent anarchy during the period when parliament is curing the constitutional defect. We ordinarily give parliament anything from six months to three years to make the necessary legislative corrections. Parliament will be invited to tell the Court about what delay might be necessary for new legislation to be adopted and we will fix the time period according to the difficulties that could be anticipated.

The framing of orders also became delicate when they were to the effect that a state or official body had failed to meet constitutional obligations. Here we had a choice between simply making a declaration and leaving it at that, or issuing a structural injunction compelling the official or body to do certain things and report back to the Court by a certain date.

In the well-known Treatment Action Campaign case, we were urge• by the successful applicants to or•er the health authorities to roll out the anti-retroviral •rug Nevirapine to expectant mothers living with HIV, an• to report back to the Court on the progress they were making. We agree• with the TAC that the Ministry of Health ha• in fact faile• to meet its constitutional obligations.

We declined to issue the structural injunction asked for, however, and made an order to that effect. We were confident that a simple deliberation of the state's constitutional obligations would be sufficient to secure compliance. We did not feel it necessary to make what could have been seen as a rather bruising order requiring the ministry to report back to the Court. And as it turned out, our expectations were justified. Indeed, many commentators have observed that the Nevirapine case proved to be a turning point in the government's movement from denialism to one of responding actively to HIV, with the result that South Africa now has the biggest anti-retroviral programme in the world.

On the other hand, in cases where there has been repeated failure to respond to declarations or orders by the courts, or where an emergency exists that requires immediate response, then we will certainly issue an order requiring the officials concerned to do certain things and report back to the Court on a stipulated date as to what they have done.

Having discussed the three Ds, I now come to the three Cs. Though my experience leads me to regard them as being essential qualities of a good judge, they are not often spoken about in treatises on judicial training. These manuals usually concentrate on a fourth C, namely, Craft. Of course, judicial craft, that is conceptualising issues, evidence-gathering and judgment-writing, are fundamental to the judicial function. And, naturally, the two Is are also vital – Independence and Integrity. But, in my view, the hallmark of a good judge is to be found not only in competence, integrity and independence but in her or his capacity to exhibit the three Cs – Civility, Collegiality and Courage.

Civility includes courtesy and politeness. It requires that the judicial officer at all times maintains a dignified and respectful posture and voice. But it goes much deeper than that. It is central to acknowledgement of diversity and equality of voice in a pluralistic society.

Ju●ges are not expecte● to be neutral in relation to the values of the Constitution. Their job is to uphol● these values, with conviction, even passion. This means that they take si●es on issues like torture, abusive behaviour, racism, sexism an● all forms of unfair ●iscrimination. But they ●o not take si●es with regar● to the parties to a ●ispute.

Here they have to be completely impartial. Civility requires respect for the dignity and right to be heard of all litigants and all witnesses, whatever their background, whoever they might be, whatever it is they might have done or be accused of having done. Civility also obliges the judicial officer to conduct proceedings in a way that is manifestly fair. Judicial officers who are rude, quick-tempered, sarcastic and imperious undermine the rule of law and besmirch the judicial function.

Collegiality. One of the greatest discoveries I made in my years on the Bench was the importance of collegiality. Collegiality is based upon the understanding that although each judge must fiercely defend her or his independence when expressing judicial conscience, at the same time all judges must acknowledge that they are members of a team involved in developing an institution. Collegiality requires showing at all times appropriate respect for colleagues as well as for the institution. Work on the Bench is frequently stressful. Judges can argue forcefully amongst themselves with regard to how matters should be handled. We all have different temperaments. Yet, both in our interpersonal dealings and in our public pronouncements, we should aim at all times at preserving the integrity of the institution to which we belong. We should avoid conduct which has the intention or effect of belittling or marginalising our colleagues. As mentioned above, on the Constitutional Court we had people of the most diverse origins and experience. Our temperaments were also very different. Yet we worked very hard and very consciously to make all members feel equally valued and respected. When criticising opinions with which we disagreed, we attempted to use measured and respectful argument. Indeed, collegiality extended to our making proposals to colleagues who disagreed with our views, which we felt would strengthen their positions against our own positions! What mattered was the quality of the Court's decision as a whole rather than who we imagined would eventually come out smelling of judicial roses.

The most elusive and yet, I believe, the most important of the three Cs, is Courage. It relates to how you connect independence of spirit with collegiality and with acknowledgement of your judicial function. It requires true fidelity to your judicial conscience. At the end of the day, although judges work in an institutionalised and collective environment, and although what they do is intrinsically public in character, there is something unusually lonely in being a judge. You have to make decisions on matters that could impact profoundly on the lives of others, indeed on the integrity of the nation. But you have to do so without fear, favour or prejudice. In some cases, having courage requires taking a stand that might be distressing to colleagues with whom you work every day. These might be colleagues whose thoughtfulness, skill and compassion you truly admire.

You might be in a tiny minority, even entirely on your own. Yet if you ‹isagree on a matter of significant principle you shoul‹ not allow yourself to sign on to something that you believe is wrong.

Equally, there might be other occasions where the pressure, consciously or unconsciously, to conform to a particular point of view comes not from people who historically have been hostile to the Constitution and its values, but from those who have fought hardest for its adoption. Thus, for example, in the case of Mr Soobramoney [*Soobramoney v Minister of Health (KwaZulu-Natal)* (CCT 32/97) [1997] ZACC 17; 1998 (1) SA 795 (CC); 1997 (12) BCLR 1696 (CC)], who was dying of renal failure, the Court declined to concede to broad public pressure to prolong his life by ordering that he receive privileged access to dialysis. Rather, it unanimously opted for a principled and sustainable approach in relation to access to scarce and expensive medical resources even if this meant that public anger would be directed at us. Our oath of office was not to strive to be popular but to uphold the Constitution and the law without fear, favour or prejudice. This did not mean that the decision should be written in cold and unsympathetic language. On the contrary, we chose language that emphasised the poignancy of a situation where resources were not coexistent with compassion. In tragic cases especially, the way the judges tell the story can be as significant as the outcome itself.

Constitutional adjudication is an ongoing project. One of the last public statements made by Pius Langa before his recent untimely death was on transformatory jurisprudence. He said that transformatory justice should not be equated with transitional justice. The transformation did not relate only to movement from racist, authoritarian South Africa to a new democratic South Africa.

It was not simply a case of five or ten years of change, an• then the transformation woul• be over. On the contrary, transformation was built into the very character an• nature of our en•uring constitutional project.

And to keep up with the new challenges that were emerging all the time, the courts constantly had to renew, renovate and transform their own thinking.

While all the members of our Court agreed on the need for transformation, we often disagreed on the way forward in particular cases: was it better to proceed by means of incremental advance through narrow interpretations sufficient to provide adequate answers to the cases before us, or was it preferable to attempt to lay down broad principles into which the particular cases could fit. Looking back, I notice that in my early years on the Court I tended to favour searching for broad principles. In my later period, I found myself favouring a more cautious, case-by-case approach. These are strategic questions that all courts have to face. I think there are some issues, some moments where you have to take a bold and sweeping philosophical stance. There are other times where it is advantageous to adopt a narrow interpretation that produces unanimity on a clear, simple and operational decision that can easily be implemented.

But whether we go for a wide-ranging or a narrowly focused approach, it is always the same project. We are part and parcel of transforming our society. It's still a very unjust society. We have made huge gains in South Africa of which we can be very, very proud. But there are many inequities and injustices that we still see all around us, all the time. And we just have to keep on keeping on engaging in enriching the texture of our jurisprudence, responding to the claims of our people, ensuring that no one is shedding a tear that needn't be shed in our society. Sadly, too many tears are being shed quite unnecessarily in our country; the courts are still being called upon to play a very, very important role.

We are not the enemy of government. We are not the opposition to any political party. We are the colleagues of the other branches of government, called upon by the Constitution to ensure it is a wonderful project that we have been involved in.

I think there is no shortcutting some of the troubles and trials we have had. Debates on the functioning of the courts can be very, very sharp, I don't think that there is any way of avoiding them. But it has been a marvellous project. I believe that all of you here in Kenya can feel proud of the fact that your judiciary can now play a role which is inspiring to society, which is operational, functional, sustainable and meaningful. As the chief justice said, the day is fast approaching, in fact it has already arrived, when decisions of the Kenyan courts are now being quoted positively in other courts on the continent. Together we are creating a new African jurisprudence. In so doing we are making a rich and original contribution to world jurisprudence of which we can justly be proud.

Equality Jurisprudence: The origin of doctrine in the South African Constitutional Court

10TH MCDONALD LECTURE | CENTRE FOR CONSTITUTIONAL STUDIES, UNIVERSITY OF ALBERTA | CANADA | 1998

Mr Hugo [*Presi*⋅*ent of the Republic of South Africa v Hugo* (CCT 11/ 96) [1997] ZACC 4; 1997 (4) SA 1 (CC); 1997 (6) BCLR 708 (CC)] was aggrieved. While sitting in prison near Durban he got to know that the newly inaugurated president, Mr Nelson Mandela, had issued what was called a 'Presidential Act' ordering the release of disabled people, children under a certain age, and mothers of children under 12. Mr Hugo said (after taking legal advice): 'I have a child under 12, whose mother is dead. Why have I been left out? That's discrimination, a violation of my rights under Section 8 of the Bill of Rights in South Africa's new Constitution'.

Mr Prinsloo [*Prinsloo v Van* ⋅*er Lin*⋅*e* (CCT 4/96) [1997] ZACC 5; 1997 (3) SA 1012 (CC); 1997 (6) BCLR 759 (CC)] was a farmer, five hundred miles away, and he was also aggrieved. A fire had spread from his land on to a neighbour's property, causing extensive damage. The Forestry Act said that if you lived in a 'non-fire controlled zone', which he happened to do, and fire spread from your land and caused damage to a neighbour's property, you had to prove that you had not been negligent. Mr Prinsloo alleged that putting the onus on him was a denial of his right to equality under Section 8. 'Why should I be treated differently from people in fire-controlled zones?' he asked (after getting a legal opinion).

These cases happened to reach the Constitutional Court at roughly the same time, and in the same way that jurisprudence sometimes has, two people who were never to meet became close accomplices in the evolution of basic doctrine. In the words of Justice Cardoso, 'The sordid controversies of litigants are the stuff out of which great and shining truths will ultimately be shaped. The accidental and transitory will yield the essential and the permanent'. So it came about that hearing these two cases in near conjunction compelled our Court to reflect on what the equality principle in our new Bill of Rights was all about. Who should be safeguarded by it? What kinds of legislation or executive action should raise questions of viewing equal protection not just as a 'good thing', but as a fundamental human right?

We began the search for answers, as our Bill of Rights encourages us to do, with a look at international jurisprudence on the question. In general terms, in interpreting our Bill of Rights we are required to apply the principles and promote the values of an 'open and democratic society based on freedom and equality'. We were trying to find basic principles, an approach, a perspective, which would guide us in our quest to protect fundamental human rights and enable us to do so in a manner which resonated with our Constitution and our historical circumstances.

A more profound contrast we could hardly have imagined: someone sitting in prison, feeling aggrieved because he was being treated differently as a man, a father, a male parent, from the way he would have been treated if he had been a female parent, as compared to somebody worried about being more at risk of paying compensation because he happened to be in a non-fire controlled zone rather than a fire-controlled one. One sensed that the distinction could be analytically useful, and the obvious thing to do was to seek direction from the jurisprudence of countries of common law background that had a Bill of Rights similar to ours.

In the United States, the equal protection clause was clearly designed to protect former slaves from being discriminated against. But brilliance of articulation does not necessarily go hand in hand with consistency of outcome; the US Supreme Court thrives on disagreement rather than agreement. To make matters worse, majorities become minorities, and minorities become majorities. Would it be helpful to us in South Africa to import all the arguments that divided American lawyers? In the end it seemed hard to get clear and convincing doctrine on equality from a deeply fissured US Supreme Court operating with a different constitution in a different historical and cultural setting.

We looked to the work of the Indian Supreme Court. It too had a coruscating and technically robust jurisprudence, developed by judges who wrote about fundamental rights in admirably passionate terms. Yet the text and the context of the Indian Constitution were different from ours. Did we want to encourage endless research and argument into what the different Indian judges had said and meant at diverse moments?

Next we looked at Canadian jurisprudence on equality, a dynamic area of Charter interpretation, and an interesting and fascinating one. For me, the *Andrews* case provided more illumination than any other I had read from any jurisdiction, and although the actual outcomes proposed by the judges were disparate, a forceful guiding principle emerged. As I understood it, the decision centred equality law on the need to overcome discrimination against groups historically subject to disadvantage. I felt: hooray, the Canadians have found the magic bullet that cures all equality-related infirmity. Of special value was the fact that like the Charter, our Bill of Rights was structured around a two-stage mode of analysis: has a right been infringed? If so, can the limitation be justified? But then I read the later judgments. And the Court divides 4:3:1, 2:3:3. Some judges agree with other judges on some aspects and not on others, and it becomes very, very difficult to extract unequivocal and easily transferrable doctrine. By a fortunate course of events, at about that time I was invited to a conference (in Halifax) of the Canadian Institute of Judicial Administration, and heard an absorbing talk on equality by Professor Lynn Smith. She summed it all up in about twenty pages, with a nice table, A, B, C, D, E, making the case law easy for outsiders. Yet, at the end, there were at least three major positions to choose from. We don't want our counsel jumping up and down saying we support this bloc in the Canadian Supreme Court or that bloc. It shouldn't be necessary in South Africa to become an expert on the intricate oscillations of the Canadian Supreme Court; that's what we expect the trade of Canadian lawyers to be about. So what do we do?

Equality by its very nature is difficult. It is difficult philosophically and difficult to apply in practice. People change, ideas change, judges change.

There are hundreds of years of experience in liberty jurisprudence and there is an even longer history of the courts wrestling with achieving an appropriate balance between the rights of the citizens and the responsibilities of those exercising public power. Yet it was only in the 1870s that equality jurisprudence started in the United States, and then with the abysmal 'separate but equal' doctrine. One can't expect clean and clear doctrine on a topic that by its very nature is messy, full of contradictions and constantly evolving. It would be illusory to think that a formula could be whipped up that would answer all questions all the time everywhere. The best we could do was to create an approach that was valid for us in South Africa, interpreting our constitutional text in the light of our reality, yet picking up from other jurisdictions those transportable ideas that were most valuable and accepted internationally.

All of law differentiates, distinguishing between one group and another; that is the nature of law: it classifies. Classifications by their nature include and exclude. The question is when does differentiation amount to unfair discrimination. Benefits and burdens are associated with classifications: a householder, a student, a patient, a litigant, as opposed to the non-householder, the non-student, the non-patient, etc. Classification is at the heart of legislation. If the courts felt compelled by equality doctrine to evaluate every piece of legislation for its reasonableness and justifiability, they would have no time left for other work. Sometimes more is less, and less is more. Good judicial resource management requires a principled pre-selection of cases (docket control) based on criteria related to why a Bill of Rights was adopted in the first place. Astute litigants should not be permitted to use mere differentiation in laws for tactical or delaying purposes, clogging up the courts so that truly meritorious cases get swamped and lost.

In theory, every case should be equal and have an equal chance of reaching the Constitutional Court; but some cases, in terms of equality principle, are more equal than others, more meritorious by their very nature. Peter Hogg, whom I find most useful as a guide to mainstream thinking in Canada on jurisprudential questions, has pointed out that in the first few years of the Charter jurisprudence of the Canadian Supreme Court, hundreds of cases were brought under the equality section, frequently, I understand, by privileged and advantaged persons. The success rate was low and the time taken high. Reading between the lines, it seems that a need was felt to separate cases that truly raised constitutional questions from those based on the ordinary differentiations that make up standard law-making, leaving some citizens aggrieved.

It was in this setting that the landmark Canadian case of *Andrews* was decided. Now it all seems so obvious – that equality jurisprudence should be based on the anti-discrimination or human rights principle. Yet nothing is obvious until attention is drawn to it, when suddenly and retrospectively it becomes self-evident. Studying the judgment brought home to me that there could be two distinct bases for judicial intervention in relation to equal protection of the law: the rational relationship rationale and the human rights rationale. Rationality review features strongly in US and Indian equality jurisprudence, though it rarely results in legislation being struck down. It requires that legislation serve some legitimate purpose, that there be some kind of discipline, or, as Cass Sunstein puts it, it mustn't represent a 'naked preference'. But it's very, very easy to pass that threshold. The main focus of equality jurisprudence is what I would call the human rights dimension.

Equality, as we understand it in the contemporary world, is associated with non-discrimination. It is designed to deal with the ways and means whereby societies marginalise, oppress, diminish, or demean people because they are what they are. That is what is generally understood by equality. That is what the international human rights instruments were designed to respond to. The Universal Declaration of Human Rights was adopted to deal with the memory of terrible genocide, racial persecution, the denial of the humanity of people simply because they were Jews, gypsies or gays, whichever it might have been. Bearing in mind our own distinctive past, this had to be the launch pad for a coherent philosophy of equality for South African jurisprudence.

The equality clause is the first substantive clause in the Bill of Rights; in our interim Constitution it comes before the right to vote or the right to free expression. It is our 'First Amendment'. Our new democratic Constitution and Bill of Rights were designed precisely to overcome apartheid, separation, inequality, to eliminate the practice of determining people's rights, duties and responsibilities simply on the basis of the colour of their skin, or the birthplace of their ancestors. It is impossible not to interpret our constitutional equality aspirations except against the background of institutionalised racism. At the same time, we have to recognise that inequality, (discrimination, subordination, treating people as inferiors, denying them full citizenship in a moral sense), isn't based simply on race. Possibly it is the awareness of the pain that people suffered under apartheid and continue to endure today because of the legacy of the past, that has made us especially sensitive to all forms of marginalisation and exclusion. In any event, our Bill of

Rights has an expansive list of categories of unlawful discrimination: discrimination on the grounds of race, colour, creed, language, disability, age, and sexual orientation are some of the grounds. Once you are aware of oppression and prejudice in one area, you extend that awareness to other categories. The underlying principle must be respect for the equal worth and dignity of all human beings.

It was relatively easy to apply rationality review coupled with a human rights approach to Mr Prinsloo in the non-fire control zone. In fire-controlled zones, express statutory duties were placed on land-owners, while in non-fire controlled zones, persons were prodded by the shifted onus of proof to take special precautions against fire-spread from their land. There was a rational purpose behind preventing those who had peculiar knowledge of what had happened on their land from simply saying: 'I don't know how it started; it is up to you to prove it was my fault'. What about the human rights dimension? Here we were able to pick up something directly from Lynn Smith's helpful analysis of the Canadian Supreme Court's approach to equality. It was a quotation from Madame Justice L'Heureux-Dubé who was in a minority of one amongst her colleagues and included in the survey, it seems, almost to complete the picture, because you can't leave out a judge! In that one paragraph – which we quoted in Prinsloo's case – she articulated much that seemed to capture the underlying thrust of our equality provisions. The emphasis, she said, is on the extent to which dignity as a human being is being assailed because of membership of a particular group. The emphasis she placed on the actual impact of a measure on the personal dignity of members of a group, appeared to be far more useful than the American strict scrutiny test, which seemed to be too formalistic and de-contextualised for South African purposes – too lax in its range and too rigid in its result. Respect for human dignity became the centrepiece of our equality analysis. Mr Prinsloo's pocket might have been affected by the special onus of proof, but his dignity was not assailed, and his equality challenge was accordingly rejected.

But what about Mr Hugo? The test was now straightforward enough, yet the context was complicated and the Court divided. This case required a close look at the actual impact of a measure, rather than the formal distinctions it drew, to see if it in reality undermined human dignity.

The first question before us was whether we coul• even review a presi•ential par•on. There was much international authority an• South African prece•ent to say that we coul• not. We •eci•e• that we coul•, hol•ing that in our new constitutional •emocracy no public official, not even the presi•ent exercising expressly conferre• presi•ential powers, coul• act outsi•e the scope of the Bill of Rights.

The fact that we could review did not, however, mean that we should review. The president had clearly differentiated on one or more of the enumerated grounds: the question was whether he had acted unfairly in doing so. One judge decided the issue was moot, so that left ten judges. Eight held that it was not unfair discrimination. Very crudely put, the argument was: Mr. Hugo had not lost any right or benefit or suffered any prejudice because an act of presidential grace had benefited the mothers; the Presidential Act was a one-off act of generosity to various vulnerable groups, not part of a patterned course of conduct marginalising men; the real choice was between releasing 440 women or freeing no one at all, since the number of fathers of children under twelve would have been about 15 000, an unacceptably high total for a crime-stricken public to accept as legitimate beneficiaries of presidential largesse; that as far as the children's' rights were concerned, to have 440 women released would benefit at least 440 children, and the president was entitled to take account of the fact that mothers tended in reality to be the primary caregivers; and that, looked at contextually, the impact on Mr Hugo had not been such as to reinforce patterns of systemic disadvantage or to impair his dignity in any way.

One judge decided it was unfair discrimination but that the measure could be justified in terms of our limitations clause, basically on the grounds mentioned above. The tenth judge said that the discrimination was both: unfair and unjustifiable. The unfairness, however, was not to Mr Hugo; he was in prison not because he was a man, but because of his crime. The unfairness was to women in general because the terms of the amnesty perpetuated the damaging stereotype of women as child-minders and of men as providers.

The dilemma facing the Court was real. On the one side was a patriarchal generalisation that was being reinforced, on the other, burdens were being lifted from 440 women, members of a group that had been historically disadvantaged and who in real life could be taken generally to have bonded more firmly with their children than the male prisoners had done. If you belonged to the school of thought that said any differentiation between men and women was objectionable because it reinforced stereotypes, then the answer was clear – the tenth judge was right. If, on the other hand, you focused on the actual lives that actual people led, and looked at women where they were in life and what their actual wants and needs were, you would end up with the majority.

The case highlighted in a vivid way the tension that can exist between a powerful broad principle and the concrete lives that people lead. I had no problem in agreeing with the notion that being kind to some women was not being cruel to all women, nor was it injurious to the self-esteem or dignity of the male prisoners. Similarly, it would have been an unconvincing form of pro-feminism to say to the women: we are not going to let you be with your kids because to do so would be paternalistic and undermine your dignity and be damaging to womanhood in general. As far as Mr Hugo himself was concerned, he wasn't being oppressed because he was a man; his dignity was not being touched in any way. He could always apply for early release, and if the relationship with his child was particularly relevant, that could be a factor to be taken into account on an individualised basis.

Theoretically a non-gendered release of all parents in an active relationship with their children would have been ideal. But, in practical terms, it was administratively just not feasible for a case-by-case enquiry to be made. It was 440 women, or nobody. Looking back, I wonder how much I might have been unconsciously influenced by what I had learnt years back from my former wife about the common law prisoners she had met while a political prisoner, namely, that the only bright and meaningful thing in their wrecked and marginalised lives had been their relationship with their children.

I will now take you quickly through some other equality cases that we have had, before concluding with the latest, and, as far as I'm concerned, the most controversial one of all.

In a matter reported as *Brink v Kitshoff* [*Brink v Kitshoff* NO (CCT 15/95) [1996] ZACC 9; 1996 (4) SA 197 (CC); 1996 (6) BCLR 752 (CC)] the estates of women married to insolvents were treated differently from the estates of men married to insolvents. That was a clear violation of the equality principle, without any justification. We struck down that particular law.

If you feel that we are completely unsympathetic to the rights of fathers, consider the *Fraser* [*Fraser v Chil•ren's Court, Pretoria North an• Others* (CCT 31/96) [1997] ZACC 1; 1997 (2) SA 218 (CC); 1997 (2) BCLR 153 (CC)] case, a poignant matter that achieved great publicity in South Africa. Laurie Fraser was living in a commune with Adriana Naude. He was a computer expert, she a violinist; she got pregnant and they split up before the child was born. When the child was born she placed the child for adoption, and he objected: 'It's my child, how can you give the child up for adoption without involving me?'

The Chil•ren's Act says that the consent of both parents is require• when the parents are marrie•, but only that of the mother if they are not marrie•. This, he conten•e•, was unfair •iscrimination against fathers. The hearing of the so-calle• fathers' rights case reveale• many contra•ictions.

One pro-feminist amicus curiae argued that there were many fathers, such as rapists, who were totally unmeritorious, with no real interest in the child, but who could nevertheless delay adoption proceedings and cause undue prejudice to the well-being of the biological mother, the child and the adoptive parents. Another pro-feminist amicus, argued to the contrary that there were many unmarried fathers who had close bonds with their children, and any blanket refusal to encourage them and all fathers to take equal responsibility for the care of their children would perpetuate stereotypes injurious to women, men and children alike. All fathers, the latter argued, should at least be heard, even if not required to give consent.

We decided the case on grounds that were narrow but technically sufficient to declare the law invalid, and then put parliament to terms to adopt a new provision that would strike the right balance between the claims of meritorious and unmeritorious fathers. We held that it was unfair to discriminate against Muslim and Hindu fathers, whose marriages were not recognised, while those of Christian fathers, were. The judgment of the Court went on strongly to emphasise the importance of encouraging paternal responsibility for and involvement in child-rearing.

In the *Harksen* case [*Harksen v Lane NO an• Others* (CCT 9/97) [1997] ZACC 12; 1998 (1) SA 300 (CC); 1997 (11) BCLR 1489 (CC)] we had to deal with a differentiation between spouses and non-spouses made by insolvency (bankruptcy) law. The law required the trustee of an insolvent to take in, as part of the insolvent estate, all the property of the solvent spouse, who then could get it back only on proof of ownership. All the judges agreed that there was discrimination on the grounds of marital status, a non-specified ground. The only issue was whether it was unfair. A majority of five judges held that because husbands and wives often merged their property, and because the process of retrieval from the insolvent estate was not unduly difficult, and bearing in mind the interest of creditors, the discrimination was not unfair. Three decided that it was indeed unfair to single out spouses for this treatment, rather than all members of a household, and that the process of vesting and retrieval – which was found nowhere else in the world, except perhaps in the Netherlands – was unduly onerous.

I was the ninth ju•ge an• went off on a tangent of my own. I sai• that what was unfair was the un•erlying concept of marriage in which only one business min• was seen to be at work. This was •emeaning to the two partners in a marriage relationship. If Jack falls •own an• breaks his financial crown, why shoul• Jill come tumbling after?

The focus on spouses rather than household family betrayed support for patriarchal notions which perpetuated disadvantage for wives. In Court, counsel always referred to the spouse as 'she, she, she', and in all of the literature it was 'she, she, she'. Interestingly, in all the articles, women authors opposed the provision while men tended to favour it. In preparing a judgment, you don't count up the number of articles for and against a position and check for the gender of the authors. Yet bells start ringing: why does an apparently innocuous and gender-free provision appear as inimical, hostile and oppressive to some people and not to others?

Is there something in live• experience which ren•ers certain phenomena sharply felt for some groups an• invisible to others, •oing so as a factor of their very membership of such groups? Can the web of •isa•vantage consist of umpteen seemingly neutral threa•s joine• by the habits of patriarchy?

And how does one prove the invisible, the experiential? Is it like the air we breathe, something of which we can take judicial notice, or must there be proof – so many parts nitrogen, so many parts oxygen?

In the *Larbi-O•am* case [*Larbi-O•am an• Others v Member of the Executive Council for E•ucation (North-West Province) an• Another* (CCT 2/97) [1997] ZACC 16; 1998 (1) SA 745 (CC); 1997 (12) BCLR 1655 (CC)] we had to deal with discrimination against non-nationals. Teachers from elsewhere on our continent, who had worked for years in South Africa, were confronted by regulations negotiated with a regional section of a teacher's union that declared they couldn't become members of the permanent teaching staff. This meant that as temporary teachers they could be replaced by South African teachers who might have qualifications far inferior to theirs. Many in fact had a right to permanent residence, and we felt it unfair to say in effect that even though they had satisfied the immigration authorities that they could stay in the country to work as teachers, they could then not be employed on the same basis as other teachers. Hovering in the background was the awareness of our past where labour was bureaucratically controlled, together with the knowledge that a tendency existed all over the world to treat foreigners as a subordinate class particularly vulnerable to abuse in the labour market.

Before discussing the most recent case, which dealt with indirect discrimination on grounds of race, I will highlight what seem to me to be six salient and inter-connected themes of our evolving jurisprudence.

The first is the need to evaluate the challenged measure in its concrete legislative and social context rather than according to abstract categories.

Second, the measuring-rod should be the extent to which substantive rather than formal equality is achieved. To treat everybody the same when they are in fact in unequal situations, is to perpetuate inequality. On the other hand, equality is promoted when special efforts are made to enable people belonging to subordinated groups to escape from circumstances that degrade and marginalise them. Such steps may expressly take account of race and gender, provided they are undertaken in a principled and not in an opportunistic or unfair manner. Equality is accordingly something still to be achieved, not something that has to be preserved. I think Ronald Dworkin got it right when he said that the essence of equal protection is not equal treatment but equal respect and concern, which might require different treatment to redress disadvantage.

Third, it is necessary to look primarily to the impact on the lives of the people actually affected, to see whether or not equality is being advanced or denied.

Fourth, special attention must be paid to the manner in which inequality systemically flows from patterns of disadvantage, subordination and dominance, which may exist outside of the measure under consideration. Thus, measures that happen to reinforce disadvantage are more likely to breach equality than those designed to overcome it. This is not to say that white men like me can't be oppressed or can't be the subject of unfair discrimination. Of course we can, but we should not be unduly ruffled by measures taken to interfere with and overcome those structured patterns of disadvantage that hold back the enjoyment by others of the many benefits of life that we may take for granted as our natural due.

Fifth, the core enquiry must always be the extent to which the measure impairs the dignity and sense of self-worth of members of the group affected, or impacts upon them in some other comparably serious manner.

Finally, in making such determination, the subjective experience or sense of injury of members of the affected group must be objectively analysed in the light of the values of the Constitution. It is not enough simply to say I feel discriminated against. The test must be whether the values protected by the Constitution have been undermined.

These ideas are in my view fully consonant with the importance attached by Canadian Chief Justice Dickson to the synergy between law, life and underlying values, and the emphasis placed by Madame Justice Bertha Wilson on impact, context and patterns of disadvantage. I won't single out any current judges for praise. I will mention, however, that shortly after the Hugo judgment was published, Madame Justice L'Heureux-Dubé accepted an invitation to come to South Africa to enjoy what we regarded as a well-deserved intellectual and moral triumph. She's a lively, bubbling, effervescent, communicative person with a sharp brain who lives the kind of philosophy that she talks about. Her visit was a great success.

I come to the last leg of this particular journey, the case of *Walker v. Pretoria Municipality* [*Pretoria City Council v Walker* (CCT 2/97) [1997] ZACC 16; 1998 (1) SA 745 (CC); 1997 (12) BCLR 1655 (CC)]. Mr Walker lived in a relatively affluent area of Pretoria, and belonged to a group that felt deeply aggrieved. His complaint was that he was being called upon to pay full metered rates for water and electricity, and was being sued when in default, while the people living in the black townships a couple of miles away firstly had their rates subsidised, secondly, were required to pay flat rate sums and, finally, were not being summonsed when in default. This, he argued, amounted to unfair discrimination against him based simply on the fact that he lived in a white suburb and not in a black one. The council, which represented a part of Pretoria that encompassed mainly affluent and overwhelmingly white suburbs but also included two black townships, had more white than black members. Nevertheless it took positions apparently sympathetic to the inhabitants of the black townships and justified them on the following grounds: a certain measure of cross-subsidisation was inevitable when it came to electricity and water charges; they could only charge lump-sum amounts in the townships, because meters still had to be installed; and summonses for non-payment were being slowly and progressively introduced, starting with the wealthier property owners. This latter process was being gently conducted so as to convert a culture of resistance and non-payment by a poverty-stricken and oppressed community into a culture of civic rights and responsibilities within a community that regards itself as part of the civic whole. And they pointed to the fact that the level of payments had in fact doubled.

Well, was it, or was it not, a case of unfair discrimination against Mr Walker? I haven't been completely fair with you in putting the question. I didn't give you the full text of Section 8 of the Equality Clause in the interim Constitution. The section provides that prima facie proof of discrimination, whether direct or indirect, gives rise to a presumption of unfairness. The case also turned to some extent on an appreciation of the facts. The whole Court accepted that the limited degree of cross-subsidisation did not amount to unfair discrimination nor, in the circumstances, did the different modes of fixing charges. But all but one of the judges agreed that issuing summonses only against defaulters in the affluent areas, amounted to indirect discrimination on the grounds of race, and that being so, the council was obliged to rebut the presumption of unfairness, which it had not done. Only one judge demurred, arguing that Mr Walker had suffered no discrimination at all, nor had he been treated unfairly; he was being asked to pay because he received water and electricity, not because he was white, and far from being a victim of prejudice, was the beneficiary of a structured system of advantage; accordingly, his dignity and sense of self-worth were not being impaired in any way, nor was any pattern of advantage or disadvantage of the group to which he belonged being reinforced or tracked by the council's conduct; if he had a complaint at all, it was not one of unfair discrimination but of unequal application of the law; his lament should not have been 'why pick on me?', but rather 'sue my neighbour as you sue myself'. Well, you might have guessed from the amount of detail given in support of his position who the lone dissenter was: it was me.

EIGHT

More than Crumbs from the Table: Enforcing Social and Economic Rights

Judge Not, Lest Ye Be Judged

COMMISSIONED BY THE FOUNDATION FOR HUMAN RIGHTS | APRIL/MAY 2014

In the beginning there was nothing. True, the constitutional text radiated with a pristine eloquence. Yet sitting up on the Bench responding to actual cases required us to go beyond simply reciting beautiful texts in resonant voice. The more important our role and the greater our authority, the stronger the need for us to be careful while we were bold. It was indeed a case of: *Hamba kahle umConstitutional Court.*

We had to establish meanings that were principled, coherent, operational and sustainable. And there was no case law and there were no textbooks to guide us. International judicial experience on the enforcement of social and economic rights was virtually non-existent. The constitutions of Ireland and India both included social and economic rights, but in each case these rights were expressly declared to be non-enforceable in courts of law. The Canadian Charter that was giving rise to extremely helpful fundamental human rights jurisprudence from the Canadian Supreme Court was completely silent on social and economic rights. The common law had nothing to say on the subject. The whole formalist and technicist mode of legal reasoning with which we were familiar was hostile to developing an appropriate form of legal discourse.

The very notion of fundamental rights was new and startling to the established South African legal mind. A young reader today could hardly imagine how revolutionary the idea was of treating the rights to health, housing, education and water, as existing on a par with the rights to speak out freely and to vote in secret. We had grown up in a legal system that gave more weight to the Oxford English Dictionary than to our country's history or its social cleavages. Moreover, the legal community of which we were a part had been so strongly imbued with notions of separation of powers that it could not even envisage judges naysaying government on questions of state policy and public spending, let alone developing an actual methodology for doing so.

How different it is today. As Chief Justice Willy Mutunga of Kenya has pointed out, the world is increasingly accepting that just as having a Bill of Rights is meant to correct deficiencies in concepts of representative democracy, so enforcing social and economic rights is intended to fill in lacunas left by the market.

Looking back, it is a tribute to the comprehensiveness and vitality of the 1996 Constitution that the jurisprudential void that existed when the Constitution was being elaborated, has now been filled. Social and economic rights were not included in the Interim Constitution with which the Constitutional Court worked in its first years. Then, even after the final Constitution came into force, cases concerning social and economic rights were slow in coming. It seemed that the legal profession was bemused by their unfamiliarity with such rights. Suddenly the *Soobramoney* [*Soobramoney v Minister of Health (KwaZulu-Natal)* 1998 (I) SA 795 (CC); 1997 (12) BCLR 1696 (CC)] case arrived, and it did so in precipitate, heart-wrenching fashion. Mr Soobramoney was dying of renal failure. After having been given emergency dialysis treatment at a state hospital, he had been informed that since his general medical condition made him a poor candidate for a renal transplant, the use of the expensive equipment would be reserved for patients whose prognoses placed them higher in line for such operations. When family funds for private treatment dried up, he returned in desperation to the state hospital, only to receive the same disheartening response. Claiming that this was denying him his constitutional rights, he went to the High Court and then, on an expedited basis, to the Constitutional Court.

These were not ideal circumstances for developing a deeply thought-through approach to the enforcement of social and economic rights. The conceptual terrain was completely unexplored. A human life literally turned on our decision. And though the oral argument in court was helpful, we had extremely limited time to do further research, engage in workshopping and write up our decision. A posthumously delivered judgment, however well articulated, would have been absurd. I do not think any of us were indifferent to Mr Soobramoney's heart-rending situation. The agony of Mr Soobramoney's counsel during argument had been palpable, as if his client's life had depended upon his persuasiveness. Remembering my days at the Bar, I had felt it appropriate to congratulate him from the Bench on the dignity of his presentation, and to add that if resources had been co-existent with compassion, the case would have been easy to resolve.

In the event, the Court went on to hold unanimously that when it came to the use of hugely expensive medical treatment, it could not fault the decision of the medical authorities, using rational and fair medical criteria, to give preference to the best candidates for renal transplants.

Mr Soobramoney ·ie· two ·ays after our ju·gment was ·elivere·.

I remember that one of our law clerks, who later went on to become a distinguished lecturer and advocate, stormed down the passage, muttering angrily: 'They could have found some money somewhere'. Sections of the press were highly critical of the decision. The human rights community in general expressed concern that through tolling the bell of lack of resources the Court would empty social and economic rights of any real meaning. I mention these circumstances to highlight some of the dilemmas built into the very heart of establishing constitutional justice in relation to competing individual and social claims to have access to extremely costly resources.

How should judges respond to the pressures placed upon them by the emotional exigencies of matters they hear? On the one hand, judges should never become machines and lose their sense of empathy and compassion for the often tragic circumstances of people who appear before them. On the other, judges must develop conceptually sustainable responses that are compatible with democratic and fair ways of allocating scarce public resources. It would be most unfortunate, for example, if persons with the best lawyers, the sharpest elbows, and the greatest contact with the media, were able to get privileged access to costly drugs and expensive medical procedures. These issues, I should add, are alive and the subject of hot debate in Latin America. In recent years courts all over that continent have intervened robustly and on a huge scale to order what they regard as just provision of medical care to litigants with persuasive claims.

Soobramoney indirectly placed on the agenda a theme which, I believe, calls for more serious reflection than it has so far received. It is a topic that human rights lawyers have regarded with alarm, not to say horror, namely the rationing of rights. At first sight the idea of rationing rights seems to challenge the very notion of their being both fundamental and deserving of equal protection. Yet, it is one thing to accept that all people are born free and equal, and that all rights are universal, indivisible, interrelated and interdependent. It is another to assume that all rights must be protected and enjoyed in the same way. Thus, any rationing of civil and political rights would strike at the very core of the right to equal protection of the law. So the fundamental principle of voting has to be 'one person, one vote'. Similarly when it comes to freedom of speech, the more voices there are the better. The same applies to the right to a fair trial which should not be enjoyed in different measure according to who the parties happen to be. In that sense, the quality of freedom, like the quality of mercy, is not strained. Of course, reasonable limitations can be placed on the enjoyment of these rights. But in our system the limitations must be imposed by a law of general application which applies equally to all affected by it. In the result, access to enjoyment of civil and political rights may be limited but will not be rationed.

> *Social an• economic rights, however, by their very nature require rationing, at least for the main part. Competition for resources is built into the DNA of social an• economic rights. They cannot be realise• by applying the principle that unless everybo•y gets everything, no one shoul• get anything.*

The jurisprudential issue is not whether the access to enjoyment should be rationed but how the rationing should be constitutionally controlled. This is implicit in the constitutional design, which is structured around the notion of progressive realisation of rights within available resources.

If the circumstances in which we heard *Soobramoney* militated against an adequately theorised approach to the enforcement of social and economic rights, the same could not be said about *Grootboom* [*Government of the Republic of South Africa an• Others v Grootboom an• Others* (CCT 11/ 00) [2000] ZACC 19; 2001 (1) SA 46 (CC); 2000 (11) BCLR 1169 (CC)]. By the time this case came to be argued before us, we knew that it was *the one*. A challenge in the Constitutional Court to the inclusion of social and economic rights in the final text of the Constitution on the grounds that this would violate the separation of powers had long been rejected. [See the *Certification* case – *In re Certification of the Constitution of the Republic of South Africa*, (CCT 23/96) [1996] ZACC 26; 1996 (4) SA 744 (CC); 1996 (10) BCLR 1253 (CC)]

> *There was no •ispute that the courts were boun• to uphol• social an• economic rights. In purely textual terms they enjoye• a status equal to that of civil an• political rights. The problem was not whether to enforce them ju•icially, but how to •o so. An•, as I have mentione•, we ha• nothing to gui•e us.*

In essence, as the winter rains were approaching, Mrs Grootboom and her children and a thousand other homeless people moved their shacks from low-lying land to a well-drained nearby hillside. Only then did they discover that the hillside had been set aside for low-cost housing, and that they were way down on the list. After mediation attempts had failed, they were evicted in a rough manner, ending up on a dusty sportsground with only plastic sheets to keep off the approaching rains. A local attorney, later supported by the Community Law Centre of the University of the Western Cape and the Legal Resources Centre, brought proceedings in the High Court to secure their constitutional right to housing. The High Court put in place an immediate temporary order providing that shelter be made available to the applicants pending the final determination of the matter. This secured sufficient time for judicial deliberation without constant references to the weather forecasts. By the time the matter reached us, we had a voluminous record and a thoughtful judgment of the High Court before us.

I kept imagining Mrs Grootboom's existential moment, lying on the groun• at night with the clou•s scu••ing overhea• an• won•ering: Why? Why? When my chil•ren an• I have •one nothing wrong an• all we want is a •ecent place to lay our hea•s, why are we sleeping out in the open with the rain about to fall? An• I, sitting in my robes on the Bench experience• my existential moment, won•ering: How? How?

How could we as judges respond to her situation in a manner that was principled, operational and sustainable, when armed only with the text of the Constitution? We looked at the relevant words once, twice, twenty times:

26. Housing
1. Everyone has the right to have access to adequate housing.
2. The state must take reasonable legislative and other measures,

within its available resources, to achieve the progressive realisation of this right.

3. No one may be evicted from their home, or have their home
   demolished, without an order of court made after considering
   all the relevant circumstances. No legislation may permit arbitrary evictions.

How did they apply to Mrs Grootboom's situation? The practice of our
Court was to workshop over and over again when issues of fundamental
importance were being considered. At each session we would go round
the table, ensuring that everybody was able to make their inputs, once,
twice, even three times. We explored many options. On the one hand,
institutional modesty and judicial prudence cautioned against asserting
an unduly aggressive and interventionist judicial posture. On the other
hand, if the rights of access to adequate housing were to have any
meaning at all, then surely there should be some judicial response to the
indignities to which Mrs Grootboom and others were being exposed.
The debates were lively. We all spoke and we all listened.

> Archimedes is reputed to have said: 'Give me a lever and
> I can lift the world'. Judges are constantly in search of
> jurisprudential equivalents. They seek organising principles
> which, faithful to the letter, purpose and spirit of the text,
> enable them to find coherent and effective ways to resolve the
> actual disputes before them.

In the end, we reached a broad consensus on what our approach should
be, and it was left to Justice Zac Yacoob to put his decisive imprint on
the judgment to be delivered. The key concept on which it relied was
the express constitutional duty of the state to take *reasonable* legislative
and other measures to realise the right. Courts were used to dealing with
the concept of what was reasonable. Thus the standard of reasonableness
was used in evaluating the amount of force that could be employed in

self-defence; the degree of care that a person should use when driving a motor car; and the degree of thoughtfulness required of someone fulfilling a function in public administration. By its very nature reasonableness was situation-based, involving elements of context and proportionality.

Furthermore, applying the test of reasonableness in scrutinising measures taken by the state, would meet separation of powers notions in two ways. First, the Court could not be said to be trespassing unduly into the heartland of the legislative and the executive functions when it was fulfilling its constitutional duty to uphold express provisions in the Bill of Rights. Second, in deciding whether or not the measures were reasonable, the judiciary would accord an appropriate degree of institutional decision-making discretion to the state. Thus, it would not assert its own opinions as to what it thought the best measures should be, but only scrutinise the measures actually adopted by the state to see if they fell within the broad parameters of reasonableness.

Turning to the facts of the case, the judgment found that by international standards the state had in fact been meeting it obligations by providing hundreds of thousands of homes free to persons living in shacks. But meritorious though it might have been, the housing programme nevertheless failed the test of reasonableness in one significant respect: it made no provision for accommodating people living in situations of crisis and extreme desperation, such as victims of eviction, fire and flood.

In deciding *Grootboom* in this way, the Court laid the first conceptual foundation stone of social and economic rights jurisprudence, namely, evaluation of the reasonableness of the measures taken by the state to fulfil its social and economic rights obligations progressively within its available resources. Internationally this approach won over many persons who had doubted the feasibility or appropriateness of courts enforcing social and economic rights. But large portions of South African academia remained unconvinced. Sandy Liebenberg, a pioneering thinker in this area, regretted the fact that the Court had failed to give any substantive normative content to the social and economic rights in question. This would have meant determining actual standards that government would have to meet. The more specific contention of many writers was that the Court should have adopted the 'minimum core' approach developed by the Committee of Economic, Social and Cultural Rights of the United Nations. They argued that evidence should have been sought to establish what the minimum core in relation to housing was. Once this had been done, then any person falling below that minimum core should have been entitled to go to court to ensure that their housing circumstances were ameliorated to reach the minimum level required. It should be mentioned that in *Grootboom* the Court did not completely close the door to the minimum core approach, but, in the social and economic rights matter to which I will refer, the *Treatment Action Campaign* (TAC) case [*MEC for Health, KwaZulu-Natal v Premier, KwaZulu-Natal: In re Minister of Health an♦ Others v Treatment Action Campaign an♦ Others* (CCT15/02) [2002] ZACC 14; 2002 (5) SA 717 (CC); 2002 (10) BCLR 1028 (CC)], it did.

The main issue in the Treatment Action Campaign case was whether, contrary to receive♦ ju♦icial wis♦om, the Court shoul♦ intru♦e on highly contentious issues of state policy. The Court graspe♦ this nettle.

It declared in general terms that it was precisely the separation of powers in the new Constitution that obliged the judiciary to check on state policies to see if they departed from the state's obligations to take reasonable measures to realise social and economic rights.

The Court hel♦ that restricting the provision of Nevirapine to only eighteen sites in the country was unreasonable an♦ represente♦ an unconstitutional violation of the rights of women living with HIV who were about to give birth in the great bulk of the country. Compliance with the Court's ecision marke• the beginning of a •ramatic change in the governmental stance on the provision of anti-retrovirals, with the result that to•ay South Africa has the largest ARV programme in the worl•, as mentione• previously.

I remember the *TAC* case vividly at a purely personal level. The Court had been filled with people wearing T-shirts saying 'HIV positive'. Young, old, female, male, black, brown and white – they remained totally silent while Arthur Chaskalson delivered a synopsis of the judgment. Then, moments after we had retired to the passage behind the Court, cheering broke out. Tears welled up in my eyes, not just because of the impact of the pandemic in our country, but because of a surge of overwhelming emotion about what it meant to be part of a court upholding fundamental rights.

Feelings of a different sort seized me when I was asked to write the lead judgment in the *Port Elizabeth Municipality* case [*Port Elizabeth Municipality v Various Occupiers* (CCT 53/03) [2004] ZACC 7; 2005 (1) SA 217 (CC); 2004 (12) BCLR 1268 (CC)]. About fifteen African families evicted from plots in another part of the city, put up their shacks on vacant land adjoining an upmarket suburb of Port Elizabeth. Under pressure from the well-housed homeowners in this suburb, the city council obtained an order in the High Court for the fifteen families to be evicted. The eviction order was overturned on technical grounds in the Supreme Court of Appeal. The council appealed to the Constitutional Court and I was asked to prepare the lead judgment. After reading the papers, I felt completely torn. The grounds on which the eviction order had been overturned appeared to be highly formalistic and not too persuasive.

My ju•icial oath of office require• me to uphol• the law without fear, favour or preju•ice, an• restore the or•er of eviction. At the same time I, as Albie, who ha• spent his whole life fighting against unjust •ispossession an• inequality, coul• not imagine myself signing an or•er compelling people ren•ere• homeless by aparthei• statutes, to give up their mo•est homes on vacant lan• owne• by people who alrea•y ha• comfortable houses of their own. I thought to myself: if I cannot uphol• my oath of office, the only course open to me is to resign.

Fortunately, I was able to convert a purely personal crisis into an objective, constitutional tension. On the one hand, the Constitution required that the landowners should not be arbitrarily deprived of their property. On the other, it declared that no one should be evicted from their homes except by court order, taking account of all circumstances, with a statute providing further that an eviction order should only be issued if it was just and equitable to do so.

Once more the Court workshopped the various dimensions of the issue. We decided that justice and equity would not be served simply by taking account of traditional land law concepts of the common law, but had also to pay regard to the history of dispossession and homelessness in South Africa. It became clear that the role of the Court went beyond merely deciding as a matter of law who was in the right and who in the wrong. As often happens in a pluralist constitutional democracy, the issue was not one of right versus wrong, but of right versus right. The Court's role was to preside over a complex and difficult social process. It was in these circumstances that we introduced a procedural element by holding that justice and equity required that there be engagement between the parties in the form of mediation. Since mediation had not been tried, the eviction had not been just and equitable and had to be set aside.

Not too long afterwards in *Olivia Mansions* [*Occupiers of 51 Olivia Roa•, Berea Township an• 197 Main Street Johannesburg v City of Johannesburg an• Others* (CCT 24/07) [2008] ZACC 1; 2008 (3) SA 208 (CC); 2008 (5) BCLR 475 (CC)], Justice Zak Yacoob took the principle a major step forward. The words 'meaningful engagement', which had appeared in passing in my judgment were made central to the remedy he proposed. In eviction cases the occupants and the governmental authorities had to engage meaningfully with each other, especially on the question of alternative accommodation.

> *Since then, the concept of meaningful engagement has become well-established in cases dealing with evictions of the poor. And so, in the incremental way in which the Court's jurisprudence has evolved, meaningful engagement took its place alongside reasonableness as the second foundation stone of social and economic rights jurisprudence.*

I conclude with one final question: what are the factors that lead courts to become actively interventionist in social and economic matters? While some who favour bolder interventions argue primarily within the framework of what they consider to be the intrinsic logic of social and economic rights realisation, my sense is that the primary determinant lies in factors outside that logic. In India it was the last generation of young lawyers who had fought for independence who re-imagined the role of the Supreme Court. It was they who pro-actively embraced the promise that the Constitution held out to advance the rights of the poor and the marginalised. In Latin America, it has been judges who cut their legal teeth in the fight against military dictatorship who moved beyond the formalism of their predecessors on the Bench to focus on social justice as an integral element of meaningful constitutional freedom. In both India and Latin America there has been an interplay between legal doctrine on the one hand, and perceived failures of representative democracy and the market, on the other. You will have to make up your own mind as to whether, when enforcing social and economic rights, South African courts have been too adventurous or too timid or have got it just about right when enforcing social and economic rights.

Liberty, Equality, Fraternity: Bringing human solidarity back into the rights equation

PUBLIC LECTURE AT THE CENTRE FOR APPLIED HUMAN RIGHTS |
UNIVERSITY OF YORK | OCTOBER 2011

I wondered why I was so keen to attend a conference in faraway Montreal to honour Charles D Gonthier, who had died two years previously and was as different to me as anyone could possibly be. I had met him only once or twice, he was a non-demonstrative person, and the sole thing we seemed to have in common was that I was a judge on the Constitutional Court in South Africa and he was a judge on the Supreme Court in Canada.

He came from a distinctively Catholic, French-speaking Quebec community, and was very family orientated. His whole worldview – and life experience – had been totally different to mine. I was a grandchild of Jewish immigrants in South Africa. My parents had fought their parents over religion and I had grown up, literally at the other end of the world, with a determinedly secular and internationalist outlook.

Why, I wondered, was I willing to undertake a long, tiring and expensive journey to a conference about the life and thought of someone whom I had barely known, and whose experiences and philosophical values had been totally different from mine? Sometimes your intuitions speed far ahead of your brain and your body, and only when I actually arrived at McGill University did I realise that what had drawn me so powerfully to honour him had been precisely the fact that we had been so far apart. The result was that in an unusually pure way we had been united solely through the fact that we shared a similar constitutional vision.

Charles was a strong exponent of the French notion of fraternity – liberty, equality, fraternity – and I had become deeply imbued with an equivalent ethos in South Africa called ubuntu. And we were reaching common conclusions about the nature of the judicial function and about how human rights should be understood. My intuition sensed, and my brain ultimately accepted, that through honouring distant Charles, I would indirectly be paying tribute to my immediate colleagues. I had in fact simply taken their virtues for granted as I had sat next to them in Court. And they would have been deeply embarrassed had I chosen publicly and to their faces to extol their virtues. We were eleven judges with very different life experiences, some religious, some non-religious, and of those who were religious, men and women of different faiths. Yet we could articulate and agree upon a strongly held vision in relation to what was meant by fundamental rights because we all acknowledged the need to look at our work through the prism of our Constitution. It was Charles Gonthier's emphasis on fraternity – in a famous paper he wrote that is now achieving considerable prominence in Canada – that triggered the theme that I'm going to explore here, of how judges on continents far apart and possessing profoundly different world views, can develop shared constitutional approaches.

In this case, the catalyst was the nee• to reintegrate the element of human soli•arity into our un•erstan•ing of the core notions of liberty an• equality.

To go back a bit in human history – autonomy, human autonomy, is one of the great achievements of humankind. Emerging in different continents at different times, the notion came to the fore in Europe during the eighteenth-century Enlightenment. The culmination of a long and hard-fought process, it established the idea that instead of human beings having their lives determined by their birth, their lineage, the family in which they grew up, the tribe they belonged to, their ethnic group or faith community, each individual had a conscience, they had choice, they had personal autonomy. I grew up with an understanding that this was an enormous breakthrough for humanity – that every individual counted as an individual, independently of birth, and station, and race, and position in family. And, as such, had inalienable rights – including the broad right to pursue happiness. Undoubtedly, the very notion of basic human rights is heavily dependent upon that achievement. It was a socio-cultural – or if you like, a socio-psychological – accomplishment, which gave rise to the idea of fundamental rights that inhered in everyone simply because you were a person. And I'm emphasising the significance and importance of this – which is well known and taken for granted – to bring out the price that we have paid for this extraordinary achievement. And the price has been the loss of the sense of organic relationship with other human beings, of community, and of human interdependence.

Previously, interdependence had been fixed. It was established by your birth – you fitted in to an allotted destiny. If you were fortunate you might have been a king. But there weren't many kings, and even fewer reigning queens, though there were more in the sequence of the entitled: in Europe, variously called princes, dukes, barons, knights and squires; in Africa and Asia, an equal number of honoured denominations.

The great majority, however, were just serfs (servants) – people tied to pieces of land somewhere, owing fealty to more privileged families. The term was European, but this wasn't by any means an exclusively European phenomenon – you found it in Africa in our traditional societies. People would be born into communities with established hierarchies and forms of responsibility, with predetermined connections, duties and loyalties – sometimes referred to as feudal. And you found it in Asia, you found it in Latin America – it was fairly universal. Its strength came from the existence of community, connection with others, a form of human interdependence. It was a solidarity based on hierarchy, on dominant groups enjoying extraordinary material and psychological benefits, with subordinate groups doing most of the work – producing most of the food, doing most of the fighting, tilling most of the land, building most of the buildings – to enable these dominant groups to survive and prosper. Yet the sense of organic connection and relationship extended powerfully downward, all the way towards the most subaltern and exploited sectors of society. Then, first with mercantile capitalism, later with the Industrial Revolution, came the extreme atomising of our world and society. It was associated in economic terms with the market, private property and globalisation, coupled with a huge expansion of productivity and creativity in all sorts of ways, as well as great daring in thought, and profound challenges to existing ways of seeing the world and imagining things.

The cost of liberation was •isintegration an• alienation; the price of the en•ing of bon•age was the en•ing of bon•ing. The French revolutionaries sought to prevent any schism between free•om an• community. Their famous cry was Liberty, Equality, Fraternity. An• Charles Gonthier, like the crow• in the street two hun•re• years before, believe• with all his heart an• imagination that fraternity represente• the sense of human inter•epen•ence that is part of the equation of liberty an• equality.

Conversely, he was equally convinced that the detachment of fraternity from the triad of human aspiration had brought about the impoverishment of both liberty and equality. In his eyes, fraternity was far from being the enemy either of liberty or of equality. The human solidarity he envisaged was quite the opposite of a terrifying and frenzied collective existence based on subordination to some notion of the popular will. Rather, he saw it as being based on a deep and gentle sense, both spiritual and practical, of human interrelationship that enriched liberty and equality.

This was not merely a private stance he adopted. It affected his constitutional gaze as he sat as a judge reflecting on how the Charter of Rights was to be interpreted and applied in Canada. I was very struck by the extent to which those of us in South Africa, picking up on the rich philosophical traditions in African society embodied in the word ubuntu, were searching for a very similar mode of – not of suppressing liberty, not of reducing equality to some kind of bland and textureless standardisation – but of reinvigorating both these concepts by locating them in the context of human solidarity. I also noticed that the discovery of the congruence of our thinking on different continents fitted in with a notion that I had found quite important for myself, that I'd like to share with you, the difference between globalisation and universalism.

Globalisation presupposes that you start with a set of significant ideas, instruments or technologies in one part of the world that you then extend throughout the whole globe, encompassing all of humanity, whether on sea or land or in the sky. Universalism proceeds in exactly the opposite direction. Things happen all over the world – and in terms of notions of human rights, people articulate claims and demands about the circumstances in which they want to live – in every continent. You then distil out of these multitudinous claims points of commonality found all over the globe which are then referred to as universal notions.

Historically, globalisation preceded universalism, often in the brutal forms of slavery and colonial domination. But ultimately they came together in the Universal Declaration of Human Rights in 1948. Primarily I see the Universal Declaration as being a representation of universalism, to the extent that the Second World War had embraced all of Europe terribly and dramatically, much of Asia catastrophically, as well as large proportions of Africa in disastrous fashion. Meanwhile, North and South America had been involved through sending troops. It was truly a world war that impacted on all of humanity, with global participation in the fight against notions of superiority of one race, or certain races, over others. There was a near universal repudiation of the claims of certain nations that in the course of warfare they were entitled to do as they wished – to dominate, to ravish, to colonise, to control, even to exterminate peoples. Huge swathes of humanity were involved in the resistance to Nazism and fascism in Europe, as well as to imperialism from Japan. And so there was a geographically and socially widely dispersed urge to get together to produce a globally agreed affirmation of the new values that had eventually won out.

From this crucible of human trage•y, there emerge• a •etermination to ensure that never again woul• human beings be subjecte• to such atrocious travail. An• so, three years after the war's en•, the Universal Declaration of Human Rights came into being.

One reason why the Universal Declaration has stood up so well over the decades is that it had that input, a universal embrace that anticipated and helped bring about decolonisation and promoted at least the formal equality of all nations. It wasn't, then, simply a case of a few lawyers and political scientists and statesmen (and a couple of stateswomen) in the West coming up with a bright idea, and then trying to impose it as a force of globalisation on the whole of the rest of the world. On the contrary, in the words of the Preamble to the Declaration, it expressed a pan-continental longing for a world in which all members of the human family would receive recognition of their inherent dignity and equal and inalienable rights, as the foundation of freedom, justice and peace in the world. In that respect, the process was far more one of universalism than of globalisation.

To say that the Declaration is universal in its ambition is not, of course, to ensure that it will be universally understood in terms of its ambit. Thus, the West is often accused of seeking to impose on the rest of the world a globalised interpretation of human rights and democracy. Critics contend that deeply embedded elements in North American and European political culture, assumed to be universal, are applied in an automatic, politically decontextualised and culturally insensitive way. One example would be after the overthrow of a dictatorship the installation of democracy is reduced simply to the single event of holding an election to choose a president or government. Of course, elections are exceptionally important to establish the legitimacy and accountability of any government. Yet, a far more profound entrenchment of fundamental ideas of democracy and human rights requires a degree of continuity, openness and popular participation. And, sadly, the point is made that when the electoral process results in the victory of persons not favoured by the West, all too often people in the West find it convenient simply to ignore the outcome.

Other critics, however, point to a strong tendency of authoritarian rulers in Africa, Asia, Latin America and the Arab world to seek to evade the principles of the Universal Declaration. Their argument has been that the Declaration ignores local systems of authority of ancient origin, disrespects indigenous religious values and generally imports alien and unrealistic notions into their countries. In practice, however, there is strong evidence that this denial of universality has been used by tyrannical regimes to perpetuate their own power and justify oppression of their own people. The pain of torture, of arbitrary detention and of being silenced has been no different in Rangoon, Cairo, Libreville or Buenos Aires than it has been in Lisbon or Athens, or, for that matter, Guantanamo Bay. Indeed, a notable feature of developments in the recent period has been the extent to which authoritarian rule in many parts of the world, defended on the basis of local exceptionalism, has given way to universal notions of openness, democracy and the rule of law. Almost invariably this has been as a result of popular local struggle.

With these introductory observations in mind, I turn to the way in which I see liberty, equality and fraternity interconnecting as values of universal application.

LIBERTY

It is difficult to convey the intensity of a debate which ten to fifteen years ago was tearing American law schools apart, namely, that between libertarianism and communitarianism. The clash is less violent today, but it still has reverberations for human rights. The libertarian approach is deeply entrenched in the notion of autonomy, of the uniqueness of each individual. It's a powerful concept and its critique of the potentially oppressive impact of communitarianism is attractive. The communitarian notion, on the other hand, is also appealing. It is based on acceptance of the idea that we don't live as isolated, atomised individuals; we live in families, neighbourhoods, communities of every kind – sporting, faith, political. To nurture our autonomy we need education, which in its essence is connective; to survive at all, the individual needs health which by its nature depends on the food we eat, the water we drink, the shelter we enjoy and the caring we have when we are ill. So the communitarians offer a persuasive critique of the cold, harsh and inhuman possibilities flowing from libertarianism.

The end result is that I find myself agreeing with the essential claims of each approach, as well as with the critique that each has of the other! I share the libertarians' fear of developing a statist or collectivist society that suppresses choice, decision-making, the uniqueness of individuals, and that submerges our individuality and diversity by converting us all into mere members of groups or communities. But I also join with the communitarians in saying that we are not isolated beings, we are not Robinson Crusoes on desert islands, and in fact it's living in communities that nurtures, strengthens, and gives vitality to the individual potential of each one of us. My preferred option, then, is to seek to combine the strengths of libertarianism and communitarianism, and this I do by supporting the principles of dignitarianism.

It is human •ignity that connects the vitality an• spark of libertarianism to the nurturing texture an• richness of communitarianism.

It's part of your dignity that you can make choices, determine your life path, be curious, create and invent – that's part of your place in the world as a unique person. But respect for human dignity also acknowledges that to do all these things in a meaningful way you are connected, involved and interactive with your fellow human beings. So human dignity becomes the key, the central, overarching or dominant notion, that ties together these two important and apparently contradictory notions – autonomy and community – producing an indivisible whole that corresponds to and enhances real lives lived by real people.

The implication, then, is to bring fraternity and ubuntu back into the constitutional equation with liberty. Extreme libertarianism, supporting an absolute exercise of autonomy detached from any social context, can be destructive rather than constitutive of freedom. This becomes evident in the area of speech, as illustrated in a recent decision by the United States Supreme Court in a matter concerning legislative regulation of the financing of political campaigns.

Senator McCain, a Republican, and Senator Feingold, a Democrat, got together to try and reduce the impact of money on elections. The law that was duly adopted by Congress was challenged by libertarians as a violation of the right to free speech guaranteed by the First Amendment, coupled with the associated right to spend your money as you liked. The avowed objective of the law was to promote democracy. Yet, by a narrow majority, the Supreme Court struck it down. Basically expressed, the majority held that Congress had no power to restrict First Amendment rights to spend your money as you liked in supporting the candidate of your choice. The minority view, strongly articulated by Justice Breyer, was (I'm paraphrasing) – that it was the undue influence of money that was in fact undermining free speech, allowing the speech of the rich and the wealthy to overwhelm and drown out the voices of those who didn't have as much money. The result was that the legislative adoption of an active notion of liberty, based on an understanding of freedom in the actual context in which people exercised their choices, expressing a bipartisan view with huge popular support, was, on purely libertarian grounds, struck down as unconstitutional.

Another example of the need to contextualise the exercise of speech in ways which ultimately allow for greater speech by more individuals arises in the case of controlling hate speech. International law actually requires the state to take action to prohibit – or to limit – speech which intensely and aggressively attacks people for being who they are, which denigrates their potential, their capacities, simply on the grounds of gender, race, or religion.

In the United States, unless the hate speech reaches the stage of inciting immediate violence or constitutes threats to the lives of others, any prohibition on it will be struck down. There was a famous case involving a constitutional challenge to a Chicago City Council regulation prohibiting Nazis from marching outside homes in a Chicago suburb where many Holocaust survivors were known to be living. American Nazis had provocatively targeted this area with a view to taunting the survivors with their avowed anti-Semitism.

The courts upheld their constitutional challenge on libertarian grounds, deciding that the regulation denied free speech and had to be struck down. In Germany, on the other hand, where free speech is also constitutionally protected, Holocaust denial is a criminal offence. It can land its author in jail because it touches on something so deep in the history of Germany, so associated with a catastrophic decade and more in the country's life, that it went far beyond simply having the right to say what you wanted, and subjecting your ridiculous ideas to the test of being refuted by better argument.

It touched on themes central to the nature of the country's new democracy; it kept atrocious memory of unspeakable indignity and extermination alive; it imposed unacceptable levels of continuing hurt on survivors of the death camps; and it threatened to provide justification in advance of new forms of extreme intolerance for future vulnerable groups.

So much depends on context. In many countries, in restricting expression that is deeply demeaning and hurtful, the law seeks to foster certain basic elements of human empathy and a vision of an inclusive and pluralistic democracy. In others, the limitation on expression is justified by an acknowledgment of the potential that fighting words have to rupture the very foundations of common citizenship and lead to deadly conflagration. Even if it doesn't incite immediate violence, divisive and hateful speech may tear the fabric of the society apart, dislocate communities and engender the kinds of enmity which at a later stage can lead to xenophobia and genocide.

Tragically, these are not just speculative or hypothetical scenarios. I once shared a platform at a book fair in Sweden with the Nobel Prize winning Nigerian writer, Wole Soyinka, and a distinguished leader of the American Civil Liberties Union, Nadine Strossen. An extremely articulate and persuasive defender of free speech, Nadine spoke forcefully and fluently in favour of virtually unlimited free speech. Wole then started his response in a way that I found surprising and disconcerting. 'We have just been listening to a white, middle-class woman from America', he told us in his deep voice, 'giving us a typical lecture of the kind we can expect from a white, middle-class American woman'. Nadine went pale. The audience was embarrassed. I felt a degree of shame that a great writer from my continent could dismiss her arguments in that shallow way. Wole paused for a moment, relaxed his stern posture, and added more quietly: 'You see, Nadine? These were just words. And they hurt, didn't they?' He then went on to tell us about somebody going around parts of northern Nigeria denouncing Christians. Many people had responded by saying, 'well, it's stupid stuff, but that's free speech'. A year later a hundred Christians were massacred. The words had acted as recipes for murder.

In Rwanda it started off with a broadcaster speaking about cockroaches. The word 'kill' wasn't used, but a million people died.

So speech then readily transforms itself into a warrant of execution.

When words are realistically capable of becoming instruments of division and death, you shouldn't have to hold back in taking action against them until the moment of actual homicide. Pre-emptive action is required rather than posthumous lamentations followed by belated prosecution.

Normally I'm a great defender of free speech against any form of control. Normally I would argue for defeating ugly speech with better argument, and contend that the law shouldn't step in and deal with every piece of obnoxious rubbish spoken over a drink in a bar – you've got to respond to it on the spot as well as you can. Normally I am concerned about censorship and thought control, about the importance in an open society of not suppressing alternative and unpopular views. Normally I side with people who demand that those who exercise power should take in their stride the slingshots and arrows of outrageous criticism, however unwholesome or unfair. But at the same time I believe that the right to say what I like, when I like, to whom I like, has to acknowledge the demeaning and destructive impact that words may have in a particular context.

Attacks based on race dig deep into the souls of human beings, denying them moral citizenship in their societies and touching on memories of their families' slavery, and various other forms of abusive domination. In similar vein, it's sad to day to read of examples of homophobic attacks that had started off with hate-filled speech and ended up with people being beaten to death. In sum, the libertarian right to speak your mind has to be balanced against profound constitutional values of shared citizenship.

I turn now to another area where liberty and empathy might collide. One of the most time-honoured bulwarks of liberty is not to be imprisoned or otherwise penalised by the state without a fair trial. And one of the principal elements of a fair trial is the right to test accusations made against you by means of cross-examining prosecution witnesses. It is easy to understand, then, how shocked civil libertarians in Canada were when, as a result of prolonged campaigning by the women's movement, the law dealing with the manner in which rape trials were conducted was changed to limit the extent to which defence counsel could cross-examine the complainant in relation to her previous sexual history. The rationales for this limitation were twofold.

In the first place, it was to avoid jury members from being unduly prejudiced against complainants through a tendency to rely on stereotyped views rather than all the actual evidence. Thus counsel could suggest or imply that because a woman has 'slept around' she was an 'easy lay' who had probably consented to intercourse in the case in question. Secondly, the administration of justice was being compromised by the unwillingness of complainants to testify in rape cases. This was because they knew that their lives would be examined in great detail in a public way on private issues bearing little direct relevance to the question as to whether the accused men had subjected them to non-consensual sexual intercourse on the occasion charged. And so the Canadian parliament introduced a law that provided restrictions on the introduction of extraneous issues which could be highly prejudicial through stereotyping, and have only minimal relevance to the actual events.

The new law locked the Trial Lawyers Association, on the one hand, and the women's movement, on the other, into bitter conflict. A great lawyer and good friend of mine, now on the Supreme Court in Canada, Rosalie Abella, gave lectures on how this new law reflected the tension between civil rights and human rights. When I first read one of these lectures I was stunned. Surely, I thought, human rights and civil rights belong to the same family, they go in the same direction. Rosalie pointed out that civil rights would emphasise the right of the accused to a fair trial, his counsel's right to cross-examine the complainant about anything that might turn out to have some bearing on her credibility. Against that, however, the human rights approach highlighted the way in which the complainant could well have suffered a grievous violation in relation to the most private aspect of herself; that sexual assaults were part and parcel of systems of male domination that have thrived in a culture that expressed itself in an assumed 'right' to bear down on women and to infer consent when it wasn't consent, even go so far as to say 'that's how women like it'. And so the clash of perspectives could best be resolved by balancing out fair trial rights for the accused, against the right to dignity of persons who might have suffered gross violations of body and spirit. How to balance out the competing interests?

The law was carefully crafted so as not unduly to limit the rights of cross-examination, and passed constitutional scrutiny by the Supreme Court. Not only the rights of the particular complainants, but the rights of women in general, were at stake. The presumption of innocence remained intact, but cross-examination was restricted to matters sufficiently proximate to the issues involved to make it fair both to the accused and the complainant to allow it to proceed. Fraternity, perhaps better expressed in non-sexist language as human solidarity, had reassumed its rightful place with liberty.

Another example of a clash between individual civil rights and a broad conception of human rights, relates to the environment. Justice Antonin Scalia of the United States Supreme Court declares firmly, certainly in his extrajudicial opinions, that all this talk about climate change is something of a hoax. He says so publicly – and he's my friend, I'm not being disrespectful to him – and he does so from a libertarian point of view. Underlying his opposition to the huge movement concerned about reversing climate change is a near absolutist notion of the freedom of the individual.

The argument is that nature has its own way of working, and people should be allowed to go ahead and do what they want without yet further restraints on free enterprise, particularly when imposed by state regulation based on dubious scientific evidence, and made even worse when cross-border controls are enforced, permitting people's rights to be determined by other countries. I would say the whole of environmental law represents a post-technological revolution in response to the enormous energy and creativity that came with individualism, autonomy, private property and scientific advance and development. It represents a shocked reaction by our present generation. Millions throughout the globe seek to reinstall a sense of humanity, and to advance the notion of the earth, if you like, having claims to be the earth, of the species to be the species, of the flora and the fauna to be flora and fauna, ideas which we as human beings have to acknowledge and protect through a system of enforceable rights and remedies. It's saying that the exercise of rights is not just dependent on individual will and personal self-determination, and it's not just those of us who are alive today who are involved – we have to look to the rights of future generations.

The notions of fiduciary responsibility, the rights of people yet to be born, the precautionary principle and the idea of trans-frontier rights all stem from an emerging legal philosophy concerned with the environment and sustainable development. And it's producing an enormous revolution, a transformation in the nature of legal thinking, which might, in fact, be exactly what most alarms Justice Scalia.

It is challenging the idea of rights as being based crucially and essentially on protection of the will and ambition of an individual. Initially, the archetype of a holder of rights was the land-holding patriarch, who dominated his family (and slaves or servants). Rights radiated around the notion of the private property owner who had occupied and laboured on a fenced-in space into which the state dared not intrude. Certainly, the idea of protected space around the individual is important – it needs to be recognised, the state can't do whatever it wants, and there are inviolable areas relating to each one of us, each human being, each person, that need to be recognised. But not in an unduly expanded manner that obliterates the fact that in reality we live in communities. We are part of humanity. Experience teaches us that the notion of liberty is enriched when you introduce the notion of fraternity (human solidarity). Our interdependence gives texture and substance to our liberty. It rescues us from loneliness and narcissism, from greed and insensitivity, and enhances our dignity as members of the human race.

EQUALITY

What about equality? The biggest debates that I've encountered in terms of how we look at equality relate first to the issue of formal equality versus substantive equality, and secondly, to how to deal with the right to be equal but at the same time be different.

The formal approach to equality simply says you treat everybody in the same situation in the same way – identical treatment. And you don't allow issues of race or gender, for example, to qualify in any way the treatment. Its supporters say that they are colour blind and gender blind. This was the approach adopted by the majority in the United States Supreme Court when it negated a decision of a primary school in Seattle to go for as much diversity as possible by facilitating entry into the school of children from minority groups. Most of the parents in the area were happy with the school programme, but a few from the white community objected and said: 'My children are being kept out of that school simply because they are white'. The minority in the Supreme Court argued forcefully, but unsuccessfully, that diversity had an important educational value in itself, even if you left out the justice aspect of redressing systematic past discrimination. Writing for the majority, however, Chief Justice Roberts said that if you want to end race discrimination, you must stop discriminating on the grounds of race. The result was that in the name of equal protection, the Court invalidated an effort by the school board, supported by the majority of parents of all backgrounds, to take a modest step to promote substantive rather than purely formal equality.

The substantive equality approach starts by looking at the way people have actually been living an• the manner in which belonging to a particular group has been use• in social an• legal practice to unfairly prevent members from enjoying the benefits of life in a full way. Substantive equality permits forms of re•ress an• reme•ial action to overcome these structure•, systemic forms of subor•ination.

And so, to achieve substantive equality, forms of affirmative action are authorised, maybe even required. The Richmond City Council had set aside a modest quota of municipal contracts for minority contractors because historically they'd been kept out – to give them the experience and opportunity to grow and develop. But the United States Supreme Court, by a slim majority, struck that affirmative action programme down as being based on race discrimination. The first African-American on the Court, Thurgood Marshall, spoke movingly on how admirable it was that the largely white council of Richmond, the capital of the Southern Confederacy, was now taking measures to bring about greater opportunities for people who remained trapped on the periphery of economic activity as a result of generations of discrimination. Yet, he pointed out, here was the Court of which he was a member, striking down a measure designed to achieve equality and doing so in the name of equal protection.

At about the same time, legal thinking of the Canadian Supreme Court was moving in the opposite direction, from a preoccupation with formal equality towards one more based on achieving substantive equality. It could be that the women's movement had much to do with this changing emphasis, whether in relation to gender, or race or disability. Applying the principles of giving equal concern and respect, takes account of the factors in people's lives which prevent them, because they are who they are, from enjoying real equality. So a substantive approach to equality ends up supporting forms of redress or remedial action that look at the actual lives that people lead, and takes account of historically constructed patterns of disadvantage connected with attributes such as colour, ethnicity, gender, religion, disability, sexual orientation or birth. And of course in South Africa our Constitution permits, and our Court supports, remedial action and redress of structured, systemic forms of discrimination.

Given the immense and pervasive inequalities created by apartheid, any other approach would have been out of the question. What remained was to ensure that the modes of redress met up with the constitutional criteria of fairness and proportionality.

*The Constitution thus facilitates re*istribution *through using the assets the state has (or acquires equitably), an*• *through the benefits it can provi*•*e, an*• *the action it can un*•*ertake, to enable people in reality to lea*• *more fulfille*• *an*• *equal lives. At the same time, it forbi*•*s arbitrary seizure of assets for* •*istribution to family or frien*•*s or political supporters of those in power.*

What about equality and difference? This was the dominant issue in the same-sex marriages case heard by our Court in South Africa. Two people met, were attracted to each other, dated, went out together, and decided to set up a joint home and live together, which they did for about ten years. Everybody regarded them as a couple, and eventually they felt they should get married. But when they went to the marriage office, the registrar said he personally had no problems, but since they were both women they could not pronounce the statutory marriage vow: I, AB, take you, CD, to be my lawful husband/wife. These words, he said, connoted the marriage of a man and a woman.

They challenged the law on the basis that it discriminated unfairly against them on the grounds of their sexual orientation. Counter arguments were forcefully advanced on behalf of faith communities, saying in effect: 'We're not against gay men and lesbian women living together and getting protection from the law. But, please, please, don't call it marriage; marriage is something that was created by our religious communities; it has a sacramental character. The state learnt about marriage from us, please leave intact an institution directed towards procreation, and intrinsically heterosexual'. They contended further that recognition of same-sex marriages would undermine traditional religious notions of marriage, and infringe religious freedom.

Yet that last argument became the very reason why the right to equality was engaged. Why should a marriage between her and her undermine respect for a marriage between her and him? Surely it would be extending rather than subverting the notion of marriage if it was expanded to enable her and her to express their love and affection for each other in a public way, and get the status, accept the responsibilities, and enjoy the benefits of their relationship in the same way that she and he could do. And central to the judgment is the notion of equality acknowledging that equal rights embraced rather than suppressed difference. It would have been absurd to say that there was nothing to stop a gay man from marrying, as long as he married a woman, or to stop a lesbian woman from marrying, as long as she married a man! You shouldn't have to suppress who you are to enjoy equal rights. So, the right to be the same, in terms of access to marriage, became meaningful to lesbian and gay people only if coupled with a right to be different in respect of sexual orientation.

FRATERNITY

Fraternity – ubuntu – human solidarity. We got our Constitution in South Africa because of ubuntu. Millions of ordinary people, particularly poor people, in spite of all the insults, humiliations, the injustices, and violence wreaked upon them, never lost their sense of ubuntu, and never gave up on the notion that even the oppressors, people who had behaved so abominably, could now be embraced and become part of that wider community of free and equal South Africans. Ubuntu, at the very least, requires listening, dialogue, speaking – it gives a voice to everybody; everybody matters. And I'm going to conclude with three cases that came to our Court where the theme of ubuntu played a central role in determining the outcome. And what unites the three cases is that by underlining the importance of human interdependence as opposed to individual isolation, they opened the way to developing creative and healing forms of restorative justice, as opposed to reliance on purely declaratory, or punitive, or compensatory justice.

The first was the *Port Elizabeth Municipality* case [discussed in the previous essay]. In coming to the conclusion that we needed to develop a procedural approach managed by the Court, rather than seek a simple determination of whose legal rights had to triumph, I found I had to refer to ubuntu. Ubuntu took account of the fact that the interested parties were simultaneously geographical neighbours and social strangers. Ubuntu went beyond the concern that any decent person should have for fellow human beings on hard times. It presupposed that not only was the dignity of the desperately poor at stake; in addition, the dignity of all South Africans was assailed by the fact that millions of our fellow human beings were compelled to live as homeless wanderers in the country of their birth. In declaring that the Bill of Rights was nothing if not ubuntu writ large, the judgment emphasised that in dealing with matters such as these, the old individualistic and highly technical notions of private land law had to be developed to embrace new concepts of land rights. This would balance out competing interests in a principled and fair manner, so as to produce as much justice and equity as possible.

The next case involving ubuntu was one dealing with damages for libel. The facts were that a manager in a local authority had been criticised by an official for overuse of a cell phone (mobile). The manager responded by saying some very rude things about his subordinate who had had the effrontery to openly criticise him. The press picked up on his denunciation, and the aggrieved official sued the manager for quite heavy damages in the High Court. The evidence showed that the manager had been wrong to impute impropriety to the official, who received substantial damages. I felt the damages were too high. But that wasn't my main concern. I felt there was something basically wrong about the emphasis our law placed on awarding money damages for loss of reputation. You don't quote someone's reputation on the stock exchange (unless, that is, you're a trader and your trading reputation is part of your goodwill). I felt the law of libel should be developed to put much more emphasis on getting an apology and reconnecting the parties, and that an apology freely offered and generously accepted could do far more to restore the reputation of the harmed person – so he or she can walk out of the court with head high – and preserve harmony, than getting a money award. The placing of a monetary value on a reputation, to my mind, is actually a denial of the intrinsic quality of what your dignity as a human being is really worth.

> *Ubuntu an♦ the African mo♦e of settling ♦isputes brings the parties together an♦ acknowle♦ges that you're all going to live together in the same community afterwar♦s. It can ♦o far more to restore ♦ignity an♦ heal the social rupture than a monetary penalty, which in fact is calculate♦ to ensure continuing antagonism.*

And I am pleased to report that what my colleague Justice Yvonne Mokgoro and I offered as a minority view in this case has since been accepted by the Court as a whole as a guide to how defamation (libel) cases should be handled in future. This would mean that the Courts' procedures, where a person's reputation has been unfairly injured, should be directed towards clarifying the truth and trying to try to get an apology rather than forcing the traducer to pay monetary compensation.

This restorative justice approach has enormous implications for criminal law. It seeks to achieve face-to-face encounters between those who have been most affected, rather than sending someone to jail, cutting them off from society and putting a brand of 'thou art a criminal' on his or her forehead. The human repair, the possibilities of actually reducing social schism and restoring equilibrium in the society, are greater if these forms of restorative justice can be achieved. It is an approach used extensively throughout the world in the case of juvenile justice. But the idea is to extend it to many other areas of criminal and civil law, particularly in rural societies where people are living close to each other and where the sense of community is great. Of course it needs to be carefully introduced in appropriate cases, and managed with sensitivity. But its potential to humanise and give agency to more people in the justice system, strengthening it and making it more effective, is unlimited.

I will conclude with a case in which restorative justice principles made it possible to secure children's rights in circumstances where a more traditional individualistic approach to punishment would have left them high and dry. M had been responsible for fraudulently using her credit card to buy food and sporting gear for her three teenage sons and liquor for herself. The total amount had not been huge, it could have reached about two hundred pounds (three hundred dollars) in all. She'd been prosecuted – it was crazy, she knew she'd be found out sooner or later – and she was given a suspended sentence – first offence, three young boys to look after. She does it again. And more than that, when she's out on bail the second time, she does it a third time! Lots of small amounts of credit card deception, maybe twenty or thirty different counts on each occasion – total amounts not very big – mainly for groceries – near certainty of being caught. She's sent to jail by the magistrate for four years. She's desperate. She's living in what's called a very fragile area socially, and knows that if she's not around her boys are going to get involved in gangs, drugs, the lot, and there's nobody else who can really look after them.

The attitude of the magistrate is, 'Well, sorry, you shouldn't have committed those offences in the first place, you knew you had those boys, you knew the danger they were in, and you were given chance after chance to correct your ways, but still you went ahead with your fraud'.

She takes the matter on appeal and manages to get one conviction knocked out, which enables the judges on appeal to reduce the sentence to two years' imprisonment, with the possibility of her becoming eligible for community service after having served four months. But four months, she felt, would be disastrous for her children to be without her. She appealed to the Constitutional Court.

When I first saw the mother's application I couldn't think of a more hopeless case. You've got a suspended sentence hanging over you, you're out on bail on further charges and you do it again. But one of my colleagues said to me: 'But Albie, you're only thinking about her, what about the children? Our Constitution says that in every case involving children, the rights of the child should be paramount, so aren't the three boys entitled to some independent consideration?'

We look at the record, see that the magistrate never considered the children's position specifically, and call for social workers' reports. In the end, our Court agreed unanimously that in all cases where a convicted person facing imprisonment is the primary caregiver of minor children, the sentencing court must make an independent investigation of the impact of a prison sentence on the children concerned. In a borderline case, the children's interests could then be enough to keep the primary caregiver, usually the mother, out of jail. But if it can't keep her out of jail, the court has to ensure that the children will be properly looked after. And so the judgment was able to emphasise that the child doesn't necessarily sink or swim with the errant parent; that the child should not be seen as a miniature adult but as somebody growing up with the rights not just to survive and not be beaten up, and not just to get food and education, but the rights to explore and to have adventure, and, finally, that the child has a right to have the best chance possible to become a future responsible adult member of society.

The question, then, was: could we substitute a community service order to keep M out of jail altogether? Time had passed, and in the several years since the offences had been committed, she had set up two successful businesses, and shown herself to be a model member of the school's parent–teacher association. The social worker's report said she was an excellent parent, and there was nobody else who could adequately look after the three boys. Our Court divided. Four of my colleagues felt M had irreversibly crossed the line after receiving so many chances, and just had to go to jail for at least four months. But seven of us opted for bringing the community into the picture through a community service order – she would repay the money so that the grocery shops and liquor stores and the others would have some sense of being involved in the process; she would receive psychological counselling because there was clearly compulsive behaviour involved; and she would do useful work in the community as indicated by social workers and probation officers. The majority view of the Court was that the community would understand this. They would rather have her doing something manifestly worthwhile, and continuing to look after her children, than have her simply sent to jail where she'd be mixed up with other crooks and criminals, with no income for that whole period, her family disrupted, and the craziness that had driven her to behave compulsively and self-destructively more likely to be intensified. Most important of all, the children would be well protected by having her present and seeing her recover her self-esteem and sense of responsibility.

Happily, the Court's decision was well received by children's rights advocates all over the world, as well as by supporters of restorative justice generally. It turned out to be a good case to be involved in near the end of my judicial career. Liberty, equality, fraternity – Justice Gonthier and I agree that the words are as relevant to epoch-making events in the streets of Paris as they are for ensuring that children in a poor neighbourhood of Cape Town can be with their mother.

NINE

Struggle Continues

Nothing About us Without us: Disability

HARVARD LAW SCHOOL PROJECT ON DISABILITY | CAMBRIDGE, MASSACHUSETTS | UNITED STATES | 17 OCTOBER 2013

It was 1990; there was great excitement. Mandela had been released and exiles, myself among them, were returning to South Africa. I was invited to meet many different groups. One of them was Disabled People South Africa (DPSA).

I was quite startled as I walked in to meet the group. The room was full of people, maybe fifteen or twenty, living with different disabilities. I was introduced to a white man who was blind. I shook his proffered hand and learnt that he was the chairperson of the DPSA. Then I met a black guy in a wheelchair, who, I was told, had been struck by a police bullet and was now the general secretary of the DPSA. I discovered that the host, who was without hearing, came from a comfortable white family, and that I knew her dad, a well-known cartoonist, and her sister, a prominent feminist law teacher. People were rushing to the kitchen for food and drinks. A black man without arms was being fed by his wife. There was a white guy with a withered leg. And there was me. They surrounded me exuberantly. Somebody said: 'We were so excited when we heard you were blown up, now we have someone on the national executive of the ANC'.

Then they asked me straight out: 'What should we do, what should our strategy be?' It was an important moment for me. What struck me straight away and became part of my emotional turbulence, was that this was South Africa. These were our people, this was our nation. Black, white, brown, young, old, poor, wealthy, all the diverse people of our country were in that room. What they had in common was the fact that they were different. They looked different, yet each was different in his/her own way. A phrase came into my head, and it has stayed there ever since: 'Here is the democracy of the disabled'.

Coupled with that was another strong, unexpected discovery – the irrelevance of the origin of the disability. It didn't matter at all how Mabuso had come to be shot by the police. Or why William was blind, whether he had lost his sight heroically in struggle, or driving when drunk, or it had been something that he had been born with or the result of disease. I wasn't even curious. It didn't matter at all. If ever there was an existential fact that equalised everyone, it was the commonality of living with disability. It was a powerful realisation. I didn't consciously take time off there and then to think about my own journey into that particular place. Each person would have had his or her own itinerary. It would have been intensively individual, as intimate and personal as any journey could be.

In my case, the route had been spectacular. I had been blown up by a bomb in the freedom struggle. Yet when it came to the issues I had to grapple with, the origin of my amputation seemed irrelevant. How do you deal with life when you wake up without an arm? How do you manage physically? And how do you deal with what the psychiatrist called 'the freak effect' of looking bizarre? I could recall my own reactions from my pre-amputation days – once I'd been on a plane and seen an amputee walking in my direction and then had felt huge relief when he had taken up a seat behind me.

I am at the end of my recovery period in London and most of the time I am feeling upbeat. Then somebody comes to me and says that he is the engineer for my prosthesis. He is keen to support me. He assiduously takes measurements of what he calls my 'stoomp'. He is from the Midlands. I don't like the word stoomp, not because of his pronunciation. It's not my stump, it's my arm. Anyway, after taking the measurement, he tells me that my stoomp was just a bit too long, and it would help them a lot if they could chop off a bit, and then the prosthesis would fit better. What? I had to fit the prosthesis, and not the prosthesis fit me? In the event he can see that I'm a difficult customer, someone to be specially careful with. Then he asks me what colour I would like my arm to be. Wow, that's fantastic! I can be the first rainbow South African, with one white arm and one black arm. But I soberly tell him to make it the same as my other arm.

I'm asked 'why do you want a prosthesis?' I've got to have an answer. I can't just say that I really don't know, and that I'm simply doing what people do. It's like when a judge asks you a question, you've got to have an answer. So I invent the answer that it would be useful for my balance and to be able to do things. Anyhow, after some time I am given the specially constructed arm. I put it on, I'm going to show the enemy and the world that I have triumphed and the bomb has failed. It is not very comfortable. It is strapped on with a claw at the end. You use your back muscles to open and close the claw.

Eventually I am transported to Roehampton, a famous rehab unit in South London that has been dealing with people injured by bombs in Northern Ireland. I enjoy my Tuesday visits to the Upper-Limb Amputation Unit. Everyone walking round has an empty sleeve, it's nice to see that we are the norm. I am asked to pick up pegs on a Chinese chequers board and move them. I am learning, manoeuvring, getting a bit faster. They praise me for doing well. I come back a few times, on each occasion becoming a bit more adept. But I am not quite sure what it is all about. There is nothing that I learn to do with my prosthesis that I cannot do far more comfortably with my left hand.

MEETING TWO WOMEN – ONE WHO LIVES IN FEAR AND ONE WHO IS FREE

One day I arrive at Roehampton to find that there is a woman ironing in the room, in my space, during my hour. It offends my patient's narcissism, the feeling that everything should be focused on me. But then I learn that she is ironing with her prosthesis, elegantly, for me to see. Gee, this is impressive, encouraging. Then she confides in me: 'The only problem is when I'm at home and the prosthesis is not on and the front door bell rings and I don't know what to do, should I delay to put on my arm or rush to open the door?' My enthusiasm collapses. I don't want to be like that, in fear of being caught without my arm.

The next week I come again and there is a little kid in the room; I think he was a thalidomide baby, no arms and legs, with a Cockney accent, as bright as anything. We speak on toy telephones, one disabled person to another. His mother comes in to fetch him. She has his same working-class accent, and presents herself with a special English working-class beauty. She stands comfortably in her summer dress, and I notice she has a smooth exposed protuberance where her one arm should have been. Probably congenital. She looks so confident, so proud on her feet, chatting so animatedly to her buoyant little kid, and immediately I know that, yes, that's what I want to be like. She walks and talks as she is, looks wonderful as she is. I am not taking a course or reading a book as part of my rehabilitation. I am learning from what I am experiencing, achieving a sense of truth through interrogating my intuitive responses.

REJECTING THE PROSTHESIS

Yet, I am still determined to show my comrades in the ANC that I can have an arm and look like everyone else. I put it on for two months, travel with it on the underground. It is as though it is my revolutionary duty to wear the arm. But I am not enjoying it, it is not helping me. It doesn't look very nice, with a claw at the end, and I wonder if I should put a glove on it. But mainly I feel it is hanging on me like a handicap rather than functioning as a boon. And I find myself discomfited, unwillingly becoming an imposter.

Two months later I put the prosthesis away in a black bag. It is doing nothing for me. I will simply go into the world as I am. I had tried, I had really tried. The occupational therapist was disappointed, another failure. I learned afterwards that ninety per cent of people with upper limb amputations don't wear their prostheses. A prosthetic leg is wonderful. It enables you to walk, even to run, to get around, be independent. And I've heard that a prosthetic arm is great for golfers. But otherwise its real role is not to help you to do things, but to make you look 'normal'.

ROSE GARDEN, CENTRAL PARK

Shortly after leaving hospital, my brother Johnny takes me to the rose garden in Central Park. I'm sitting on a bench enjoying the sun for the first time in months. Johnny wanders off and I sit enjoying the warmth. I'm there to let the sun fall on me and to see roses. It's getting hot and I begin to feel uncomfortable. Can I take my top off? No, I say to myself – I'm full of scars, people are coming to see beautiful flowers, to enjoy themselves with their families; they don't want to see a chopped-off arm and a mutilated body. Then I reply to myself: 'Albie, take off your top'. The debate in my head goes on. 'You can'. 'You mustn't'. And eventually I find myself grasping the sleeve with my teeth, and pulling the top up till it's over my head, and it's off!

People are walking by. No one cares tuppence. They are enjoying the roses. I'm sitting there, feeling fantastic. And when I come to write it up afterwards I write how happy I was, taking possibly the most important decision in my life surrounded by roses.

SUITCASE ON A TRAIN

Now I am on a train wondering what to do with my medium-size suitcase. I want to put it on a rack at the top. How can I get it up there? The English are looking at me without looking, as only the English can do. I sense that I can do it, but don't know how. I'm not strong enough to lift it right up with my left hand. I think I have the solution. So, I lift the case on to a table. Then from the table I raise it to my shoulder. Then from my shoulder I place it on my head, and then I manoeuvre it on to the rack. The whole carriage applauds without applauding, as only the English can do.

One very important moment for me came later when I was about to start my first post-bomb job teaching at Columbia University. I was just out of hospital, learning to use a computer, wondering if I could type with one hand as effectively as I had been able to do with two.

Ten minutes later I knew: I was okay, I coul♦ type as fast with one finger as I ha♦ been ♦oing before with two. I write, therefore I am.

For nearly a year my short right arm lay inert at my side, physically part of me, but quite expressionless. Then, one day without any warning it suddenly sprang to life and joined energetically in the conversation. (Today 'short arm' is extremely active, not only gesticulating as I speak, but carrying groceries as I leave the shopping centre, and helping me keep the page down as I ink in directions in this manuscript).

It took me two years to get over another problem. What to do about people who want to help me in circumstances where I don't want assistance? At first I would get huffy and mumble, 'I'm fine, OK?' Everybody would feel awkward. I once even responded quite heatedly after a host had cut my meat into tiny baby bites – just as I had used to do for my kids when they had been toddlers. And then happily one day I found the answer, it was simply to say: 'No, but thanks for offering. So easy, so natural, so gracious. 'I'm OK, but thanks for offering'.

I DON'T THINK OF MYSELF AS DISABLED

In those early years I never referred to myself as disabled. I hated the word 'crippled' and felt uncomfortable with 'handicapped'. The description 'disabled' didn't bother me. I felt I was getting on with my life, triumphing over the bomb, and just was not disabled.

Meanwhile two relevant experiences were to affect me in different ways. The first was a fundraiser on my behalf put on at the Young Vic Theatre in London. Four actors who had played me previously took various parts in a special performance of the *Jail Diary of Albie Sachs*. The audience knew that the actors knew that I knew that they knew that I was in the audience. After the performance was over I decided to add to the theatricality. I walked up to the stage and told the audience that I had wanted spontaneously to applaud by clapping, but realised I couldn't do so. So I started clapping with my left hand against my cheek. Tears flowed.

The second encounter with my disability came when I was walking one day in bright sunshine and I suddenly noticed my shadow moving on the ground next to me – the shape looked so odd, quite freaky without a right arm – I was quite startled, even disconcerted.

The only time I directly encountered the disability movement as such was when April De Angelis wrote a play based on my book *The Soft Vengeance of a Freedom Fighter*. She did it to be performed by a disabled theatre company in London. The play was developed around the idea of dividing the narrator of the story into two persons: the good Albie, played by a young Caribbean British guy who was completely without hearing, and the bad-tempered Albie, played by April's white British actor husband, who happened to be an amputee. I found I loved being interviewed on a special BBC programme by a woman in a wheelchair, and was thrilled by the seriousness and good humour of the diversely disabled cast. The production itself was intensely moving. To get to my seat I had to lift my legs carefully over a large guide dog. All the actors and about half the audience were disabled. The play was about learning to live with dignity as a disabled person. Without realising it I was being prepared by the disabled community in London for my encounter with the disabled community in Johannesburg.

'WHAT SHALL WE DO?'

I don't remember what advice I gave to the DPSA, but I do recall my hesitation over the right words to use: what 'you' should do, I told them, what 'we' should do, what 'you' should do, what 'we' should do.

More and more I found myself saying 'we'. The word was just slipping easily in to my consciousness. And that was the

beginning of my being an active an∙ prou∙ member of the
Disable∙ People of South Africa network.

My main activity was still in the ranks of the general struggle for democracy. But I felt that working with DPSA was a very specific and meaningful part of the broad anti-apartheid movement. It contributed its own special dynamic. 'Nothing about us without us'. A powerful slogan. Throughout the country people were speaking out in all their different formations about what the new society should be like, using their own voice, making demands that could never have been made before. DPSA was a strong example of unity across race and class and language and gender. We were of the nation, for the nation.

I don't remember all the different meetings I attended, but I do recall travelling throughout the country and speaking to many people at various conferences. I was identifying with the movement, and proud to be in its ranks.

There was one session that was particularly intense. Two medical personnel spoke at a large conference about an injection that could be given to paraplegic and quadriplegic men that enabled them to have erections. This was so personal, so intimate, so direct, the kind of thing you don't normally discuss at a conference. People were putting up their hands to speak. One young African guy asked insecurely, 'After I have the injection and have the erection, what do I do?' The doctors were so absorbed by the technical side that they just had not dealt with the emotional and relational aspect at all, let alone the physical movements to bring pleasure and release.

These meetings went well beyond determining what words we wanted to see in the Constitution. We were the most diverse people imaginable, working together to achieve a better life for all, a paradigm for the nation.

DISABILITY IN THE SOUTH AFRICAN CONSTITUTION
We did in fact succeed in getting the theme of dignity for the disabled into the Constitution. There had been a strong move to simply have

a general clause outlawing all forms of unfair discrimination, thus avoiding the danger of establishing an apparently closed list. The idea was that the courts would then decide on a case-by-case basis when discrimination would be unfair.

> *I oppose• this approach. Vulnerable groups wishe• to see themselves expressly protecte•. It was necessary to mark out •isability expressly an• clearly.*

The equality clause in the Bill of Rights went on, in fact, to prohibit unfair discrimination on a number of specified grounds, including race, colour, sex, language, sexual orientation and disability.

It was important to have these categories expressly identified. They were more than just springboards for litigation. They signalled the existence of fundamental features of life in the world. Where people's dignity was being infringed, where there was unnecessary pain, the Constitution had to serve as a beacon of hope and aspiration. The issue was not just one about policies a progressive government should have. It related to a fundamental right, the right not to be discriminated against, in this case, on grounds of disability.

AFFIRMATIVE ACTION

There is considerable legislation in South Africa about affirmative action. Forms of affirmative action are required in a number of areas, with special emphasis on race, gender and disability. In practice, only in the case of disability is a quota used, not a huge quota, but something tangible. At the very least, it gives to those employers who do want to hire disabled people, a tool to overcome the active or unconscious resistance of their colleagues. They can point to the Constitution to justify what they are doing as the right thing. And in many cases they get excellent workers who do more than pull their own weight to get and retain the job.

WORKING ON THE CONSTITUTIONAL COURT

What about the Constitutional Court? The fact I had one long and one short arm turned out not to be a factor at all in my being appointed to the Court. From a functional point of view it was quite irrelevant to my work on the Court. Yet I believe it played a valuable if very indirect role in helping me develop ideas on the right to be different.

One of my ten colleagues, Zak Yacoob, had been blind since he was a toddler. Practitioners and the public got used to seeing me with one long and one short arm, dispensing justice while seated near to Zak Yacoob. Zak was brilliant, funny and smart. He would love saying 'Counsel, at page 726 of the record ...' He had an extraordinary ability to identify the place where things appeared on the record. And to add to the diversity of our Court, we were joined by Edwin Cameron, an openly gay man who had declared his HIV-positive status when applying to become a member of the Court.

I wish this presentation could include examples of how we applied the law in relation to the rights of the disabled. But no case on the subject came our way. Maybe this was because we had good legislation so people didn't need to go to court to establish the rights of the disabled. Perhaps it was in part because members of the DPSA were in government and could exercise influence directly. I was particularly pleased when I learnt recently that Michael Masutha, a visually impaired senior official of DPSA, had been appointed as a deputy minister, and later as minister of justice. So, we got used to seeing sign language used in various public proceedings, to noticing wheelchairs in parliament.

Somehow people ∎on't speak about ∎isability in quite the same way if someone ∎isable∎ is there; you ∎on't speak about the ∎isable∎, you speak to an∎ with the ∎isable∎. Disable∎ people are seen not as a section apart from the nation, but as an active an∎ constitutive part of the nation.

CONCLUSIONS FROM THE SOUTH AFRICAN EXPERIENCE

To my mind an expansive and broadly based vision is crucial for the development of disability rights. People in the human rights community do wonderful work expressing indignation at oppressive and discriminatory conduct – the world indeed needs committed namers and dedicated shamers. But there's a risk of saddling human rights work with a permanently long face. Happily, in the anti-apartheid struggle in South Africa we never lost the capacity to sing and dance and crack jokes.

Disability law is clearly based on enhancing human dignity. Thus dignity can be undermined by laws which force you to be unduly dependent on, say, social workers who deprive you unnecessarily of your autonomy. On the other hand, claims based on the human right to have your dignity respected can be enormously useful in enabling disabled people to be active, productive, loving and caring members of society. Accordingly, we cannot underestimate the practical utility that disability law can have for disabled persons. And the enforcement of social and economic rights can be particularly valuable. But to my mind, the importance of disability law goes well beyond its instrumental utility. Indeed, there are few other areas of law where both the tangible and instrumental, and the intangible and symbolic, impacts of the law can be so significant.

IT IS IMPORTANT TO BE NAMED IN THE CONSTITUTION

It is important to have constitutional and statutory texts that bear your name and tell your story. Being identified expressly becomes a symbol of participating in a shared citizenship. Then, it is extremely meaningful to be directly involved in the making of legislation. 'Nothing about us without us'. That is all part of the process of inclusion that is central to disability law. Moreover, the disability movement has a role to play in relation to how law generally, and not only that which bears directly on disability rights, impacts on disabled people. Law that is apparently neutral can in fact bear with great exclusionary severity on disabled people. Conversely, disability-sensitive law can do much to facilitate the possibilities of disabled people leading full and fruitful lives.

If there is one thing that the struggle against aparthei♦ has taught us, it is how important it is to manage ♦ifference in society. Difference was use♦ as the basis for aparthei♦. Difference became an instrument of ♦omination an♦ control. What if we can turn ♦ifference aroun♦ to become a source of vitality, of variability, of richness?

So while disability law may help people get access to a bus, it does much more than that. It says that everyone matters, that society cares about the well-being of each and every one of us, that we are all living in an interdependent society. Indeed, public awareness of the rights of the disabled is important not only for disabled people, but for society as a whole. If society is intolerant, embarrassed, exclusionary, its own imaginative heart is being restricted. Its capacity for human empathy is being denied. Exclusion damages the way we understand and characterise the world we live in. Inclusion enhances our humanity.

DISABILITY LAW CAN HAVE AN IMPACT BEYOND THE LAW OF DISABILITY

One of the striking features of legal activity and thinking over the past decades has been the way that creative legal endeavours in certain areas have gone beyond advancing the initiating cause to develop and enrich legal thinking and practice generally.

Thus, the women's movement helpe♦ transform many fun♦amental features of law. For one, it challenge♦ the whole ♦istinction between the public an♦ the private spheres of law.

If you want to eradicate torture, you don't simply denounce it when practised by state agents, you repudiate it when it takes place in the privacy of people's homes, where people are in fact being subjected to it on a daily basis. Thus, under the South African Constitution the clause in the Bill of Rights dealing with freedom refers to the duty to prohibit violence from any source, public or private. This represents a major reconfiguration and enlargement of the role of the law. The state is not only obliged to ensure that state agencies do not themselves abuse the rights of the people. It is required to create protective and remedial measures to prevent private actors from denying people in the private sphere their rights to bodily and psychological integrity. The gaze of the law expands to take in millions, mainly women, but men as well, for whom the rule of law had hitherto been a chimera.

> *The same can be said of the green movement. Its objective was to get changes in the law to protect the environment, the earth. But it is far more than just that. It introduces new philosophies into the law, new ways of looking at it. Thus, the ordinary land law rights and expectations that go with ownership had to be conjugated with new theories of stewardship of land and non-renewable resources, as well as flora and fauna. Unborn generations had to come into the picture.*

Standing to bring cases needed to be enlarged, generational and national boundaries had to be re-thought, and where particularly severe threats to the human and natural environments appeared on the horizon, the ordinary principles of negligence had to take account of the higher standard of care implicit in the precautionary principle. A dream becomes a declaration which becomes soft law which becomes hard law and new energies radiate through the body of law as a whole. My view is that disability law too, has fertilised the law in areas that go well beyond the rights of the disabled.

From Refugee to Judge
on Refugee Law

CRITICAL ISSUES IN INTERNATIONAL REFUGEE LAW |
EDITED BY JAMES SIMEON | CAMBRIDGE UNIVERSITY PRESS | 2010

The first time I arrived in England as a refugee I was something of an emotional and psychological wreck. While practising at the Bar in Cape Town I had been locked up in solitary confinement for 168 days. The isolation was punishing, unbelievably so. It was so strict that I might possibly have been the only person in the world who did not know for quite a while that Kennedy had been assassinated.

But I held out, and on my release ran twelve kilometres from the detention centre in the heart of the city, and flung myself fully clothed into the sea. Outwardly, I was strong, even triumphant, but in reality I was crushed. Two years later I was again detained in solitary confinement, this time for three months in an awaiting-trial jail where I had frequently interviewed clients. The authorities referred to me as a terrorist, and I was subjected to torture by sleep deprivation. On this occasion, when I was released I did not run to the sea, or even climb Table Mountain. I slouched home.

The resistance to apartheid was being severely battered. It was difficult to escape from Cape Town, which was a thousand kilometres from the nearest land border. My clients expected me to keep them out of jail, not to go to jail myself. So it was either go underground fulltime, or leave the country. We didn't have the structures, and I didn't have the courage, to go underground. So, sick at heart, I became a partner in my own humiliation, and applied for what was called an 'exit permit'. After a long delay I was allowed to leave with a document that said I was stripping myself forever of my citizenship, and would be committing a criminal offence under South African law if ever I returned.

At that time I was subjected to a 'banning order' that restricted me from leaving the portion of Cape Town reserved for only white occupation, and forbade me on pain of imprisonment from entering the harbour area. So I had to suffer the further indignity of entreating the authorities to give me written permission to board the ship that was to take me from the country of my soul and deposit me, perhaps for the rest of my life, into a stateless limbo. When I got to my cabin, there was one farewell phone call I needed to make. Knowing that the phone would be bugged, I spoke carefully to a lawyer friend: 'Dullah, I am on the Cape Town Castle (ocean liner), this is my last phone call before I go into exile … I just wanted to say goodbye. … I will be back one day' (Dullah Omar went on to become the first minister of justice in democratic South Africa, responsible for the law that set up the Truth Commission). As the ship steamed out and passengers joyously threw streamers to friends at the dockside, I just stared numbly at the disappearing quayside. Part of me was jubilant, I was safe, safe, safe. And a week later when we were in the middle of the Atlantic and England scored a goal in overtime and won the World Cup, and a below-deck roar seemed to lift the boat out of the ocean, I smiled with delight like everybody else on board. How most forced migrants would love to depart from their countries in an ocean liner!

Yet each refugee makes his or her own journey, and while I happily played ping-pong, tenniquoits and bridge, and dressed up for the fancy-dress ball, the spikes of my pain and humiliation never stopped tearing at my insides.

Just as a diver must rise slowly from the ocean depths to the surface, so do victims of repression need to emerge gradually into freedom. It is not just the need to come to terms with the separation anxiety that most people feel when they move from their customary habitat to a place where everything is unfamiliar. There is the trauma that preceded the compelled departure; the loss of autonomy and sense of defeat at having been overwhelmed by irresistible forces beyond your control; and finally there is the emotion of doom at not being able to return. Asylum may save you from continued persecution. It may even permit your courage to resurge. But it does not in itself repair the damage that accompanied being extruded against your will from the land of your birth. Two weeks cruising through the waves did allow some of the trauma to abate.

Yet when I arrive♦ in Englan♦ I was still in turmoil. Day after ♦ay, almost obsessively, I woul♦ lie on my back on Hampstea♦ Heath an♦ stare up at the kites flying peacefully, this way an♦ that, overhea♦. I became a♦♦icte♦ to serenity. Yet I felt existentially ♦e-centre♦.

There was a total disjuncture between the over-turbulent character of life in South Africa, and the over-stolid way in which people seemed to get on with their lives in England. The very placidity that gave me a sense of security there seemed to mock all our passionate endeavour in South Africa. As a child I had read in weekly comics about the brave exploits of pilots in the Battle of Britain. The war was far away, something 'in the news'. Then, as the war neared its end, we were told to eat up all our food and remember the poor starving children of Europe. Now all was reversed. I was in Britain, a country that shook its head in disbelief at the violence, suffering and hunger in faraway South Africa.

Although I could control my movements, I could not regulate my emotions. At the simplest level, the sense of trust that I would survive through the day, and the night, and the next day, without being locked up, was ineffable. Yet, however marvellous it was to be living far away from terror, I could not subdue a degree of wild anger against the country to whose shores I had come.

> *An irrational rage, flowing from my helplessness, projected itself onto my hosts. Had it not been Britain that had finally subjugated indigenous African resistance in southern Africa, and gone on to 'unite the white races' to create the Union of South Africa in 1910? And who, if not British investors, had been the greatest beneficiaries of the exploitation of cheap black labour? Feelings of grievance went forth and multiplied.*

Who was now using a veto to prevent sanctions from being applied to bring apartheid to an end, and who was calling Nelson Mandela a 'terrorist'? I particularly hated us being called 'terrorists'. We were fighting for freedom, and only after all other avenues to get the vote had been firmly closed, had we reluctantly included armed struggle as part of our campaign for liberation. Yet we had specifically refused to use terrorism directed at civilians, just as we had decided resolutely against employing torture to get information from people sent to kill our leadership and destroy our organisation. A deep sense of morality and respect for human life lay at the core of all our endeavours. How dare they call us terrorists – how dare they!

It was all so confusing. There were many people and organisations in the UK who received us with understanding and love. I was able to complete a doctorate at Sussex University, have three books published and even take part in an interview on the first night that colour television was broadcast in London. And I spent many productive years as a law lecturer at Southampton University (having been taken on, I suspected, on the basis that, because I came from overseas, I should be able to teach International Law.)

Many people who migrate feel uncertain about the extent to which they should immerse themselves in the culture of their new country and risk giving up the identity they had developed in their country of origin. In my case, the process went the other way. I engaged as much as I could with British society, always intending to take home with me whatever could enrich the new democracy we were going to build in South Africa one day. So the more I plunged into British life, the more South African did I feel. Similarly, I always had the idea that I was not only receiving opportunities but giving something to the society I was now in. I think of the strange experience of being at the Donmar Theatre, with an American tourist at my side, watching the Royal Shakespeare Company putting on a beautifully modulated version of the *Jail Diary of Albie Sachs*, and being too timid to nudge him and say: 'You know something … ?' Then the law faculty allowed me to put together the first full academic course in the UK on Law and Discrimination. And later I was able to get a book on sexism and the law published. As ANC choirs always sang so beautifully in our places of exile: 'When freedom comes along, we shall ever remember the things you've done for us'.

In 1977, I moved to Maputo in newly independent Mozambique, where I took up a position as professor of Law at the recently established law faculty [Faculdade de Direito] at the University of Eduardo Mondlane. By now I had learned something about International Law, but I did not teach refugee law, because it simply did not exist as an area of academic study, not there, nor anywhere else in the world. Refugee law in fact came to me in a purely practical form. The United Nations High Commission for Refugees in Mozambique required people like myself to complete application forms to enable us to be classified as refugees. Although the objective was primarily to provide us with protection against cross-border raids by South African commandos, I was reluctant to fill in the forms. I wondered why I felt uncomfortable being called a refugee, and came to the conclusion that, as so much in law, the significance of the term depended on the context in which it was used.

In some circumstances receiving the label 'refugee' coul•literally save your life. In others it consigne• you to being a ∙isempowere∙ member of an anonymous mass, whose existence woul∙ be ∙etermine∙ by classification an∙ controlle∙ by the will of others.

I believed that I and others who had been displaced from our country because of our actions in compliance with United Nations calls to end apartheid, should be treated as freedom fighters, and not as refugees. Yet, out of respect for my hosts, I signed the forms and identified myself as a refugee, without for a moment feeling I was one.

The secon∙ time I arrive∙ in Englan∙ as a refugee, I came as a physical wreck on a stretcher.

In 1988, as I was about to go to a beach on the outskirts of Maputo, a bomb placed in my car by South African agents exploded, and I lost my right arm and the sight of an eye, and had my right heel shattered. Ten days later, to protect me from a further attempt on my life, I was flown to London. For the first time in my life I travelled first class, but sadly I was virtually unconscious the whole way. Then I was taken semi-comatose by ambulance to the London Hospital, where my brother was a doctor. The National Health Service had changed, and I had to pay a full fee for the ambulance and partial fees for my stay at the hospital. But I did not feel aggrieved. To this day I recall the touch of the hands of my nurses as they removed my blood-stained bandages, cleaned my body and put fresh bandages on again. And I remember with continued amazement and gratitude the way in which the physiotherapists encouraged me to find strength in myself, first, to wriggle my backside from my bed to the commode, later, to stand, quite literally, on my own two feet, then, to walk, and finally, go up and down stairs leading with the correct foot ('good foot up to heaven, bad foot down to hell'). Somehow the organised love of the hospital staff bound me more directly, intimately and unambiguously to my host country than all the multifarious forms of support and solidarity had done on my previous sojourn. And, to complete the transformation, I had the unexpected experience of being visited from time to time by a Special Branch officer from Scotland Yard, who kept me under surveillance, not to report on my activities, but to ensure that no harm came to me.

In the public mind I was always regarded as a refugee from apartheid violence. Yet in purely technical terms that status got disqualified. After polite but very intensive questioning by a security official, and a long delay during which there was an opportune change of government, I received British citizenship and a UK passport. During seven lean years of statelessness, I had travelled with some difficulty on a 'Travel Document'. But now I could move around the world freely until one day, I was sure, I would recover my South African passport.

Of all the journeys I was to make, undoubtedly the most wonderful was the one I undertook twenty-three years, eight months, two weeks and a day after the day I departed from the dockside in Cape Town. It took me by plane to Johannesburg International Airport, where I arrived joyously as a free person bursting with knowledge to be used in transforming the land of apartheid into a non-racial democracy.

When I got off the plane an Afrikaans-speaking airport security official took me aside and said: 'Welcome home, Albie'. This unexpected greeting somehow helped me become aware of a thread that had connected up all the different experiences of exile over nearly a quarter of a century. The connecting element was my participation in the freedom struggle.

My expulsion from the country had been brought about not by some malign, irrational and irresistible calamity, but as a consequence of voluntary adherence to certain beliefs. The years of displacement which followed were tied in with these beliefs. And my immersion in British and Mozambican life served to re-enforce rather than undermine my South African identity. I would tell people that I never considered myself to be 'an exile', but rather to be a person 'living in exile'. Living in exile located me but did not determine who I was; exile was as much a presence as an absence.

So all the way through I was able to be both an intensely patriotic South African, and, like Tom Paine, a proud citizen of the world. Thus, 'the reason for everything' that many people believe in, was not for me some occult force beyond human understanding. It was a core choice in my life which provided significance and continuity to the long years of my comity lost and my country re-gained.

And one of the key experiences that I took home with me was speaking at the Centre for Refugee Studies at Oxford University, newly founded by Dr Barbara Harrell-Bond. For the first time, refugee law was being developed as an independent, multidisciplinary area of study. I had just come out of hospital, and had been asked to talk about the way the law had impacted on my life as a refugee. Still physically frail, my leg gave way while I was giving my presentation and I collapsed to the ground. Consternation! But my mind was still robust. I was rapidly learning some of the key characteristics of refugee law. At its heart lay not systems of classification and structures of administration, important though these were. The core binding elements were respect for human dignity and insistence on fairness of procedure and respectfulness of outcome.

I ‎iscovere‎ that ‎ignifie‎ ‎ialogue was the key to the relationship between those offering help an‎ those receiving it, an‎ central to ensuring that people ‎isplace‎ by persecution were able to speak in their own voices. An‎ I learnt about the role that law coul‎ play in encouraging self-reliance rather than ‎epen‎ence, an‎ integration rather than segregation.

Perhaps it was our experience as South Africans that had made my generation particularly averse to seeing refugees in prototypical terms. We certainly did not regard ourselves as constituting forlorn families huddled in camps waiting for handouts from benefactors. And we had no doubt that host countries benefitted from the skills, song, business acumen, political ideas, music and cuisine we brought with us. Similarly, we constantly envisaged one day taking back home with us some of the multitude of riches we had found in our host countries. Properly configured and applied, then, the law could transform refugees from being objects of pity into participants in processes of humane good-neighbourliness.

Finally, I discovered that refugee law focused on the creation of legal and other mechanisms to anticipate and prevent forced migrations, if possible, and to repair and heal, or at least to mitigate, their effects. As the African proverb puts it, 'the foot has no nose', that is, we must look after each other because we never know where our own life journeys could one day lead us to.

THE *UNION OF REFUGEE WOMEN* CASE: BACKGROUND

I had been a member of the Constitutional Court for ten years when the first case dealing with refugee law came before us. Brought by a body called Union of Refugee Women, which had the support of civil society organisations, it concerned the treatment of refugees in South Africa, more especially in the area of employment. Literature presented to the Court asserted that while the provisions of the Refugees Act were notably progressive, their implementation left much to be desired. This particular matter had in fact started off simply as a complaint about implementation. It concerned the rights of refugees to work in the private security industry, and was triggered by a suddenly imposed blanket exclusion in the Private Security Act that barred all refugees from working in that industry. Refugees who had previously been given permits to work in private security had their permits suddenly withdrawn. During the course of the litigation the applicants broadened their challenge and sought a declaration that the relevant section in the Private Security Act was unconstitutional. The Act stated broadly that non-nationals who were not permanent residents could not enter the security industry unless they were given special exemption. The Refugees Act, on the other hand, declared in unqualified terms that accredited refugees could seek employment. How could these provisions be reconciled?

All ten judges who sat in the matter agreed that the blanket exclusion was unlawful, and that each applicant should have had his or her case reviewed on an individual basis. We also all emphasised that refugees should be assisted in understanding the processes involved. A costs award was made in favour of the applicants. The Court divided, however, on the question of the constitutionality of the relevant section of the Private Security Act.

Four of the members of the Court stated that refugees were a group vulnerable to discrimination. Though the exclusionary provision in the section had a legitimate and laudable purpose, its terms were not narrowly tailored to that purpose. They accordingly held that, taking account of South Africa's international obligations, the overbroad exclusion was unfairly discriminatory and inconsistent with the Constitution. Six judges, however, felt that unconstitutionality could be avoided if the provisions of the Private Security Industry Act were applied in a way that was consistent with South Africa's international obligations. In particular, the exemption powers should be applied in an individualised manner which gives due recognition to the status and entitlements of refugees.

It should be noted that after five years' residence in South Africa, refugees were entitled to become permanent residents. So the exclusion applied only to refugees who had been in the country for less than five years.

Which group did I belong to? The reader would correctly assume that life experiences sharpen and intensify judicial instincts. But sitting on the Bench one realises that these experiences are strongly mediated by the legal culture within which we operate. Our Constitution is overtly value-laden. The matters that reach us are rarely solved simply by textual analysis. We spend much time balancing competing interests, relying heavily on the principle of proportionality. For this very reason we aim as much as possible to achieve principled and fully articulated solutions to problems. Analysts have battled without success to find discernible ideological blocs in our Court. None of us could simply be categorised as pro- or anti- either refugees or the executive. In one way or another, all of us had taken part in the struggle against apartheid. We all shared the view stated in the preamble to the Constitution that we came from a past of great injustice, and that our Constitution was aimed at transforming our country rather than protecting an unfair status quo. Yet, as in this case, we often disagreed on precisely how the Constitution should be applied in a particular set of circumstances. And as this case also demonstrated, sometimes the tenor of the language used and the socio-juridical vision emanating from a judgment can be as meaningful as its technical outcome.

Thus, although the remedies we proposed were different, in practice the divergence was small. All the members of the Court agreed on the importance of applying relevant international law principles, and ensuring that the Refugees Act be implemented in a humane and supportive way. And all of us, I believe, adopted an approach that emphasised the human dimension of what was at stake. Where we differed was over the most appropriate technical ways of achieving respect for the dignity of those affected.

In formal legal terms, the issue was whether the constitutionality of the exclusionary provision could be saved by requiring the exemption clause to be applied in a manner that fully acknowledged the rights of refugees, and could this be done without completely destroying legitimate legislative objectives concerning regulation of the private security industry? The reader will see from extracts from the conclusion to a separate judgment I wrote on which side I came out in this case, and will possibly be surprised.

CONCLUSION

The culture of providing hospitality to bereft strangers seeking a fresh and secure life for themselves is not something new in our country. As Professor Hammond-Tooke has pointed out, in traditional society:

'The hospitality universally enjoine• towar•s strangers, [is] capture• in the Xhosa proverb Unyawo alunompumlo *('The foot has no nose'). Strangers, being isolate• from their kin, an• thus •efenceless, were particularly un•er the protection of the chief an• were accor•e• special privileges'.*

Today the concept of human interdependence and burden-sharing in relation to catastrophe is associated with the spirit of ubuntu-botho. The reminder that we are not islands unto ourselves, however, must be applied to our relationship with the rest of the continent. The applicants in this matter all came from African countries. They had been granted refugee status because instability and bloodshed in their home countries had rendered life there intolerable. Their states of origin had either set out to persecute them or else been unable to provide them with the protection that citizens should be able to demand from their government. Two examples illustrate this. The tenth applicant, whose father was a schoolteacher, stated that:

'It was alleged by the [Rwandan Patriotic Front] that all Hutus were involved in the genocide which occurred in my country during 1994. During the period 1994 to 1998 all my husband's family members were killed and two of my sisters, one of my brothers and a host of other family members were killed'.

The twelfth applicant told a similarly tragic story:

'I have been a resident and citizen of the Democratic Republic of the Congo ... My father was a king in Bukavu, South Kivu. He was killed by rebel soldiers who were in the process of fighting a civil war against the government on or about April 2001. At the time of my father's death I was a student. The rebel soldiers killed my father because he refused to sign a proposition document'.

One was the child of a schoolteacher, the other of a king. Both had been students when forced to flee to South Africa. They were not seeking handouts from the state, but simply the opportunity to work and earn a living. They had organised themselves into groups and received training as security guards, which capacitated them to do relatively humble tasks, such as guarding parked cars or patrolling shopping malls.

I saw no reason why access to employment in the security industry by persons in their situation should not be permitted in relation to sectors such as these, where no high-security interests were at stake. To bar them would have been to discriminate against them unfairly. At the same time I would not have regarded it as unfair to keep them from guarding installations and persons where particularly high security considerations come into play.

'The greater power of officials to grant unqualified exemptions to enter the industry should not exclude a lesser power to grant a restricted exemption, the only proviso being that the basis for the qualification be fair and reasonable in the circumstances. Indeed, it would be dangerous and self-defeating for the public administration to function on the basis that if officials cannot grant everything an applicant might seek, they cannot grant anything at all. The converse should also apply: officials should not be required to accede to everything refugees may ask for on the basis that in fairness the applicants are entitled at least to something. The principle of 'all or nothing' is frequently dangerous in administrative law. It disregards the notion of proportionality that lies at the heart of fairness of treatment. Experience warns that because cautious administrators might be fearful of being regarded as unduly generous, in practice this principle will usually lead to nothing.

In summary: the applicants had been correct in their initial approach to Court when they had challenged the criteria used by officials who had excluded them in blanket fashion from the security industry, in some cases withdrawing permits already granted. However, the applicants' subsequent challenge to the constitutionality of the relevant section was over-ambitious. The mere fact of being refugees did not entitle them to be admitted by right to all spheres of the private security industry. The key factor was that being an accredited refugee went a long way in itself to establishing that there was 'good cause' for exempting an applicant from the prohibition against non-nationals and non-permanent residents entering the security industry. Bearing in mind the special status that accredited refugees enjoy under our law, I hoped that the clarifications given by the Court would assist both refugees and officials in streamlining the processes involved, engaging with each other in a mutually respectful manner, and achieving outcomes that were objectively grounded, fair and reasonable.

A Conversation about the Sacred and the Secular: Same-sex marriage

2ND CONFERENCE OF THE AFRICAN CONSORTIUM FOR LAW AND RELIGIOUS STUDIES (ACLARS) | STELLENBOSCH, SOUTH AFRICA | 26–28 MAY 2014

By way of preamble to our Constitution's Preamble, let me start by telling you how I nearly became a hero.

It was 1991, and the leader of a very big evangelical church in Natal [as the province was then called], Michael Cassidy, came down to Cape Town on a special mission to speak to me. I was a bit curious about the purpose of his visit. He quickly asked, 'Albie Sachs, would you like to be a hero to millions?' Now that's a wonderful offer, so my ears went up. 'Uh-huh, what do I have to do?' He told me that we were entering into negotiations for a new democratic dispensation in South Africa, and he personally, along with members of his church, thought very favourably of these developments. But they had one big concern, and that's why he was speaking to me. Was it possible, he asked, could I do something to bring about a Preamble to the Constitution that began, 'In humble submission to Almighty God'? 'If you do that,' he concluded, 'you'll be a hero to millions'.

His request was difficult. Not because becoming a hero to millions was within my grasp and I might lose the opportunity. And not because I had any doubts about his sincerity. Indeed, I was sure he was speaking not only for his congregation but for millions of other Christians in the country, as well as for believers from other faiths. Yet, I personally, the one to whom he had appealed, had grown up in an expressly secular home – not by accident, not by a lapsing of religion, not by having a greater interest in other things so that the spiritual didn't matter. I did so because my parents had taken a stand against their parents that had become part of their self-identification and of the world I had grown up in. They wanted to storm heaven. They fought for human emancipation. And they saw the religion that was being imposed upon them, was expected of them, as a barrier to the kind of liberation they were imagining and fighting for. In my case, it started when I was very young, aged about four in a kindergarten, and my mother asked the principal of the kindergarten, 'Can Albie keep his eyes open during prayers?' And the tolerant kindergarten head said, 'Of course he can keep his eyes open during prayers'. And I kept my eyes open during prayers, and to my amazement half of the other kids also opened their eyes though they didn't have that permission, and I felt that was very wrong of them!

Later on, it became a little tougher. I'm turning eleven, twelve, the phase when a bar mitzvah is coming, and all my pals at school – half of the kids at the boys' school were Jews, half were Christian – were saying, 'Albie, when's your barmi?' And I was two years younger than any of the others, because during World War II a lot of the teachers had gone 'up North', the way it was put, to fight Hitler in North Africa. Married women weren't allowed to teach then, so there was a great shortage of teachers. They pushed the brighter kids into higher classes, and I found myself two years younger than my peers. Some years later, one by one, my Jewish peers had their bar mitzvahs, and I wondered, 'What am I going to do?' And my parents said, 'It's up to you. If you want a bar mitzvah, we'll support you. If you don't want a bar mitzvah, we'll support you'. And my thinking, and it was very difficult, very personal, was that if I was to pretend a belief in God that I didn't have as mine, as real, it would be disrespectful to me, and disrespectful to God, if God exists, and I felt I couldn't go along with that. Now, looking back, that's quite tough for an eleven- or twelve-year-old, but the consequence of that is that, for me, conscience is number one.

Conscience is what is in your hea•, conscience is what you •etermine for yourself as the most central aspect of your being. An• the para•oxical result of that was that fighting for my secular belief system as a young chil• in an intensely, at least overtly, religious an• pious environment, went on to make me extremely respectful of an• conscientious towar•s the consciences of others, inclu•ing religious beliefs an• consciences.

Now that's the preamble to the Preamble.

One more little but important biographical discovery. At age seventeen, at the time when I joined the Defiance of Unjust Laws Campaign, we used to hold weekly meetings on the Grand Parade in Cape Town, in front of the City Hall, sometimes fifty people, sometimes five hundred, sometimes five thousand, and to sing songs, 'Volunteers, obey the orders, volunteers obey' and being quite dramatic. And one of the speakers, Johnson Ngwevela, whom we knew to be what we called a 'big Communist', an African man who had belonged to the Communist Party before it was driven underground and who worked for an attorney, Sam Kahn, who was well known as a Communist, said: 'One day, the Red Sea will open for us, like it opened for the people of Israel, and we will walk to freedom'. I went to him afterwards, and I said, 'Comrade Johnson, how come that you're using a parable from the Bible in terms of us achieving our freedom?' And he said, 'Comrade Albie, there are some things that politics can reach, and there are some things that can't be reached by politics'.

The Bible was as meaningful for him as the Communist Manifesto, an• he was somebo•y long in the struggle, whose chil•ren were active in the struggle, whose gran•chil•ren went on to join the arme• struggle, someone as •eeply committe• as I ever wante• an• preten•e• to be.

For him, there was space for both politics and religion, each was part of his make-up, of the way he saw the world. It was one of those intellectual shocks that I think everybody should have fairly early on in their life, a shock to a formal, philosophical system that you are absolutely certain about, that you would defend with your life, and your absolute certainty is undermined, not through some persuasive logical argument, but by the words of somebody whom you admire and respect who shows that there's another way of looking at the fundamentals of the world.

This was the background then to Michael Cassidy's request, which I found to be very moving. Yet I didn't see that we could open our Constitution with the phrase 'In humble submission to Almighty God'. The words were just too powerful, too overwhelming. They could even have had a constitutional significance and contribute a certain religiosity to everything that followed in the text, which would be extremely oppressive to people who didn't share that belief. At the same time, it was clear to me the great majority of South Africans were religious. If democracy could be associated with a form of comfort, of accommodation, of not being threatening to or hostile to or separate from religious belief that would help integrate democracy into their lives, especially for African people, but also for Afrikaners, for many English-speakers, as well – that would be a gain. That would mean democracy would be more strongly implanted. It would be more welcome, it would be seen as something natural for us as a society, rather than something that lawyers have invented as some sort of a compact that's being imposed on society.

And so I was able to make a recommendation when it came to looking at the Preamble. It was not to say, 'In humble submission to Almighty God' right at the beginning, but to say in isiXhosa, *'Nkosi Sikelel' iAfrika'* (Lord bless Africa), at the end of the Preamble. We sing this anthem, believers and nonbelievers alike, Christians, Muslims, Hindus, Jews, agnostics, pantheists, atheists, we all sing *Nkosi Sikelel' iAfrika*, and that would be a phrase that would unite us, that would bring us together. It was the hymn of the oppressed, and so the Preamble in our Constitution sets out that 'South Africa belongs to all who live in it, united in our diversity', and so on and so forth. That was my recommendation. Then the next words: 'May God protect our people. *Nkosi Sikelel' iAfrika. Morena boloka setjhaba sa heso. Go• seën Sui•-Afrika*. God bless South Africa'. But Cyril Ramaphosa, chief negotiator for the ANC, insisted that that was not enough – what about Tshivenda and Xitsonga, which were not included, and so they added the words in these languages as well, and it fitted. '*Mu•zimu fhatutshe•za Afurika. Hosi katekisa Afrika*'. What could have been an issue that divided people – that kept us apart and segregated us – was turned around into a theme that brought us closer together and helped to create that sense of unity in diversity, or diversity in unity, that's foundational to the South African vision.

I never went to Mike Cassidy afterwards to claim my certificate of heroism, but I was glad that he'd spoken to me because he had underlined the importance of finding a place and a space for religion in our constitutional order, but one that would not be competitive, jarring, oppressive, imposing or harsh to anybody, rather one that could slip naturally into our culture, our history and our sense of identity.

I now turn directly to the question of the sacred, the secular and the Constitution. I'll start by running through four cases we had while I was a judge on the Constitutional Court, before dealing a little more extensively with the recent case before the Court on the question of same-sex marriage. These cases tie in beautifully with the theme of the sacred and the secular, law, religion and the common good in pluralistic societies.

THE LAWRENCE CASE: LIQUOR LAWS, RELIGIOUS HOLIDAYS AND LEGACIES OF PAST DISCRIMINATION

The first case we had on religious freedom in South Africa, *S v Lawrence* [*S v Lawrence; S v Negal; S v Solberg* (CCT 38/96, CCT 39/96, CCT 40/96) [1997] ZACC 11; 1997 (4) SA 1176 (CC); 1997 (10) BCLR 1348 (CC)], dealt with a claim by 7-Eleven, the grocery chain, to be able to sell booze on Sundays, Good Friday, and Christmas Day. Now that's a hell of a claim for freedom of religion! To sell more liquor on these singled-out days. But our law allows that even if you don't show that your own personal rights to religious freedom are directly affected, you can still come to court to say this is a violation of religious freedom, because, objectively, it's unconstitutionally singling out three religious days associated with Christianity.

Four of my colleagues said – I'm putting it in very non-legal language – 'Come on, this has got nothing to do with freedom of religion. You can pray, you can go to the temples, churches, synagogues, the lot. It's not inhibiting any religious practice'. But three of my colleagues said in effect, 'No, this is elevating Christianity above other religions, and if you prohibit the sale of liquor on Diwali, and other important sacred days to members of the Hindu faith, on Fridays for Muslims (who shouldn't be drinking on any day in the week,) on Saturdays for Jews, that would be different. Then they wouldn't be discriminating by favouring one religion over another'.

I was tending to go with the first group. I just couldn't believe the claim of 7-Eleven. Come on, it had nothing to do with religious freedom – but everything to do with making money out of selling liquor. I was moving in the direction of saying that it was a purely trivial form of singling out Christian specials days, and the law really doesn't want to take account of trivialities. And my colleague, my law clerk, Fatima, the name tells you something, her eyebrows went up just a little bit – it's the only time I've changed my point of view because of a clerk's eyebrow going up – and I said, 'Fatima, what's the matter?' And she said, 'Albie, it's these little things that make many of us feel we are not full citizens of this country'.

This made me really realise that, although a small detail, it was one of those signals coming from the law that showed ignorance of the experience of life in our country of Muslims and Hindus who had originated from the Indian subcontinent, who'd been subjected to race discrimination, whose marriages hadn't been recognised, who'd been subordinated in all sorts of different ways – a tiny relic perhaps, but a relic of a very painful past. You couldn't just say, it's so small, it doesn't matter. And so I wrote a separate judgment which was joined in by one colleague, Justice Yvonne Mokgoro. So the result, at that stage, was that our two voices, coupled with the three who found unfair discrimination in favour of Christianity, made a majority in favour of – well, let me not get there too quickly.

Should the law be upheld or struck down? I asked the question: from whose point of view do you decide whether or not it's infringing religious freedom? From a Christian point of view? If so, where's the problem? From an atheist point of view? Well, all religions are equally bizarre. From a Muslim point view, a Hindu point of view? And clearly under our Constitution, it can't be from any particular faith or belief point of view. It's from the point of view of a believer of any faith, or a non-believer without particular confession, sensitive to the values of the Constitution. You've got to imagine not what you yourself think personally, given your background, but imagine yourself into the position of that ideal-type individual, and be somebody who is not so thin-skinned that the slightest affront gets the hackles to rise, nor so thick-skinned as to be insensitive to things that can be wounding to others.

And that's when I went back to the importance of the impact on ordinary people of the hegemony of Christian values built into the law. It had denied non-Christians respect for their dignity, their sense of self, the significance of their family life – it had called their children illegitimate, and declared their wives to be concubines. These values were coupled with racial discrimination against people who inhabited the ghettoes of our society in a 'Go back to India' kind of approach. You never tell people to go back to Holland or go back to England, but you say: 'Go back to India!' It's these kinds of things, accumulated, that were very insulting and led to Gandhi taking action – and he used a beautiful phrase: 'Our wives, our sisters, our daughters, armed only with the patriotism of faith, went to jail,' he said, 'their sacrifice was greater than our sacrifice'. So that is why, in the end, I said 'What limited religious freedom, was the singling-out of one religious faith

– Christianity, Christian holidays – above others, the state endorsement of a particular worldview.'

> *In our constitutional or*er, I observe*, the state *oes not elevate any particular worl*view – neither Christianity, or Islam, or Ju*aism, or Marxism-Leninism, or free market neo-liberal capitalism, or any other worl*view or ortho*oxy, as a state worl*view to be impose* upon the whole of society.*

So that was my first finding in *Lawrence*, a tiny case in the legal firmament, but important to me. That, however, was not the end of the matter. I went on to say that the infringement is so slight, it's merely a relic of a fading form of hegemony, and even though it is an unacceptable endorsement of Christianity, the effect of the law can be justified on secular grounds. It didn't seem right that the first case on religious freedom should be one using the principle as the basis for allowing 7-Eleven to be able to sell liquor on Sundays. I noted that the prohibition could be justified because it reduces drinking, boozing on double holidays. And that was a secular foundation for the law, a meaningful practical justification for upholding what was a very slight invasion of religious freedom. And the net result was that the four judges said 'there's no invasion at all', three said 'there is an invasion', and two of us said 'it is an invasion, but it is a justifiable invasion, a justifiable limitation'. So by a vote of six to three, for different reasons, the provision banning the sale of liquor by 7-Eleven on Sundays was upheld by the Constitutional Court. Just two Sundays later, I went to my local supermarket to buy some beer, and I was told, 'Sorry,' – they didn't actually put it like this – 'but some damn fool up in Johannesburg in the Constitutional Court upheld the law and we still can't sell it to you'.

THE *DANIELS* CASE: THE RIGHT OF MUSLIM WIDOWS TO BE REGARDED AS WIVES

Daniels [Daniels v Campbell an Others* (CCT 40/03) [2004] ZACC 14;

2004 (5) SA 331 (CC); 2004 (7) BCLR 735 (CC)] was a case where a widow of a Muslim marriage wanted the local housing council to give her the right to continue to live in a house that it had allocated to her late husband. The regulation said that the surviving wife could take over the property. But she was told, 'You're not a wife as far as the law is concerned'. Writing for the majority of the court, I said, 'Why aren't you a wife in terms of the law?'

> The old interpretations, given by the colonial and postcolonial judges in the Cape and in the Union of South Africa, had represented anti-Indian prejudice, a colonial/imperial sense of domination and hegemony of the Anglo-type world view. The notion was that all these 'tribal' kinds of unions were not real marriages, because they were potentially polygamous.

The case relied upon by the courts then was that of *Hyde*, decided in the High Court in England, dealing with a Mormon marriage. The judge in that matter declared that a purported marriage of the Latter-Day Saints could not be recognised for the purpose of divorce in the English High Court, because it was potentially polygamous, and therefore not a marriage as recognised in Christendom. The *Hyde* decision was picked up by South African courts to invalidate marriages of Hindus and Muslims in South Africa. Even though actually monogamous, they were held to be potentially polygamous.

The Constitutional Court rejected this approach. It held that in terms of both the English language and general public acceptance, let alone the egalitarian requirements of the Constitution, Mrs Daniels was indeed the wife of the deceased. As such she was entitled to succeed to ownership of the house.

THE CHRISTIAN EDUCATION SCHOOLS CASE: RELIGION, CORPORAL PUNISHMENT AND THE RIGHTS OF THE CHILD

The next case, the *Christian E•ucation Schools* case [*Christian E•ucation South Africa v Minister of E•ucation* (CCT 4/00) [2000] ZACC 11; 2000 (4) SA 757 (CC); 2000 (10) BCLR 1051 (CC)], turned out to be much tougher. After finding that it had been increasingly difficult to apply corporal correction to kids in the United States to fulfil the Biblical command that to spare the rod was to spoil the child, teachers had moved their Christian education schools from America to apartheid South Africa. And to their credit, in the apartheid days they hit black bums as well as white bums – the school was non-racial in that respect. They regarded it as a central tenet of their religion to administer corporal correction to errant boys. They didn't call it punishment, they called it corporal correction. When I first read the record, I thought, 'Can they seriously claim a constitutional right to beat children? Come on'. It just seemed ludicrous. They would hug the boy, tell him to bend over, hit him with the paddle, hug the boy again, and say, 'It's for your own good'. I found that kind of freaky. But when the case actually came before us, and I was asked to prepare the judgment, I realised that the case raised a profound and complicated question of conscience. The schools were being set up by people precisely because of their beliefs.

I'd been caned as a child at school, unjustly, for months. We didn't know about psychosexual things in those days, but for three months, every single day, Monday to Friday, a teacher would find some alleged breach of a rule by me to order me to bend over and whack my bum six times. I cried for the first few weeks. Then one day I decided not to cry any more, and I didn't cry again for about ten years. These things have an effect on you. It was unjust, but you put up with injustice at school, you didn't 'blub'. The worst thing a boy could do was to cry. And the second-worst thing to do was to 'split', to report on somebody. So you were learning these masculine values: first, you sustain pain without flinching, you grit your teeth; and second, you don't complain to anybody. Terrible. And when, years later, I was locked up in solitary confinement in police cells next to a court, I would hear kids getting juvenile whipping, and screaming and screaming. So I had a loathing, a physical loathing, horror, at the idea of beating children. And yet, I had this belief in conscience, the importance of conscience. The question was how do you reconcile the two?

Ironically, secular Albie was on the side of those supporting exemptions in favour of the rights of religious freedom. Writing for a unanimous Court, I held that when an apparently neutral law in fact impacted in a significant and negative way on religious freedom, then a balancing exercise had to be done. The object of the balancing was to see if the public purpose served by the law justified the limitation of religious freedom. I decided, in the end, given the rights of the child involved, that the generalised prohibition of corporal correction in the relatively public domain of the school, could be justified in an open and democratic society. The law didn't prevent the parents from exercising their religious relationships with their kids in the environment of the home. It didn't block out completely what they wanted to do, provided that the correction did not exceed what the criminal law permitted in terms of reasonable chastisement. It was a difficult case, far more difficult than I'd imagined.

THE *PRINCE* CASE: RASTAFARIANS, MARIJUANA AND THE LAW

The next case was that of Gareth Enver Prince [*Prince v President of the Law Society of the Cape of Good Hope* (CCT 36/00) [2002] ZACC 1; 2002 (2) SA 794 (CC); 2002 (3) BCLR 231 (CC)]. Prince was a talented law student who had passed all his exams, applied to be admitted as a lawyer, and the Law Society had said, 'No, you've got two convictions for smoking marijuana (dagga)'. He challenged the law prohibiting anyone from smoking marijuana on the grounds that it should have included an exemption in favour of Rastafarians exercising their religious freedom. I don't know why I felt so much for Prince. A group of Rastafarians were standing at the back of the Court with their dreadlocks, kind of uncomfortable. They wear funny clothing, they have long hair, and they say, 'Why is everybody looking at us?' And worse than that for me, they get up my nose. They're saying, 'Albie, people like you, what's the matter with you? You're so driven. Take it easy! Tomorrow is another day! Relax!' They're undermining me, they're challenging me! But I just felt, this guy is fighting for his beliefs. He's willing to sacrifice his career as a lawyer because of his beliefs. It is not for me to say if they are sensible or crazy beliefs.

If you're secular, all religious beliefs are equally irrational. None is more sensible or credible than the other. Rastafari have their own way of seeing the world, one with a strong African dimension. Dagga was being smoked in this country long before the colonists came. And yet it was prohibited and banned, research showed, because whites were worried too many white kids were smoking it together with black kids. Before then, it had been tolerated.

Whisky imported from Scotland, you can drink as much as you like, and get as drunk as you like, and then smash up your cars and cause all sorts of damage and get punished for that and not for taking alcohol as such. But you can't smoke dagga, even if you cause no damage.

The Rastafari were an interesting group. They modelled themselves on Jamaicans who were in turn modelling themselves on an imagined Ras Tafari in Ethiopia. Now, the Capetonian Rastafari were doing something similar. But they were identifying strongly in their own specific way with Africa. I referred to them as a diaspora of a diaspora.

In the end, our Court divided by five to four against granting them a religious exemption. We all accepted that balancing was required. The majority said that even if smoking marijuana was not a serious form of drug-taking compared to other drugs, the state had included it in a general ban on narcotic drugs, and it would be impossible to police the ban if you allowed this one exemption for religious purposes. The minority, of which I was one, said the authorities could take confiscated dagga and give it to the priests of the Rastafari to dispense like communal wine on sacramental occasions. This would give at least a glimmer of recognition to seriously held religious beliefs, without threatening the general prohibition on dangerous drugs. But in any event, we lost.

THE *FOURIE* CASE: SAME-SEX MARRIAGE IN SOUTH AFRICA

I now come to the more recent case of *Fourie* [*Fourie an• Another v Minister of Home Affairs an• Another* (CCT 25/03) [2003] ZACC 11; 2003 (5) SA 301 (CC); 2003 (10) BCLR 1092 (CC)], the same-sex marriage case. And I think it is important for me to start with a personal preamble. I'm just back in South Africa after two decades in exile. I'm driving towards the centre of Cape Town, and I'm sweating. I'm sweating because it's a hot, early summer day. I'm sweating because I'm driving with my left arm, and I haven't been driving for very long since losing most of my right arm in a bomb blast just a couple of years previously. I'm sweating because I don't know the roads really well. But above all, I'm sweating because I'm going to go on a gay pride march. I so wish there would be a poster that says, 'Straights for gays'. And then I feel ashamed. If you're gonna go, you go! And eventually, I see the group, I'm late, and they're marching towards me, and the first poster says, 'Suck, don't swallow'. Oh no, my picture will be next to it in the newspaper tomorrow, for sure. I stop the car, get out and rush to join the group. I find myself marching next to Edwin Cameron, then a law professor, now a regarded member of the Constitutional Court. And I feel proud. I feel proud of myself because I've broken through a barrier of embarrassment and confusion, and I am marching with people fighting for their basic rights and dignity. We stop at a little park, and they ask me to say a few words.

I point out that the issue of rights for gays an• lesbians is important for a section of our community that's been marginalise• an• •enie• basic rights. But it's important too

*for the whole of South Africa. If we cannot manage ⸱iffer-
ence, we're finishe⸱ as a country.*

Difference has been used to divide us in the past, to elevate some people over others. So acknowledging and protecting gay and lesbian rights becomes a touchstone of our capacity to manage difference independently of inherited racial, cultural, religious and other views.

Fast forward fourteen years. I'm sitting at the Constitutional Court conference table and Pius Langa, chief justice, tells us there's a body called Christian Lawyers for Africa who will be having a gathering outside Johannesburg soon, they have invited him to attend. Is there anybody who can go? He adds that it would be during court recess when he would be away. I put up my hand very tentatively: 'Pius, I am on recess duty, but I don't think I am the right person'. He replied, 'Albie, you're just the right person'. And I knew what he meant. Pius was a Christian, a lawyer from Africa; if he attended it could be taken as a form of sectarian identification with the group. If I go, I'm simply representing the Court. So a few weeks later, I'm being driven to the meeting. I'm not sweating this time; it's cooler, but I'm worried. What do I say to them? I can say, 'On behalf of the Court, I welcome you, have a good conference'. And I think, 'That's not right. These are people of conscience. I want them to get some sense, some flavour of what it means to have a Constitutional Court in South Africa'. So I decide to tell them the story about my taking the oath and being sworn in as a judge.

I'm the last judge to be sworn in, 'Sachs' – alphabetically challenged. Since then there's been a Van der Westhuizen and a Yacoob, but then I was the last. Some of my colleagues affirm. They don't take the oath but simply say, 'I affirm that I will uphold the law and the Constitution, etc.' Those who swear the oath say, 'So help me God', and raise their right arm when doing so. And I want to raise my shortened right arm. This is the arm of sacrifice, of struggle, of Ruth First and Joe Qabi, and the other comrades of mine who had been assassinated in the struggle. Raising my shortened right arm means that this is the most solemn oath that I could make to the Constitution, even if doing so requires me to say 'So help me God'. And I tell the Christian Lawyers that I come from a very secular background, but in the end, for purely personal purposes, and without religious belief, I raised my right arm and said, 'So help me God'. And I get a standing ovation. I feel uncomfortable, with my instrumental, personal purposes on the one side, and the people of faith on the other.

The next day we do a tour of the Court and about seventy Christian lawyers are following me on an emotional tour through a very beautiful building. As we get to the end of the tour I'm eager to rush off, to speak at a meeting at the Women's Jail. But before I can leave, the Christian lawyers insist: 'We must say a prayer'. Some prayers are very short, and some go round the world a few times, and this turns out to be one of the latter. And I'm late. But I delay my departure to receive their prayer with an open heart. They are giving what they have to give. They are offering the gift of their good wishes for me in the form that means the most to them, and I am happy to receive it in the same spirit.

The prayer over, I'm about to rush off, an• they say, 'We must lay on han•s'. An• that's what they •i•, seventy pairs of han•s being lai• on my secular bo•y. It took time, but what they •i• was given an• receive• with love. It was very, very meaningful to me.

I mention this because later that year I'm asked to write the judgment on same-sex marriages. I'm not consciously thinking about the gay pride march. Nor am I consciously thinking about the Christian lawyers laying on their hands. But I'm aware that they're all part of our nation. They're all going to read the judgment. They all want to feel acknowledged and recognised in it. Surely, I don't have to choose which 'side' I'm on. I have to find a way, *we* have to find a way. Our Constitution has to be articulated in a manner that speaks to the whole nation in a coherent language that's meaningful to everybody.

In the end, the Court's decision came down in sections. We declared that the marriage law was unconstitutional to the extent that its effect was to render homosexual couples legally invisible. We accordingly ordered that the law be changed so as to acknowledge the right of homosexual couples to marriage equality and sent the matter to parliament to make the necessary correction within one year. We added that if parliament didn't make the correction timeously, then automatically the vow in the Marriage Act would be altered so that the words, 'I, AB, take you, CD, to be my lawful husband/wife', would have added to them the word 'spouse', a gender-neutral term.

It was important for parliament and the nation to think and talk about what the Constitution required. It shouldn't be seen as a sleight-of-hand kind of legal device created by progressive judges and imposed on the nation. The expectation of serious national engagement turned out to be fulfilled, and in a most positive way. The nation did talk. Parliament eventually, by a huge majority, accepted the notion of same-sex marriage. In a rather strangely worded law it permitted same-sex couples either to register a domestic partnership or else to say: 'I, AB, marry you, CD'. The m-word was used. The constitutional rights of same-sex couples were vindicated.

But what about the rights of people like Christian Lawyers for Africa? A few of them might have supported same-sex marriages, but the majority almost certainly did not. This led to a significant part of the judgment dealing with the relationship between the sacred and the secular. Possibly the strongest statement in any legal decision in recent years on religion being significant for public life, and not just something you can do in private, was written by Albie Sachs. The secular Albie said that religion is not restricted to something you practise in private; it's part of the being of individuals and the temper of the nation. Religion has given rise to cultural development for many people; the beliefs of many in human rights spring from religion. It's got an enormous significance in our society that's got to be recognised and respected. And we don't gain anything by saying that opponents of same-sex marriages are bigots. This caution I took from words in a judgment of the Court delivered several years earlier. We didn't want a cultural war. We didn't want a dividing line between those we regard as 'the tolerant' and those we condemn as 'the bigoted'. We wanted everybody to feel they are recognised, envisaged by the Constitution. It doesn't help to castigate people who have a different world view. Rather, I believe, we should allow for the coexistence of different world views.

The judgment goes on [as mentioned in an earlier section] to point out that the very Constitution that protects the rights of same-sex couples publicly to celebrate their marriage, protects the rights of faith communities not to be compelled to perform marriages that could go against their beliefs. The motivation was partly to prevent people rallying around self-proclaimed martyrs who might wish to undermine the whole process and taint it with untoward controversy. But it wasn't just that. I do worry about people being compelled when serving the public to go against their own particular deep moral convictions, particularly if they had accepted the job long before and are now struggling to accept an evolving reality. And as far as same-sex couples are concerned, I can't help wondering what it means to feel you are being married at this great moment in your life by somebody who's loathing what's happening. The vibes would be all wrong. It would be incompatible with the very celebratory function that marriage is designed to perform. The central point though is that the public administration is obliged to ensure that there are always marriage officers available to preside with appropriate dignity and decorum over same-sex marriages.

Getting the Last Laugh on Rhodes

'THE RHODES DEBATE: HOW WE CAN HAVE THE LAST LAUGH' | *CITY PRESS* | SOUTH AFRICA | 29 MARCH 2015

Rushing up the steps of UCT so as not to be late for my early morning lectures, I always winced as I passed the statue of Cecil John Rhodes. What a way to start the day, to be reminded of the persuasive power not of reason, but of what had been the newly invented machine gun boastfully used by Rhodes to suppress resistance to conquest in Pondoland and Matabeleland. But politically we had more important fish to fry.

Off the campus I was waiting to hear if I, as a white, could join the Defiance of Unjust Laws Campaign, until then restricted to black volunteers. On the campus we were fighting to destroy the rule that barred black students from participating in social life at the university. My first public speech was to a thousand highly vocal students in Jameson Hall. My heart beat with terror and exhilaration as I felt myself issuing what I thought were thunderous denunciations of the ban against black students playing tennis or attending dances, only to be told afterwards: That's just what we needed, Albie, a nice, quiet argument. We weren't just acquiring knowledge and skills at UCT. We were learning about how to express ourselves, what it meant to be a human being and how best to struggle for a better society.

Just like today.

At that time, I would have supported melting down the statue and selling the bronze to support scholarships for students from the Eastern Cape and Zimbabwe.

I can give two examples of how this was managed in similar situations. The first related to the question of what to do about historically offensive murals in South Africa House, Trafalgar Square, London. One showed Jan van Riebeeck hoisting the Dutch East India flag, another depicted a bucolic wine farm, no slaves, no workers paid with bottles of wine, no dop system. The great majority of South Africans were either rendered invisible or at best portrayed as smiling natives. Slavery, dispossession and disenfranchisement were simply not there. As I recall, the high commissioner (Lindiwe Mabuza or Cheryl Carolus, both of whom had great cultural sensibility), confronted the issue. My tentative proposal had been that instead of trying to blot out our history, we place batiks or other interesting artworks over the murals. In this way the originals would not be destroyed and could even be exhibited from time to time to demonstrate the way white domination had been glorified in the past.

The artist Willem Boshoff came up with a far more meaningful idea: to cover the murals with transparent glass panels that recorded the names of the indigenous people and slaves whose voices had been silenced in the past. The result is striking: the viewer is compelled to look at and interpret the murals with present-day eyes and sensibility. A visually arresting and historically powerful new artwork has emerged, based on seeking transformation rather than obliteration.

The second example concerns the Old Fort prison in Johannesburg, where the new Constitutional Court was to be built. Some people said the prison was a site of humiliation and despair that ought to be razed to the ground to make way for a hospital or school. We said 'No. There was too much history in those cells'. We organised an international competition for the new Court building to be put up in the heart of the old prison. The result: a sharp and memorable interaction has been set up between then and now. Constitution Hill has become one of the most widely acknowledged and admired sites of memory and conscience in the country, indeed, in the world.

My proposal, then, is that UCT lay down the principles based on the anti-racist values of our Constitution which should guide the transformation of the Rhodes statue; invite the public and professionals to produce designs for the creation of an imaginative and renovated space in which the statue should be located, and, finally, establish a broadly based panel, in which the present generation of students would have a strong voice, to choose the most appropriate entry.

In this way we could have the last laugh on Rhodes.

TEN

Are the Beautiful People Born?

United in Diversity

FW DE KLERK FOUNDATION CONFERENCE | CAPE TOWN | 2 FEBRUARY 2016

The Constitution places much emphasis on the 3 Ds: Dignity, Diversity and Difference. I have already cited the ringing phrase 'South Africa belongs to all who live in it, united in our diversity'. That is the motto for our country. The qualities of being united and diverse are not seen as antagonistic, as mutually incompatible. On the contrary, they are regarded as producing a potentially productive tension.

As I look at it, we are united in our right to be the same, to have the same fundamental rights, yet we are diverse in enjoying our right to be different, in terms of how we express ourselves and exercise our rights.

A similar note is struck with regard to *language rights*. I still remember when the negotiators met on language rights in a room in Kempton Park. It was just the two of us, Baleka Mbete and myself, sitting on the one side, and a huge team of professors and even Neil Barnard, the top security official, on the other. Clearly this was going to be extremely important for the National Party. They would be fearful that the Afrikaans language would be submerged under majority rule as it had been after the South African War when the British had imposed a policy of Anglicisation on the defeated Boers. Indeed, it was clear that the whole negotiation process would be jeopardised if an appropriate place for the Afrikaans language could not be found.

But the approach that Baleka and I had been mandated to adopt had not been governed only by a need to find accommodation with 'the other side.' Our mandate came from a conference which the ANC had organised in Lusaka on the question of developing a principled approach to language rights in a democratic South Africa. Baleka and I had been among the principal speakers at that conference. My views on language rights had been strongly shaped by my experience in Mozambique. It had been wonderful to be in the newly independent country in 1976. It was the time of the Revolution, full of *joie ɩe vivre* and transformatory energy. We sang songs of freedom. Everything seemed possible.

Samora Machel came out with a viviɩ phrase, 'For the nation to live, the tribe must ɩie'. It was very powerful. But it was wrong. For sure, tribalism as an iɩeology of separation, of ethnic exclusion, haɩ to ɩie. But many of the customs, cultural formations anɩ languages associateɩ with the tribes haɩ not only to survive but to flourish.

At the time, however, the prevailing idea was that Portuguese should serve as the language of national unity, and that its extended use would unite all Mozambicans. It didn't, and the policy of making Portuguese the supreme language and treating other national languages as subaltern, didn't work. Thus, President Machel would deliberately send a person who had grown up speaking Ronga, to be governor in Cabo Delgado where the mother tongue was Makonde. The object was to discourage regionalism and promote the idea of the nation. The governor would address the people in Portuguese, the language of struggle, the language of national unity. It didn't work. We could see the results in practice and came to the conclusion that promoting multilingualism rather than the predominance of one language as the official language, was the way to go. So for me the idea of equal respect, now in our Constitution it is called 'the equal esteem', of all languages, was born in Mozambique.

Baleka came to a similar conclusion after seeing how the relationship between English and Kiswahili was evolving in Tanzania. Baleka spent a number of years connected to the University of Dar es Salaam. Living in an independent African country she learnt that language couldn't be looked at simply in purely instrumental or quantitative terms. Language was intensely meaningful to people, to their sense of self. Kiswahili had been developed over centuries as a language of common usage in large portions of the east coast of Africa, freely spoken by everybody in the region. English had come later as the language of colonial domination and even later been appropriated by a section of the people in their struggle for independence. Yet exclusive use of English for all official business in independent Tanzania would disempower the great majority of people. Conversely, extensive use of Kiswahili would literally give voice to everyone and make everyone feel part of the national polity.

Now the idea of equal esteem for all languages – how do you achieve that? If you make English the dominant language and you subordinate Kiswahili, there is no equal esteem. National unity is not furthered.

In a sense, in all former parts of the British Empire language rights are rights against English. English doesn't need rights and protection. It's powerful, it's overwhelming, it's the air you breathe. But it needn't suffocate other languages.

It is convenient as an international means of communication; it is the mother tongue of millions in South Africa, and the second or third language of millions more. But it should not be like the eucalyptus tree that sucks up all the water for metres around, preventing any other growth within its radius.

So, based on what we had learnt in Mozambique and Tanzania, Baleka and I both made strong interventions at the Conference on Language Rights in Lusaka before we returned home from exile: Make English *an* official language in a future democratic South Africa, not *the* official language. The ANC in fact officially adopted a policy aimed at achieving equal respect for all languages that were deeply implanted in our country. This did not require reducing the status of Afrikaans and English. Rather, it called for upgrading the African languages that had been marginalised first by the British and then under apartheid. Instead of undermining English and Afrikaans, it presupposed freeing the marginalised languages of their subaltern status and facilitating their emergence as flourishing means of expression and communication enjoying equal recognition in the new society. In other words, the idea was to achieve equality of the vineyard by upgrading the suppressed languages rather than equality of the graveyard by downgrading the dominant ones.

So we came up with the concept at the constitutional negotiations of coupling upgrading of marginalised languages with non-diminution of existing language rights.

Looking at the language provisions in the final text, one in fact notices something textually quite odd: though all the eleven official languages are declared to enjoy parity of esteem, they are not listed in simple alphabetical order. So, instead of starting alphabetically with Afrikaans followed by English and ending with isiZulu, the list begins with Sepedi followed by Sesotho. To have begun with Afrikaans and English would indeed have looked as though these two languages still enjoyed precedence. So, wisely I believe, the drafters broke alphabetical ranks and tucked these two languages in about two thirds of the way through, with isiZulu still coming in proudly at the end. Oddity may not be out of place in constitutional texts.

The language clauses are comprehensive and sophisticated. They deliberately leave open quite a few issues for future balancing and interpretation. There is not one single official language requirement that runs through every aspect of public life. Thus language policies at the national, provincial and local government levels can be different; and language in education is treated with specific care in the Bill of Rights. You disaggregate the issues and they become less contentious.

In terms of legal developments it is the Bill of Rights itself that has probably had more direct impact on public life. The Bill of Rights gives considerable attention to religious, cultural and language rights. It does so without involving group rights as constituent elements of constitutional structures. Rather, it protects the rights of individuals, on their own or in community with others, to express themselves in terms of language, culture and religion. Thus freedom of religion, belief and opinion goes beyond simply protecting belief, conscience, the right to worship, and so on. The Constitution acknowledges a degree of legal pluralism by permitting legislation to recognise marriages concluded under any tradition or system of religious, personal or family law. The one proviso is that the legislation must be consistent with the Constitution. This area is very sensitive. To this day there has been no consensus reached in the Muslim community as to whether Islamic family law presided over by Muslim clerics should be officially recognised as part of the state judicial system.

Meanwhile the Courts have moved cautiously in the area of recognising Muslim marriages as part of the state system of law. On the one hand, there are a number of decisions which uphold the status and dignity of Muslim marriages for the purposes of entitlement to receive state benefits. Similarly, in keeping with the spirit and letter of the Bill of Rights, the courts have provided legal support for vulnerable parties in Muslim marriages. But the courts have refrained from engaging with questions concerning the way Muslim marriages are entered into or ended. Similarly, they have not pronounced on the legal status of polygamous Muslim marriages as such. Parliament and the courts have, however, dealt with African customary law marriages that might or might not be polygamous.

One of the most commented-on features of the Constitution is the express recognition it gives to customary law as an original source of law. This is contained in the shortest chapter in the Constitution, which is headed Traditional Leaders. Here once again a limited form of legal pluralism is permitted. The institution, status and role of traditional leadership, according to customary law, are recognised subject to the Constitution. A traditional authority that observes a system of customary law, may function according to legislation and customs as amended over time. And the courts must apply customary law when applicable, subject to the Constitution, including the Bill of Rights and any legislation specifically dealing with customary law. Finally, provision is made for legislation which would permit traditional leaders to have a role at the local level, as well as to set up a national council of traditional leaders and provincial houses of traditional leaders.

Thus, traditional leadership is recognised, but not as a source of political power competing with democratic power, but rather as a significant institution in the cultural life, if you like, the spiritual life, of considerable sections of the nation. At the same time, customary law now takes its place as an original, indigenous source of law on a par with the common law, that is, with Roman Dutch law and those aspects of the English common law that were received with colonisation into South African law. But as with the common law, customary law is subject to the Constitution and legislation. Furthermore, when developing the common law or customary law, the courts must promote the spirit, purport and objects of the Bill of Rights. Thus customary law is not seen as an autonomous system to be applied by autonomous courts to communities subject to it according to what we lawyers call choice of law principles. It is instead regarded as part and parcel of the national legal system, operating within the matrix of legislation and being infused with constitutional values. At the same time, themes consonant with customary law have been influential in the interpretation of the Constitution, as will be seen below.

Amongst the many notable features of our Constitution is the establishment of a number of bodies with special responsibilities for supporting constitutional democracy. Popularly referred to as Chapter 9 institutions, some, like the Public Protector, the Electoral Commission and the Auditor-General, are very well known. Others, like the Commission for the Promotion and Protection of the Rights of Cultural, Religious and Linguistic Communities (CPPRCRLC), are much less so. Sadly for the CPPRCRLC, it would seem that the weightier the title and the more widely stated the objectives, the more slender the resources and the less the public profile.

The priority objects of the CPPRCRLC are firstly to promote respect for the rights of cultural, religious and language communities; secondly to promote and develop peace, friendship, humanity, tolerance and national unity among cultural, religious and linguistic communities, on the basis of equality, non-discrimination and free association. It may recommend the establishment of a council for any community or communities. Its membership must be broadly representative of the main cultural, religious and language communities, and, interestingly, broadly reflect the gender composition of South Africa. I say interestingly, because the constitution-makers were clearly aware of the manner in which many people use cultural identification as a means of perpetuating patriarchal domination.

The voice of the CPPRCRLC has been directly heard at this conference, so I will say nothing more about its impact on national life, save to mention that as with the Language Board the issues it has to deal with tend to be too politically loaded for it to have great impact. I do get the impression, however, that at the internal level interesting and valuable interactions take place.

CASES ON MULTICULTURALISM IN THE CONSTITUTIONAL COURT

How did the fact that South Africa is a multicultural society play itself out in the Constitutional Court? We judges don't look for cases in order to make points about how the Constitution should be interpreted. I remember once being full of expectation about us receiving a case dealing with the way that intellectual property rights of giant pharmas were being asserted to prevent South Africa from importing generic anti-retrovirals at a tenth of the price. But the pharmas capitulated in the High Court, so we never pronounced. We could only resolve particular disputes as they reached us. I will mention a number of cases involving disputes centred around multiculturalism that did in fact reach us.

A challenge to the constitutionality of the *Gauteng School E•ucation Bill* [*Gauteng Provincial Legislature In re: Gauteng School E•ucation Bill* of 1995 (CCT 39/95) [1996] ZACC 4; 1996 (3) SA 165 (CC); 1996 (4) BCLR 537 (CC)] was heard fairly early on in my term on the Court. I might mention that, contrary to expectations, the provinces have passed very few laws of their own, their main function being to manage the delivery on the ground of nationally determined laws and policies. In any event, this was a law adopted by the Gauteng legislature which included a provision to the effect that no child should be denied access to a public school, a state school, on grounds of language. The background was the refusal of some formerly whites-only Afrikaans-medium schools to admit black kids who could understand English but not Afrikaans. The schools insisted that black children were now most welcome, and that the children who were being turned away were not being excluded because of their race but because the school was an Afrikaans-medium one. The provision was challenged by some Afrikaans-medium state schools as well as by an NGO that promoted the Afrikaans language. The gist of their argument was that to protect the future of the Afrikaans language it was necessary to have Afrikaans-medium schools.

I found it to be a poignant case. I could feel the anguish of counsel arguing for what amounted to a form of group rights in a constitutional context that was heavily weighted towards individual rights and non-discrimination. I recalled the days of my anguish as an advocate arguing in a court where many of the basic assumptions were totally against the philosophical framework within which my mind functioned. And I recalled the intense anxiety I would have that my inadequate contentions would be disastrous for the client or cause I was representing.

Ismail Mahomed wrote a judgment very, very quickly for the Court based on the text of the interim Constitution, which made it very clear: you could have single-medium schools in the private sphere, but there was nothing to justify an exclusively single-medium school in the public sphere.

That has been changed; the final Constitution allows a measure of flexibility in this respect. I strongly supported Justice Mahomed's reasoning, but felt something had to be added to it. The application to the Court was a cry from the heart. People were indeed fearful that the Afrikaans language would be suppressed after the victory of democracy, as it had been under Lord Milner after the victory of the British against the Boers.

I think that the first statement in our post-democracy jurisprudence explaining the importance of Afrikaans in our country was written by me. And it was easy for me to do so. Uys Krige, Gregoire Boonzaier – I grew up with them. They were Boere with a sense of humour, vitality and energy.

My dad was the General Secretary of the Garment Workers Union – Anna Scheepers, Johanna and Hester Cornelius; they all seemed six feet tall, full of brightness and energy and fun. The kind of English disdain for Afrikaners that was so strong in my school – I didn't have that. One had to acknowledge that Afrikaans – and it is in the judgment – is one of the treasures of South Africa. The literature, the culture, the very name Afrikaans – African – it was born here in the Cape. It had input from slaves and Khoi people, as well as the Dutch language. As part of the context for interpreting the multicultural thrust of the Constitution we had to acknowledge the harsh impact of Milner and the forced imposition of English on people with a view to destroying their sense of independence, their pride, their sense of community – that's part of our history, part of why we had a Constitution.

At the same time we also had to acknowledge that there were black kids living in the suburbs of Johannesburg who didn't have a school they could go to. The nearest school – their mother might be a domestic worker – would be an Afrikaans-medium school. We had to balance out these different aspects, develop an appropriately balanced constitutional vision derived from the text of the Constitution itself.

I cannot help thinking that the very points our Court was ●ealing with alrea●y in 1996, are the issues playing themselves out in Stellenbosch, in the universities, elsewhere, to●ay. It is not a question of the one principle trumping the other, but of reconciling the principles as fairly an● harmoniously as possible. It is respecting, acknowle●ging, accommo●ating, listening to the Other, an● seeking joint solutions that accor● with the letter an● spirit of the Constitution. Human ●ignity, equality an● free●om must always be the touchstones.

The *Shilubana* case [*Shilubana an● Others v Nwamitwa* (CCT 3/07) [2008] ZACC 9; 2009 (2) SA 66 (CC); 2008 (9) BCLR 914 (CC)] raised the issue of whether a woman could be chosen as a traditional leader. The Hosi (traditional leader) of the Baloyi community was not well. He and the royal family decided that his successor should be his cousin, Ms Shilubana, then a member of parliament. This decision was endorsed at a public meeting of the community. But shortly before his death the incumbent said, 'No, no, it's got to be my son'. After his death, the government appointed Ms Shilubana, and the son went to court. The High Court ruled in his favour, saying you can't be elected a traditional leader; you are born a traditional leader. The matter went to the Supreme Court of Appeal. They said the same thing. It came to us and we said, 'No, customary law had to be looked at as a living body of law, not an ossified set of rules'.

Ms Shilubana was not being foiste● on the Baloyi community in the name of gen●er justice. Rather, she was being calle● to occupy her post by the overwhelming majority of the community. It was gen●er injustice that ha● kept her out of that position in aparthei● times. Now the community wishe● to correct that injustice an● restore her to the position she shoul● have occupie● ●eca●es before. This is what the community wante♦, an♦ so Ms Shilubana now is the Hosi of that community.

The theme of customary law being living customary law that incorporates and embraces the Constitution, and the values of the Constitution, is now firmly established as part and parcel of our constitutional jurisprudence. My personal view is that this will strengthen rather than weaken customary law, ensuring for it both vitality and widespread legitimacy.

I should add two more cases. In *Bhe* [*Bhe an♦ Others v Khayelitsha Magistrate an♦ Others* (CCT 49/03) [2004] ZACC 17; 2005 (1) SA 580 (CC); 2005 (1) BCLR 1 (CC)] the Court struck down primogeniture as an element of customary law, namely the principle found in many feudal societies throughout the world that the eldest male relative of a deceased person succeeds to title and estate. My colleague Sandile Ngcobo felt that the answer was to make the eldest descendant, whether female or male, the heir. The majority, however, decided that the issues were so multiple and complex that parliament should decide through properly thought-through legislation. In *Richtersvel♦* [*Alexkor Lt♦ an♦ Another v Richtersvel♦ Community an♦ Others* (CCT19/03) [2003] ZACC 18; 2004 (5) SA 460 (CC); 2003 (12) BCLR 1301 (CC)], the Court accepted that under customary law indigenous communities did indeed have aboriginal rights in relation to the land on which their goats had eked out survival. This meant that their racially motivated expulsion from the land to make way for lucrative diamond-mining should be classified as a deprivation of property rights entitling them to appropriate compensation.

I end by returning to an aspect of traditional values and ways of doing things that moves from customary law to our legal system as a whole: ubuntu. Ubuntu is not a principle reserved for customary law, but a philosophy coming from African society that should humanise the whole of our law. And if ever there was someone who embodied the spirit of ubuntu in everything he thought and did, even in the midst of one of the most strenuous and prolonged struggles for freedom in our era, it was

Oliver Tambo. The story never ends, but the telling of it does; in this case where it began in this book.

Are the Beautiful People Born?

IMAM HARON 4TH ANNUAL MEMORIAL LECTURE | UNIVERSITY OF CAPE
TOWN | 28 SEPTEMBER 2011

Cape Town was on the boil. May 1961, and the City Hall was jam-
packed. Nelson Mandela had gone underground and called for a
general strike. Declaring that the majority of the people had not
been consulted about South Africa becoming a Republic outside
of the Commonwealth, he had combined a stay-away call with
the demand that a national convention be held to draft a new
constitution.

The year before, following the massacre of Sharpeville, tens of thousands
of African people had marched from Langa and Nyanga to the centre of
Cape Town. A state of emergency had been declared, and the army and the
navy had been called in to surround what were then called the 'locations'.
Thousands of people had been detained. And a feeling had grown in
nearby communities on the Cape Flats and in District Six: 'Where were
we from the coloured community? Why hadn't we participated en masse
as well?' And so now, a year later, the majority of people then classified as
coloured in Cape Town were throwing their weight behind a struggle that
was to be for total emancipation of all our people.

As it happened, the response in Cape Town to Mandela's call was
powerful. An estimated fifty per cent of the workers of this city stayed

home in the biggest general strike Cape Town has known to this day. And right at the heart of the mobilisation a meeting of popular protest was held at the City Hall. The government had declared a mini state of emergency, placing all sorts of specific restrictions on different individuals. It was now flying military aeroplanes overhead, bringing tanks and armoured cars to parade in the streets. The City Hall was to be our answer. And in the middle of all the excitement, the one big question on everybody's mind was: would George Peake be there?

The government had prohibited Councillor George Peake from attending any meetings during the period of the mini-emergency. He was now in hiding. The Hall was jam-packed – even if it hadn't been filled with his supporters, there were enough security police to make quite sure no seats would be left empty. Those of us sitting up on the platform were tense. I think I was in the chair and I remember Achmat Osman was up on the platform as well, together with several other leaders. We knew the security police were waiting for George. The situation was explosive, the expectancy palpable: would George come?

George Peake was the only person not white on the City Council of Cape Town. A powerful speaker in the working-class tradition, he was the greatest orator of us all. Another leader, Alex La Guma, was a brilliant writer but a quiet, thoughtful person not too comfortable behind the microphone. Barney Desai was a great, uninhibited speaker. Reggie September. Tofie Bardien, Hettie September, many names come to mind. From time to time, Dick van der Ross would speak out. From the African community, I recall Zoli Malindi, Letitia Malindi, Elijah Loza, Oscar Mpetha, Annie Silinga, Joseph Morolong, Mildred Lesia, Archie Sibeko, the marvellous Dora Tamana, and the young Christmas Tinto. And among the white comrades, Ray Alexander, Brian Bunting, Fred Carneson, Amy Rietstein, Denis Goldberg, Ben Turok, and Mary Butcher. Almost all of these people, like George, were restricted.

And increasingly in those days we would hear the name of Imam Haron. It wasn't very common then for people holding religious office in any of the faiths to actually stand up and denounce apartheid, and to do so not simply in the relatively safe space of a sermon or a letter to the editor, but directly in public life. The Imam was one of the few exceptions, and we honoured him for this.

To return to the City Hall. We were talking away, in good old meeting fashion – you might have heard it all before, sometimes you even enjoyed hearing the same people saying the same things, like when a singer comes up with an old favourite and everybody cheers ... and suddenly there's commotion! We are transfixed.

We see this figure wearing a white jacket an• a kappie moving slowly forwar• from the back ... then in a flash he's •ashing to reach the platform. It's George! It's George! Everybo•y's stan•ing up, trying to impe•e the security police.

And the only question was: would George make the platform? And as he got about two yards away from the platform, honestly, it's like Habana on the wing, he was actually dive-tackled and brought down by one of the security cops. Tofie Bardien, a taxi driver, had evidently lent George his white taxi coat, to make him look nondescript. I think George managed to touch the platform, but we couldn't claim it as a try since he hadn't got onto the platform itself. Of course, it wouldn't have brought the ramparts of apartheid down if George had made it all the way, but it was a very Cape Town kind of defiance, and we all cheered ourselves hoarse at his daring dash.

Then, as the police were hauling George off, the cheering turned to agitation. Some people were shouting that we must go to Caledon Square police station and free George from the cops. The statements were fiery. We up on the platform were concerned, sensing a trap waiting for us, concerned that provocateurs were trying to lead us into the arms of the police. And we managed to calm the people down, so that hundreds of us marched in small groups in a disciplined way up to Caledon Square. When we got there, I was able, as an advocate, to quietly arrange for

George to be released on bail. We learnt afterwards that in fact the police had been lurking around the corner with their batons at the ready, no doubt waiting for the order to wade into us and smash some heads. Quite possibly some looting could have been provoked, a few people killed, with a massacre of Caledon Square serving as the government's response to the immense anti-apartheid emotion in Cape Town at the time. After all, it had been events of this kind that had given the government the pretext to introduce draconian measures to crush the Defiance of Unjust Laws Campaign a decade earlier.

DEATH OF THE IMAM

The awful, incredible, news comes – I'm in exile in London, towards the end of a decade of terrible repression – the Imam is dead, killed in detention, his body covered in bruises. We can hardly believe it. The Imam. How they must have beaten him for information. And how bravely he must have resisted. The shock was followed by a further shock – the inquest magistrate accepted police testimony that he had slipped down some stairs, with no one to blame. Such a ludicrous, pathetic, undignified, ridiculous finding, a further blot on a judiciary that, with honourable exceptions, had increasingly aligned itself with or turned a blind eye to the atrocious practices of racist rule.

> *What a disgrace, that the Imam should be killed so grotesquely precisely because of his belief in freedom and justice, and then have his death glossed over so casually by the state. I think Chris van Wyk's famous poem about a man hanging himself on a piece of soap, was initially inspired by the gruesome cover-up of the Imam's murder.*

And it wasn't just the police and the magistrate who connived at the cover-up. Where were the investigative journalists, the thunderous editorials? For each brave newsperson trying to expose these crimes, there were ten others blithely parroting the disinformation given out by the authorities. (When I was blown up, nearly two decades later, the story carried by the press was that it had been as a result of an internal ANC feud).

> *Yet the truth ♦oes come out. Imam Haron's story was finally recor♦e♦ in the most honourable fashion, firstly in a book by his comra♦e Barney Desai, an♦ then in a film by his gran♦son. An♦ the meaning of his life an♦ ♦eath has been subsume♦ into the very core of our new Constitution.*

Indeed, it is precisely to avoid repetition of the brutalities he suffered that we have a Constitution with an entrenched Bill of Rights. That is why certain deep foundational, fundamental principles now have to be respected in fair weather and foul, for good days and bad, and for all of us, whoever we are, whoever our parents were, whatever our appearance, whether in office or in opposition or not politically involved at all, for everyone in the nation. The Constitution says 'Never Again'. Never again should people suffer the worst pains, the deepest insults, the most terrible degradations of the past. And sadly, Imam Haron was just one of a multitude. Among close friends of mine who were murdered by security agents, there was Looksmart Ngudle, the first of the detainees to die in detention. Despite bruises all over his body, the magistrate accepted that he had hanged himself. Elijah Loza died in detention in Cape Town; Ruth First, whose bomb-blasted body we carried to the crowded ANC graveyard in Maputo; Joe Qabi, journalist and freedom fighter, assassinated in Harare; and Gilbert, a radio journalist who had so many 'travelling names' I can't remember his surname, who died having been given a final dose of poison while recovering from a mysterious disease in the Maputo Central Hospital.

Never, never, never again. These were the words used by President Nelson Mandela in his first address to parliament. When preparing early drafts of the Constitution, many of us insisted that never, never again in this country should the state use its resources to try and exterminate its opponents; should the instruments of the judiciary and the media be used to cover up, to deny the truth, to hide facts, and to lie. Indeed, our Constitution is unique in the world in expressly incorporating the words 'no detention without trial'. Detention without trial was the basis of all the cruelties: the tortures, the manipulation of witnesses, and the total undermining of the possibility of political suspects getting a fair trial. It is a matter of some pride for all the survivors, then, that the lives and deaths of their loved ones are permanently memorialised in the most enduring monument to the sacrifices of generations of freedom fighters, the Constitution of South Africa.

THE DIRECTION THIS COUNTRY IS GOING IN

I will ask a difficult question: given that we have a wonderful Constitution, given the nature of the sacrifice of Imam Haron and so many others, and given the many confusions of public life today, was it worth it? For decades, many of us lived for that wonderful thing called 'The Future'. Now we are living in that future. The certainties of hope have been overtaken by the ambiguities and perplexities of the present. I am sure there are people in this room asking themselves the question stated above. In their day, joining the struggle was not a good career move – you risked detention, torture, imprisonment, exile or death. Today, becoming politically involved is viewed by many as a shrewd step up the ladder of personal advancement. Over long years of struggle, building unity on the basis of non-racialism was central to the liberation movement; nowadays many people who spent their lives fighting for non-racialism feel dismayed at what they consider to be opportunistic and disrespectful attitudes of certain prominent personalities towards the communities to which they belong.

There is widespread concern about the huge gap that exists, and is even growing, between the very rich and the very poor; the doggedly resistant patterns of massive unemployment; the extent of crime and sexual violence.

*Experience tells us that poor people are capable of extra-
ordinary patience when it comes to the step-by-step
improvement of their lives. Their emotions boil over,
however, when they see former neighbours in informal
settlements abusing newly occupied public positions to take
bribes and favour family and friends when distributing
public goods. And people from all walks of life, including
many in this room who have undoubtedly benefited from
the opportunities opened up to them by the new democratic
dispensation, are deeply shaken by tales of corruption in
public life.*

It is not just the waste of resources, the shoddy performance and the
parallel demoralisation of law-enforcement agencies. The distress comes
from the sense that the ethical core of the whole project of democratic
transformation is being undermined. After all, the cynics say, why bother
to spend hours in arduous study or to perfect performance at work, when
the one proven skill that will secure advancement is a master's degree in
the art of getting in with the right people, and a doctorate in the science
of corruption?

The most profound unease, therefore, comes not simply from the
apparent intractability of the problems of continuing inequality besetting
our country. It flows from a fear that in the evolution of our new
constitutional order, the moral purpose that enabled us to overcome
apparently insuperable obstacles is being dissipated, and the perfectibility
for which we strived is giving way to corruptibility to which too many
of us are prone.

PERFECTIBILITY AND CORRUPTIBILITY

In 1991 or 1992, I gave my inaugural lecture as an honorary professor
at the University of Cape Town on the theme of perfectibility and
corruptibility, and it began with the words: 'The beautiful people are not
yet born'. I picked this statement up from a Zimbabwean writer who had

himself been quoting a Ghanaian writer, both concerned by the failure of their countries to live up to the high hopes generated by independence. The basis of the lecture was the notion that all constitutions are based on the tension between perfectibility and corruptibility. Perfectibility drew upon hope, idealism and the expectation that people could live together with dignity, comfort and honour. Corruptibility, on the other hand, stemmed from the capacity of all of us to do things that are wrong, and sometimes evil and cruel. That lecture was given in the spirited but confusing period after the unbanning of the ANC, PAC and SACP, the release of Mandela and other political prisoners and the return of exiles, but before the start of actual constitutional negotiations. Many of my colleagues and comrades and friends had been envisaging some kind of beautiful ideal society 'when freedom comes along, when freedom comes along'. Some had spent all their adult lives preparing for the revolution. Now it seemed that in front of their very eyes, prospects of a Revolution were being snatched away. Instead, we were going to negotiate a new Constitution, which many of them might not have known had been the very thing that Mandela had called for thirty years earlier. And in my own case, it was not just the memory of Mandela's call that made me an ardent proponent of negotiations. It was my experience of living in revolutionary Mozambique.

HARD LESSONS OF THE MOZAMBICAN REVOLUTION

I had had eleven productive years in exile in England, got a PhD, had books published, become father to two children. But in England even when I had been happy, I had been unhappy. For all the anti-apartheid work, and the great personal kindness I received, I had felt detached, dislocated, far away. And when we had ANC meetings, usually in some small hall with broken windows, and stood up to sing the national anthem, sometimes in our overcoats, the right arm that I then still had, had not gone up with fist clenched. After solitary confinement and sleep deprivation back home, my courage had fled, and my arm, having a mind of its own, just stayed down while all the other right arms in the room were proudly aloft.

In 1976, after a wondrous spell of teaching law in Dar es Salaam during the time of Julius Nyerere and Ujamaa, I visit newly independent Mozambique. On a public holiday to mark the launch of the armed struggle, I go to Machava Stadium and join 60 000 people waiting for Samora Machel to arrive. 'Samora, there's Samora', I hear, and I see this little figure far away going to the microphone. 'Viva o povo Mozambicano unido do Rovuma ao Maputo!' ['Long live the people of Mozambique united from the Rovuma to Maputo'] and 60 000 arms go up in the air – my arm included. I got my courage back in Mozambique; so even when I was unhappy there, I was happy. This was the Revolution, and we were the beautiful people. The Revolution ... the Revolution. I went up with the Revolution. It played itself out in many marvellous ways. One example was a big, open prison outside Maputo. It had no walls, and I would drive past, and have to turn around, and eventually after finding it, have to ask a prisoner to take me to the warders because the prisoners were running the place. A senior prisoner, serving ten years for fraud, once proudly told me of the maize they grew for themselves, their families and the market; the only problem was that people in the neighbourhood would walk into their fields and steal the mealies, showing no respect whatsoever for other people's property!

Though the first words in the Portuguese-language primer were about how to get to the bank or a railway station or a taxi, the first phrases I actually learnt were about the emancipation of women, and the need to combat racialism, regionalism and tribalism. Every single institution, place, factory, or school had a cultural unit that would have choral singing and group dancing and put on plays.

We painte• murals on walls all over the city. Extraor•inary work was being •one in anthropology an• archaeology, recuperating African history not just by stu•ying the lives of the kings an• the rulers, but by examining social structures an• the lives of or•inary people. The researchers rejecte• the

notion of a marvellous African past that has been without
class formation and exploitation.

They were underlining the fact that there were new forms of exploitation in Africa today. Indeed, the danger of a new class of oppressors emerging from the ranks of the Mozambique Liberation Front (FRELIMO) had been highlighted during the liberation struggle itself. After Eduardo Mondlane, its founder, was assassinated, FRELIMO had been riven in two. One source of division was over what to do with captured Portuguese soldiers. 'Kill them', one group said, while the section headed by Samora said, 'no, they are children of Portuguese peasants who should be encouraged to understand the values FRELIMO was fighting for'. Another question had been whether women should be allowed to take part in the armed struggle. The reactionaries, as they were called, said, 'no, their job is to look after male fighters', while the Women's Detachment, headed by Josina Machel, insisted on going into combat. A third issue was whether there was a place for non-Africans in the struggle.

Samora followed Mondlane's principle of working with
people of mixed origin as well as with those of Indian and
European descent. And it had been the section headed by
Samora, which had actually done most of the fighting, that
had won out. And now, after triumphantly becoming presi-
dent of newly independent Mozambique, Samora would say
that some people refused to be killed by a foreign tiger but
didn't mind being eaten by a local lion.

The battle cry in the newly independent People's Republic, accordingly, was to reconstruct the country to further the interests of workers and peasants. It was formidable and inspiring. The owners of beautiful high-rise apartments had fled and the balconies now contained the washing lines of people who had previously only entered as cleaners and cooks. A poem I wrote went more or less along the following lines, 'Of all the banners in Maputo/of all the flags that fly/the ones that stir me most of all/are the clothing out to dry'. Special classes had to be given to the new occupants: if all the women stamped their mielies at the same time, the walls would crack!

And then when things began to get more difficult at a material level, we all lined up happily in the same queues for our rations: rice, cooking oil, bread, occasionally eggs or fish, and even some meat. There was a strong sense of equality based on a vision of uniting the working people under the leadership of FRELIMO to propel the whole nation forward.

> *It seeme♦ beautiful, it felt beautiful. But it coul♦n't be sustaine♦. Just as I went up with the Revolution, so I came ♦own with the Revolution.*

The electricity went off for some hours in Cape Town today, and we were all irritated. In Mozambique we would comment if the electricity stayed on for a week. South African commandos were hitting the electricity lines all the time. One simple consequence was that petrol pumps couldn't work, and we couldn't even print the coupons for rationing. I was fortunate – with the few dollars I had I could buy gas for cooking, but living on the eleventh floor of one of those beautiful high-rise buildings, I had to lug the big canister up seemingly endless sets of steps in the dark.

> *Africa an♦ especially Angola an♦ Mozambique, pai♦ a bitter price for supporting the struggle against aparthei♦. The continent was sucke♦ into the Col♦ War. A week after Ronal♦ Reagan took office as presi♦ent of the USA in January 1980, South African comman♦os massacre♦ a number of ANC people in Matola.*

But external attack was not the only reason for the country's difficulties. The deepest cause of problems was the colonial inheritance. After five hundred years of colonial rule, only a handful of indigenous people had been able to acquire the skills needed to run a modern public administration. Thus, at the time of independence, there were only four qualified Mozambican lawyers in the country. In every field, it was the same. And the combination of war and severe underdevelopment proved devastating.

Yet war and underdevelopment were not the only sources of difficulty. The country's problems were compounded by what turned out to be serious errors of policy. I remember Samora telling the shoemakers of Mozambique that instead of each having his or her own little corner shop, the leather would now be given out to cooperatives so that they could all work together. It sounded great, but simply didn't function. Then shoe designers of middle-class background produced sturdy shoes in the factories, which they were sure the masses would appreciate, oblivious to the fact that the masses didn't want robust but inelegant footwear, they longed for a nice pair of shoes for Sunday best.

There was a poignant story doing the rounds about an interchange between Samora and his father. In the colonial period Samora's father had been expelled from a small piece of land along the Limpopo River to make way for Portuguese peasants to grow rice there. After independence the colonists return to Portugal, and Papa Machel asks his son, the president, when he could start growing rice there again. To his dismay, and our delight, Samora replies that FRELIMO had not been fighting for the president's father to get land, but for the nation to get food. And with Bulgarian help the FRELIMO government created a huge and expensive state farm on the banks of the Limpopo. The tractors came to till the soil, which was good, but they put in too much fertiliser, which was bad. The rice grew too quickly, and they had to get volunteers from the towns to cut it. Now, if anybody asks me to come and cut rice, even if I still had two arms, I would know they are in desperate straits. Though it was fantastic for me to be with the workers cutting rice, for the country it was a disaster. Vast sums of money went fruitlessly into the project. Our delight turned to dismay. The objective was beautiful, food for everybody; the water was there and the willingness and the capacity to introduce science were there. And given the absence of an indigenous managerial class, the temptation to place everything in state hands was understandable. But the result was calamitous. In a country at peace, you can learn from failure and bounce back with productive corrections. But when everything is disrupted by civil war, there are no second chances.

Perhaps the greatest lesson we South Africans who lived there learnt was that there was a deep flaw at the very heart of the country's political system. There was no space for legitimate opposition. Opposition to FRELIMO did not just fade away. It went underground, and was picked up by powerful regional and international forces that were quite happy to maintain white supremacy in the region as long as the reds could be kept firmly under the bed. Suddenly war raged everywhere. We heard the guns from across the bay, while refugees streamed in. Staff, students and workers at the university had to give up their prized 'July Activities', the month we all spent in rural areas every year doing research, getting to know the country. We could only leave Maputo by plane.

In a macabre way, it was the extent of the war that probably saved my life. After hearing the explosion that wrecked my car, a young Mozambican surgeon with whom I used to play bridge, went, without being called, straight to the hospital. There he saw my unconscious body and operated on it with a speed and skill that was to amaze the doctors in London. And after I came to, and the bandages covering my eyes were removed, I was able to see that they had been using the same bandages over and over again, washing and boiling them each time, and sterilising the same needle for injections. Thanks to the high consciousness of the medical staff, I received top class treatment in the top hospital in the country, in minimalist conditions. I will long remember the warmth of the people, their non-racism, their creative and inclusive approach to culture, their solidarity with us in South Africa.

But, from being the beautiful people in the beautiful country,
fille• with inspiration, we came to have thousan•s of persons

315

like me without limbs; millions of refugees in neighbouring
countries; brother fighting brother, sister fighting sister.

When I had first landed at the Maputo airport and seen a sign: 'Welcome to the liberated zone of humanity', I had noticed an armed FRELIMO soldier standing guard, I had felt filled with joy – guns had always been pointed at us, and now there was a gun on our side! But when I was wheeled out, semi-comatose to catch a plane to recover in London, I didn't want to see another gun, not another gun; too many guns, too many deaths.

It is sad to acknowledge that in the 25th year after Samora's plane crashed, the pulverisation of Mozambique that resulted basically from FRELIMO's support for us in the freedom struggle in South Africa, is barely appreciated in South Africa today. And it should be noted that before his plane was fatefully lured by a false signal to crash into a hillside in South Africa, Samora himself had strongly urged the leaders of newly independent Zimbabwe not to follow the path of swift and radical change mapped out by FRELIMO. Rather, he counselled them, they should aim to use all the skills of all the people living in Zimbabwe in order to build a more equitable society progressively. I make these points not to comment on current debates on nationalisation in South Africa – I strictly refrain from doing so. My purpose is simply to explain the thoughts that were going through my head at the time of my inaugural lecture in 1991. The key element was that I didn't regard the idea of a negotiated settlement as something forced on us because we hadn't had enough physical power to overcome the enemy and seize power. It was, as Shakespeare says, 'a consummation devoutly to be wished'.

A negotiated revolution rather than a seizure of power,
would enable us to retain the physical fabric of the country.
But more important, it would prevent the terrible scarring
and hatred that goes from generation to generation when
you establish power against the will of another group, and
crush and conquer them.

Furthermore, when you storm, take power and remove everything in your way, you don't have to think about the best forms of governing. You simply legitimise the government that you've installed, and then rely on the continuation of your power to stay in control.

And after years of devastating conflict, Mozambique itself ceased to be a 'People's Republic', and negotiated a new constitution based on principles of openness and political pluralism and a less dominant role for the state in the economy.

MYTHS ABOUT THE CONSTITUTION-MAKING PROCESS

Before answering the question of whether the sacrifices made in struggle are being honoured or disregarded by the country we have created, I believe it is necessary to dispel three myths about the constitution-making process. By distorting our history they make it difficult to make a correct appreciation of where we stand now.

The first myth is that the won•erful Nelson Man•ela an• the wise FW •e Klerk put their hea•s together an• plucke• the miracle of a new non-racial •emocratic constitution out of a hat. How wrong an• mislea•ing!

Though they both undoubtedly played an important role in keeping their respective sides steady, their personal chemistry was bad and their involvement individually in the actual drafting of the document very limited. In reality, literally hundreds of people participated in a protracted, procedurally complex and unusually creative process that endured for more than six years.

To say this is not to belittle the importance of the broad political leadership displayed respectively by Madiba and FW. It is to emphasise that we should not be longing for a new Mandela-like figure to lead us miraculously out of our problems. As before, what is needed is an immense amount of hard work and a huge amount of hard talking by hundreds and thousands of people.

The second myth is that National Party and ANC elites cynically did a sweetheart deal to ensure that both would end up in office, without in any way disturbing existing property relations. Thus, Nelson Mandela has been accused by some within his organisation of having been 'too nice to the whites', while FW de Klerk has correspondingly been charged by conservative Afrikaners with having 'rolled over' to please the ANC. The reality just wasn't like that at all. The constitution-making process was rough. Everything was contested. There were breakdowns, rolling mass action, massacres. We fought over process, how parties should be represented, how decisions should be taken, and whether the Constitution should be written at Kempton Park or by a democratically elected Constitutional Assembly. And we fought over substance: whether there should be a white veto, a government of national unity, about provincial powers, the army, the police, local government, the Constitutional Court, and customary law, not to mention gender equality, gay rights, capital punishment and single-medium schools.

An• the hottest issue, the one in the Bill of Rights over which we fought the longest, was the property clause. It is to•ay the subject of extensive litigation, so it woul• be inappropriate for me to comment on it. What I can say, however, is that the Constitutional Court has frequently hel• that our Constitution requires property law in our country to be interprete• on the basis that there has been massive an• unjust •ispossession of people from lan•, that restitution is constitutionally require• an• that lan• reform an• upgra•ing of precarious tenure have to be facilitate•.

At the same time, and not losing sight of these principles, the Constitution insists that redistribution should not be done in an arbitrary fashion. The third myth that needs to be dispelled is the assertion, beloved by many commentators, that at the time of the achievement of democracy and the first democratic elections, there was a halcyon period of public peace and euphoria in South Africa, as contrasted with the confusion, and dissatisfactions, and disillusion of today. The fact is that more people died in the low-grade civil war in KwaZulu-Natal in the four years preceding the first elections than in all the political violence of the rest of the twentieth century. The conflict between so-called ANC and AZAPO (Azanian People's Organisation) self-defence units on the East Rand was deadly, as was that between different forces in the former Bophuthatswana. Chris Hani was murdered. The country almost erupted then. The massacre in St James Church shook all of us in Cape Town, and we had the daily shock of scores of people being thrown to their deaths off trains in various parts of the country. Even during those first wonderful elections, bombs went off claiming many lives. And after 1994, the Government of National Unity foundered and FW de Klerk pulled his team out, while the media were filled with complaints about the gravy train and the Arms Deal.

Once more, the point is that an ano•yne view of the past will not help us •eal with the travails of the present.

SALAAM, IMAM HARON

I remember the Imam vividly as a brave and thoughtful participant in particularly harsh days of struggle. He had strong energy and a strong will, and wasn't somebody who just blended in. In his quiet way he was very forceful and committed. And the pain of his death has a permanence that we continue to feel in our souls. The justification for his life and the risks that he took, and his willingness to expose himself to what ultimately happened to him, lies in the real and massive achievements I have spoken of. We should not denigrate those achievements, but take pride in and build on them.

And though in dealing with the serious challenges we now face, we need the same courage and determination we had in the days of the struggle, the energy has got to be different. It can't be the fiery, intensely focused energy of the liberation movement, one that required enormous courage and willingness to endure pain. It's got to be an energy appropriate for an open, democratic society, with clearly established principles of justice and equity as our guide. The intense, vigorous comradeship in the struggle has to give way to gentler expressions of ubuntu in daily dealings – valuing interconnectedness, and promoting humanity and respect for all. We need fewer shrill, self-serving polemics and greater civility towards each other, as well as more openness on the side of ourselves, the former freedom fighters, to challenging and even disconcerting ideas coming from others.

What worries me now is that millions of people who are doing the hard work of keeping the country going are so preoccupied with their day-to-day concerns that very little of an overall vision comes out from them. At the same time, people who project beautiful visions don't seem to be doing any of the hard work needed to solve the actual problems of our society. So it seems that what we need now is to reconnect the hard work that thousands and thousands, indeed millions, of people are doing decently and honourably inside government, in the private sector, in public life, in the schools, in all areas of life, with a refreshed vision of how our new democratic society can advance. All honour, then, to the Imam, whose fusion of practicality, wisdom, integrity and idealism serves as an eternal beacon for us all.

THEN AND NOW

I turn now to answering directly the question of whether the sacrifices made by people like Imam Haron were in vain. Reflecting on the differences between our country then and our country now, I find myself coming to the emphatic but not unqualified answer that the sacrifices were not in vain.

Then we had detention without trial. Now we have a Constitution that expressly outlaws such detention. And people have rights of access to a lawyer and to appear in court. The Constitution also guarantees a free press and a right to information. And the public is alert. Can you imagine what would happen if someone today died in detention with her or his body full of bruises, and a magistrate said it was an accidental death? There would be an outcry. In this respect we are living in a completely different country from the one in which the Imam died.

Then we had censorship and thought control on a massive basis. My thesis, a scholarly dissertation for a PhD at Sussex University, was banned in South Africa. Not once, but three times: because I was banned; because it quoted other banned people; and because it was expressly banned in its own right! Sadly for me, as soon as it was unbanned, people took off the false covers and stopped reading it. We don't have that now. We don't have the Censorship Board banning masses and masses of books and films. People speak out forcefully on questions of threats to press freedoms and the right to information. We know about these possible threats because the press reminds us about them 24/7. I'm not going to comment on any actual measures before us now that could impact on press freedom or the right to information. I simply make two broad comments. The first is that we South Africans have won our right to know what is going on and to speak our minds, and I can't see South Africans, whether inside or outside government, easily giving up these rights. The second is that we have a Constitution that is taken very seriously, and if it comes down to that, it will be the Constitutional Court that will decide whether any measure intrudes unjustifiably on our protected rights.

So, we might not have anything like the jobs, housing, health and education that we want. But we do have our freedom.

People speak out, an• they protest. We are not a scare• society. We are not •own-tro••en. We know about injustices because people are speaking about them in their own voice, insi•e an• outsi•e political parties, through NGOs, in the courts, outsi•e of the courts, in the press.

Sometimes we can't even imagine now, let alone remember, the things we lived through as ordinary features of daily life. They seem quite incredible. I can recall a banal little example of the impact of the Group

Areas Act on me, a privileged white. When I was practising at the Bar and had chambers in Dorp Street near what we then called the Supreme Court, I used to park my car a couple of blocks away in Bloem Street. Then my second banning order restricted me to white areas only. So I had to park in a white area – even my car had to be forcibly removed from Bloem Street! At a far more serious level, Imam Haron couldn't live in any of the beautiful areas of Cape Town reserved for whites only. He didn't have the vote. He couldn't stand for parliament. He couldn't become a cabinet minister.

A month or two ago, I'm speaking in Boston and the South African Ambassador to the USA comes to the platform, Ebrahim Rasool. He gives a beautiful address, and I feel so proud to see the audience soaking up his spontaneously delivered and eloquent words. And he'd been the premier in the Western Cape. Now some people think he was a brilliant premier, some people think that he was terrible. It's a part of our freedom that people can have and express different views. But the idea of somebody from the Muslim community being the premier, not of some tiny little group area council, but of the whole Western Cape, was just unthinkable in the time of Imam Haron. Now we take it for granted.

There are many things we just take for granted. Our elections are free and fair. The average term of office of our first three presidents has been five years, not forty-one or thirty-nine, as elsewhere in Africa. It is good and bad that we take these aspects of our democracy for granted. It is good that they have become so normal that they are now part of our everyday culture. It is bad that we forget the significance of our achievements, and the difficulties we overcame to realise them. It didn't just happen. We re-made our country. And the result of the endeavours of which the Imam was a part, is that a resolute and deeply spiritual person like Imam Haron can live freely today as religious leader, as a citizen, as a Muslim, as a human being.

It's another country, and even with all its imperfections and grotesqueries, a hugely better one. And we have a Consti-

*tution that allows for the further transformations necessary
for thorough-going equalisation of life chances for all.*

If government hasn't done as much as it could have done, that's a valid
point. But we can't put the blame on the Constitution. And we should be
very wary of tinkering with it. Some of the structural details can perhaps
be changed – we have, for example, already altered provincial boundaries
and banned floor-crossing. But its basic elements and foundational
values should not be touched. The Constitution is our country's greatest
tribute to the people who died in the struggle [and to the names of
the Cape Town heroes I mentioned earlier, let me add those of Ashley
Kriel, Basil February, and, of course, Chris Hani, who worked quietly
and tirelessly with us here in the underground before slipping out of
the country in the early 1960s]. The Constitution recognises that they
suffered because they were who they were, fighters for liberation. It
incorporates and memorialises their highest ideals and finds a way of
speaking to everyone in the nation. It's a beautifully crafted document,
referred to with enormous admiration throughout the world. And, it's
ours. We made it; we wrote it; and we are applying it today.

Up to an important point, then, we can say mission accomplished. I
do so not to imply that we have wiped out all the problems that we have
inherited, or to suggest we do not create new problems for ourselves.
We have won our freedom, but we haven't won nearly enough personal
security. The inequalities that continue in our society are intolerable.
And the failures of public morality are totally, totally unacceptable. But
for all that, our accomplishments have been of historic proportions.

We achieved the impossible when the world didn't give us a chance.
I think most South Africans didn't feel that we could live together as
equals in one country. And we achieved it. And who achieved it? We
achieved it. Not beautiful people. It was us.

*If you are waiting for the beautiful people, or even a
beautiful lea•er, it won't happen. It's always got to be us*

an• the people like us an• our neighbours an• our parents an• our chil•ren an• gran•chil•ren. An• it's us with all our limitations an• ambitions an• pettiness an• gree• an• impatience, an• all our perfectibility an• corruptibility. The same us who brought about the •ownfall of aparthei•. It's that same us, an• maybe the chil•ren of us, an• even the gran•chil•ren of us, who now have to create that more beautiful society that we long for an• still have to achieve.

Cases Cited

Alexkor Lt• an• Another v Richtersvel• Community an• Others (CCT 19/ 03) [2003] ZACC 18; 2004 (5) SA 460 (CC); 2003 (12) BCLR 1301 (CC)

Bhe an• Others v Khayelitsha Magistrate an• Others (CCT 49/03) [2004] ZACC 17; 2005 (1) SA 580 (CC); 2005 (1) BCLR 1 (CC)

Brink v Kitshoff NO (CCT 15/95) [1996] ZACC 9; 1996 (4) SA 197 (CC); 1996 (6) BCLR 752 (CC)

City Council of Pretoria v Walker (CCT 8/97) [1998] ZACC 1; 1998 (2) SA 363 (CC); 1998 (3) BCLR 275 (CC)

Christian E•ucation South Africa v Minister of E•ucation (CCT 4/00) [2000] ZACC 11; 2000 (4) SA 757 (CC); 2000 (10) BCLR 1051 (CC)

Daniels v Campbell an• Others (CCT 40/03) [2004] ZACC 14; 2004 (5) SA 331 (CC); 2004 (7) BCLR 735 (CC)

Doctors for Life International v Speaker of the National Assembly an• Others (CCT 12/05) [2006] ZACC 11; 2006 (6) SA 416 (CC); 2006 (12) BCLR 1399 (CC)

Executive Council of the Western Cape Legislature an• Others v Presi•ent of the Republic of South Africa an• Others (CCT 27/95) [1995] ZACC 8; 1995 (4) SA 877 (CC); 1995 (10) BCLR 1289 (CC)

Fraser v Chil•ren's Court, Pretoria North an• Others (CCT 31/96) [1997] ZACC 1; 1997 (2) SA 218 (CC); 1997 (2) BCLR 153 (CC)

Fourie an• Another v Minister of Home Affairs an• Another (CCT 25/03) [2003] ZACC 11; 2003 (5) SA 301 (CC); 2003 (10) BCLR 1092 (CC)

Gauteng Provincial Legislature In re: Gauteng School E•ucation Bill of 1995 (CCT 39/95) [1996] ZACC 4; 1996 (3) SA 165 (CC); 1996 (4) BCLR 537 (CC)

Government of the Republic of South Africa an• Others v Grootboom an• Others (CCT 11/00) [2000] ZACC 19; 2001 (1) SA 46 (CC); 2000 (11) BCLR 1169 (CC)

Harksen v Lane NO an• Others (CCT 9/97) [1997] ZACC 12; 1998 (1) SA
    300 (CC); 1997 (11) BCLR 1489 (CC)

In re: Certification of the Constitution of the Republic of South Africa (CCT
    23/96) [1996] ZACC 26; 1996 (4) SA 744 (CC); 1996 (10) BCLR
    1253 (CC)

*Larbi-O•am an• Others v Member of the Executive Council for E•ucation
    (North-West Province) an• Another* (CCT 2/97) [1997] ZACC 16; 1998
    (1) SA 745 (CC); 1997 (12) BCLR 1655 (CC)

MEC for E•ucation: KwaZulu-Natal an• Others v Pillay (CCT 51/06)
    [2007] ZACC 21; 2008 (1) SA 474 (CC); 2008 (2) BCLR 99 (CC)

*MEC for Health, KwaZulu-Natal v Premier, KwaZulu-Natal: In re: Minister
    of Health an• Others v Treatment Action Campaign an• Others* (CCT
    15/02) [2002] ZACC 14; 2002 (5) SA 717 (CC); 2002 (10) BCLR
    1028 (CC)

Minister of Finance an• Other v Van Heer•en (CCT 63/03) [2004] ZACC
    3; 2004 (6) SA 121 (CC); 2004 (11) BCLR 1125 (CC); [2004] 12
    BLLR 1181 (CC)

*Occupiers of 51 Olivia Roa•, Berea Township an• 197 Main Street
    Johannesburg v City of Johannesburg an• Others* (CCT 24/07) [2008]
    ZACC 1; 2008 (3) SA 208 (CC); 2008 (5) BCLR 475 (CC)

Port Elizabeth Municipality v Various Occupiers (CCT 53/03) [2004] ZACC
    7; 2005 (1) SA 217 (CC); 2004 (12) BCLR 1268 (CC)

Presi•ent of the Republic of South Africa v Hugo (CCT 11/96) [1997] ZACC
    4; 1997 (4) SA 1 (CC); 1997 (6) BCLR 708 (CC)

Prince v Presi•ent of the Law Society of the Cape of Goo• Hope (CCT 36/00)
    [2002] ZACC 1; 2002 (2) SA 794 (CC); 2002 (3) BCLR 231 (CC)

Prinsloo v Van •er Lin•e (CCT 4/96) [1997] ZACC 5; 1997 (3) SA 1012
    (CC); 1997 (6) BCLR 759 (CC)

Rossouw v Sachs 1964 (2) SA 551 (A)

S v Makwanyane an• Another (CCT 3/94) [1995] ZACC 3; 1995 (3) SA
    391 (CC); 1995 (6) BCLR 665 (CC)

S v Mhlungu an• Others (CCT 25/94) [1995] ZACC 4; 1995 (3) SA 867
    (CC); 1995 (7) BCLR 793 (CC)

S v Lawrence, S v Negal; S v Solberg (CCT 38/96, CCT 39/96, CCT 40/96) [1997] ZACC 11; 1997 (4) SA 1176 (CC); 1997 (10) BCLR 1348 (CC)

Shilubana an• Others v Nwamitwa (CCT 3/07) [2008] ZACC 9; 2009 (2) SA 66 (CC); 2008 (9) BCLR 914 (CC)

Soobramoney v Minister of Health (KwaZulu-Natal) (CCT 32/97) [1997] ZACC 17; 1998 (1) SA 795 (CC); 1997 (12) BCLR 1696 (CC)

Sources

1. In the Beginning

The Future of Multiculturalism in South Africa: The vision of the Constitution
Extract from Sachs, Albie. 2016. 'The Future of Multiculturalism in South Africa: The vision of the Constitution', in The Future of Multiculturalism in South Africa, Conference to Commemorate the 26th Anniversary of FW de Klerk's Speech that Initiated South Africa's Constitutional Transformation Process, Cape Town, 2 February 2016. FW de Klerk Foundation in conjunction with the Konrad Adenauer Foundation, pp. 24–27. Available online at http://www.fwdeklerk.org/index.php/en/latest/news/538-publication-the-future-of-multiculturalism-in-south-africa (Accessed 3 June 2016).

The Original 'Pinch-me' Moment
Extract from keynote lecture at the launch of the Kader Asmal Human Rights Award, hosted by the Council for the Advancement of the South African Constitution (CASAC), University of the Western Cape, Cape Town, 28 May 2013. Reprinted with permission.

2. Hope and Caution

The First an◦ Last Wor◦ – Free◦om
Published in Sachs, Albie. *Protecting Human Rights in a New South Africa*, Cape Town: Oxford University Press, 1990.

3. We Have to Mistrust Ourselves

Preparing Ourselves for Power
Published in Sachs, Albie. *A*•*vancing Human Rights in South Africa*, Cape
Town: Oxford University Press, 1992.

Perfectibility an• *Corruptibility*
Published in Sachs, Albie. *A*•*vancing Human Rights in South Africa*, Cape
Town: Oxford University Press, 1992.

4. Inventing a Constitution

South Africa's Unconstitutional Constitution: The transition from power to lawful power
Sachs, Albie. 'South Africa's Unconstitutional Constitution: The
transition from power to lawful power', *Saint Louis University Law
Journal*, Vol. 41, Fall 1997, pp. 1249–1258. Reprinted with permission.

5. With Clean Hands and Without Secrets

Why I Supporte• *Amnesty*
Sachs, Albie. 'Honouring the Truth in Post-Apartheid South Africa',
North Carolina Journal of International Law an• *Commercial Regulation*,
Vol. 26, No. 3, Summer 2001, pp. 799–810.

Meeting the Man who Organise• *a Bomb in my Car*
Speech presented at From Violent Conflict to Peaceful Coexistence
Conference, International Centre for Ethnic Studies Colombo, Sri
Lanka, 27 February 2014.

Soft Vengeance
Keynote address delivered at African Literature Association (ALA) Conference, Charleston, March 2013.
Published in the *Journal of the African Literature Association (JALA)*, Vol. 8, No. 2, Winter/Spring 2014, pp. 258–264. Reprinted with permission.

6. Reconciling the Past and the Future

Archives, Truth an◆ Reconciliation
Sachs, Albie. 'Archives, Truth, and Reconciliation', *Archivaria*, 62 [S. l.], January 2007, ISSN 1923-6409. Available at: http://archivaria.ca/ index.php/archivaria/article/view/12887/14118 (Accessed 3 June 2016). Originally delivered as the 1st National Archives Lecture on 24 October 2005 in Beveridge Hall, Senate House, University of London, convened by The National Archives (TNA), London and the School of Advanced Study at the University of London.

The Place Next Door to Number Four
Niederhuber, Margit and Sachs, Albie. *My/Mein Johannesburg*. Wien: Mandelbaum Verlag, 2014, pp. 9–16. Reprinted with permission.

Free Spirits an◆ Ravage◆ Souls
Keynote address at the Time of the Writer festival, Durban, South Africa, 4 May 2011. Published in *Africa Insi◆e Out – Stories, Tales an◆ Testimonies: A Time of the Writer anthology*, edited by Michael Chapman, Scottsville: University of KwaZulu-Natal Press, 2012.

Towar◆s the Liberation an◆ Revitalisation of Customary Law
Sachs, Albie. 1999. Towards the Liberation and Revitalisation of Customary Law. Pre-dinner address at the Southern African Society of Legal Historians Conference on Law in Africa: New perspectives on

origins, foundations and transition, Roodevallei Country Lodge, Pretoria, 13–15 January 1999.

Values, Nation Formation an• Social Compacting
Sachs, Albie. 2014. Values, Nation Formation and Social Compacting. Paper presented at 20 Years of South African Democracy: So where to now? Conference, hosted by the Mapungubwe Institute for Strategic Reflection (MISTRA) and the Thabo Mbeki African Leadership Institute, University of South Africa, 2014. Published in *20 Years of South African Democracy: So where to now?*, Johannesburg: Real African Publishers, 2015, on behalf of the Mapungubwe Institute for Strategic Reflection (MISTRA).

7. Living Constitutional Law and Ubuntu

Constitutional Court Simulation, Case No. 2: The constitutionality of the •eath penalty
Sachs, Albie. 2015. *Constitutional Court Simulation, Case No. 2: The constitutionality of the •eath penalty.*
Presentation as invited expert witness to a simulated Constitutional Court hearing on the constitutionality of capital punishment, Taipei Bar Association, Taipei, May 2015. Published in *Civilization without Capital Punishment – Procee•ings of Constitutional Court Simulation, Case No. 2: The constitutionality of the •eath penalty.* Taipei: Taipei Bar Association, September 2015.

A New African Jurispru•ence: From abstract ju•icial rulings to purposive transformative jurispru•ence
Sachs, Albie. A New African Jurisprudence: From abstract judicial rulings to purposive transformative jurisprudence. Paper presented at the International Conference on Interpreting and Shaping a Transformative Constitution, hosted by the Katiba Institute, the British

Institute for Eastern Africa, the Judicial Training Institute and the
Kenya Human Rights Commission, Nairobi, Kenya, June 2014.

*Equality Jurispru•ence: The origin of •octrine in the South African
Constitutional Court*
10th Annual McDonald Lecture, Centre for Constitutional Studies,
University of Alberta, 1998. Published in *Review of Constitutional Stu•ies*,
Vol. 5, No. 1, 1999, pp. 76–103. Available online at
http://ualawccsprod.srv.ualberta.ca/images/journals/review/
Review5.1.pdf. Reprinted with permission.

8. More than Crumbs from the Table: Enforcing Social and Economic Rights

Ju•ge Not, Lest Ye Be Ju•ge•
Commissioned by the Foundation for Human Rights, April/May 2014.
To be published in *Socio-economic Rights: Progressive realisation?* edited by
David le Page, Johannesburg: Foundation for Human Rights, November
2016. Reprinted with permission.

*Liberty, Equality, Fraternity: Bringing human soli•arity back into the
rights equation*
Public lecture presented at the Centre for Applied Human Rights,
University of York, October 2011. Published in Sachs, Albie, 'Liberty,
Equality, Fraternity: Bringing human solidarity back into the rights
equation', *Journal of Human Rights Practice*, 2012, Vol. 4, No. 3, pp.
365–383. Reprinted with permission.

9. Struggle Continues

Nothing About us Without us: Disability
Keynote address at The Annual Harvard Law School Project on
Disability (HPOD) Open House, Cambridge, MA, United States, 17
October 2013. Amended version to be published in *Disability Social
Rights*, edited by Malcolm Langford and Michael Stein, Cambridge MA:
Cambridge University Press, 2016.

From Refugee to Ju•ge on Refugee Law
Published in James Simeon (ed.), *Critical Issues in International Refugee
Law: Strategies Towar• Interpretative Harmony*, Cambridge MA:
Cambridge University Press, 2010, pp. 40–58. Reprinted with
permission.

A Conversation about the Sacre• an• the Secular: Same-sex marriage
Papers presented at the 2nd Conference of the African Consortium for
Law and Religious Studies (ACLARS), Stellenbosch, South Africa,
26–28 May 2014. Published in *Law an• Religion in Africa: The Quest for
the Common Goo• in Pluralistic Societies*, edited by Pieter Coertzen, M
Christian Green and Len Hansen, Stellenbosch: SUN MeDIA (under the
Conference–RAP imprint), 2015, pp. 247–260. Copyright © 2015
ACLARS. Available online at www.africansunmedia.co.za www.sun-e-
shop.co.za. Reprinted with permission.

Getting the Last Laugh on Rho•es
Extract from Sachs, Albie. 'The Rhodes Debate: How we can have the
last laugh', *City Press*, 29 March 2015. Available online at
http://www.news24.com/Archives/City-Press/The-Rhodes-debate-
How-we-can-have-the-last-laugh-20150429 (Accessed 3 June 2016).
Reprinted with permission.

10. Are the Beautiful People Born?

Unite♦ in Diversity

Extract from Sachs, Albie. 2016. *The Future of Multiculturalism in South Africa: The vision of the constitution,* in The Future of Multiculturalism in South Africa, Conference to Commemorate the 26th Anniversary of FW de Klerk's Speech that Initiated South Africa's Constitutional Transformation Process, Cape Town, 2 February 2016. FW de Klerk Foundation, in conjunction with the Konrad Adenauer Foundation, pp. 27–31. Available online at http://www.fwdeklerk.org/index.php/en/latest/news/538-publication-the-future-of-multiculturalism-in-south-africa. (Accessed 3 June 2016).

Are the Beautiful People Born?

Lecture delivered at the 4th Annual Imam Haron Memorial Lecture, Kramer Law Building, Middle Campus, University of Cape Town, 28 September 2011, organised by the Imam Abdullah Haron Education Trust (IAHET) (unpublished).

Index

Printed and bound by CPI Group (UK) Ltd, Croydon, CR0 4YY

09/06/2025

14685830-0001